Communism:
The Great
Misunderstanding

second edition

Gennady Ermak, Ph.D.

2019

Contents

Introduction

What if someone told you that, after over a century of bitter fights, both pro- and anti-communists got communism wrong? That is exactly what this book finds. Moreover, this book reveals that Marxism was also misconceived, and that the misunderstanding of communism resulted largely from the misunderstanding of Marxism.

This book was written neither to promote nor to defeat communism, but rather was written to clarify its tenets and to promote understanding between the opposed camps of pro- and anti-communists. Having grown up in the former USSR, I was forced, like many, to study communist ideas at school and at the university level. However, following advanced study of the subject, I couldn't shake the persistent feeling that something wasn't right. For example, the philosophy behind communism (dialectic materialism) suggests that one can move toward communism but never reach it, but the Soviet leadership projected that the USSR would enter communism soon, before the year 2000. This feeling lay in a dormant state for decades until I finally decided to address it. That's when I wrote this book.

When we take a look at the modern world, we may be surprised to find that many countries that tried to build communism have failed miserably. On the other hand, the nations that are currently closest to communism are capitalist countries such as Denmark and Norway, which have not claimed to build a communist system. How this happened, where we are now, and where the world will go from here – these are the questions to which the book will attempt to find answers. Of course, this field is so inundated with polemics and confusing pronouncements that we can justify nearly any conclusion that we want – and this is exactly what has happened. When I began writing this book, I had no idea where it would take me. I tried to keep my mind open and used my background in scientific research to remain objective and unbiased. In the process, I learned and discovered a great deal. Hopefully, you will too.

Please note that the book is comprised of 12 chapters which do not have to be followed chronologically, allowing readers flexibility to skip a chapter or select their own order. References, therefore, are provided at the end of each chapter rather than at the end of the book. Also, I remember all too well how my university classmates struggled in their homework to extract the main ideas from the works of Marx and Lenin. These were intellectual people acquiring a higher education – what about an average person? Most literature in this field is written in a complicated and often confusing language, which is one of the factors contributing to the misunderstanding. Therefore, I've put forth an effort to write the book in simple language and to make this subject understandable to a wide audience.

Chapter 1

What is Communism?

Imagine no possessions
I wonder if you can
No need for greed or hunger
A brotherhood of man
Imagine all the people sharing all the world...

These are lyrics from the best-selling single "Imagine" by John Lennon. The song plays every year in Times Square in New York City – the heart of capitalism – just before the famous Times Square Ball drops on New Year's Eve. Thousands come to the square and millions watch the event on TV. But little do they know that they are enjoying a song about something that resembles communism – a classless, stateless, and moneyless (yet rich) society. And who can blame them for not knowing this? Living in the modern Western world – and especially in the U.S. – individuals are conditioned to believe that communism is freedom-limiting and terrible, something along the lines of fascism.

Photo-Illustration. How the West normally reacts to the word "communism."

And it gets even better. In general, Americans hate and fear communism but are in love with the *Star Trek* TV show and movie franchise, in which money and classes don't exist, where people are altruistic and work not for financial gain, but rather to achieve something, to be useful, to strive for greatness and to be "the captain." In other words, *Star Trek* characters live in a communist-like world. If only Americans knew...

Western media is flooded with communism-related titles like *The Great Terror: A Reassessment* and *The Black Book of Communism: Crimes, Terror, Repression*. Scary memories of the USSR are still fresh, and modern media still associate communism with them. But what did the former Soviet Union have in common with communism? The answer is: not much, if anything at all. As we will see below (Chapter 7), the Bolshevik Revolution and the rise of the USSR were nothing more than a distortion of this ideal. What then, is communism?

Some theorists simply say that "there is no single theory of communism." [1] This is probably where the misunderstanding begins. Does it mean that communism cannot be defined? Why can feudalism, capitalism or virtually anything in the world be defined but not communism? What is so mysterious about it? In fact, there is no mystery: communism has a definition, but that definition has been lost due to too many interpretations and misinterpretations in modern time.

The word communism derives from the Latin *communis*, which means "shared by or belonging to all." The idea of a communist society has existed in human minds and actions for thousands of years, but was scientifically defined only in the 19th century by Karl Marx and his colleague, Friedrich Engels.

Currently, there are numerous definitions of communism. These can be divided into two contradicting groups: a) the traditional definition originally proposed by French socialists of the 18th century and later developed by Marx and Engels, and b) a new definition developed by modern Western ideologists. According to the former (original) definition, the goal of communism is complete freedom and equality, with equality connoting fairness in all aspects of human life, such as gender and race but primarily wealth. According to the latter (modern) definition, communism is a system in which all economic and social activity is controlled by a totalitarian state. In other words, the goal of communism is to limit freedom. Why this contradiction?

The new understanding of communism came from the observation of self-proclaimed communist states such as the former USSR. The systems of these states provided neither much freedom nor equality, and did not fit into the traditional definition. Hence, the new definition was developed. However, if we accept the new definition, then how can we reconcile hundreds of years of human history? We will be forced to accept that virtually all free thinkers of the past – Marxists, social democrats, *et al.* – fought to limit freedom and install totalitarian regimes. This would be a gross falsification of history and maligning some of the best minds of humanity. To reduce communism to such a definition would, of course, be ridiculous, which is why it's essential that we adhere to the traditional definition of communism.

How, then, can we reconcile the traditional definition with the reality of self-proclaimed "communist" states? If not communist, what are they? This problem was actually solved a long time ago. Roughly a century ago, Russian revolutionary Nikolai Bukharin understood that the system of the USSR did not fit into the existing definition of communism and termed it "bureaucratic collectivism." More recently, this idea was further developed by American author Michael Harrington in the book *Socialism: Past and Future.* Unfortunately, this solution did not become widely known.

Having settled that the definition should be traditional and as originally intended, let's try to figure out which definition of communism would be the best. Like capitalism, feudalism, or slavery, communism is a social and economic system (some use the word "formation"). Hence, its definition must reflect two parts: economic and social. Economically, communism is predicated on the equal division of wealth among all citizens depending on each individual's needs, insofar as not all people have equal needs (for example, a single mother with a baby has more needs than a single healthy man). Socially, communism means complete freedom, not just democracy, since democracy only protects the interests of the majority. Thus, communism calls for the highest degree of equality and freedom. Any system that limits either equality or freedom cannot be classified as communist. Therefore, communism can be defined as a socioeconomic system in which material distribution is based on equality and need, while social relations are based on freely associating individuals.

And yet, not everybody might agree. One of the main ideas of Marxism is that all socioeconomic systems are based on economy and ownership of the means of production (equipment, tools, buildings, technologies, materials, etc.). According to Marxism, complete equality and freedom are only possible when the means of production are owned by all people publicly/socially/collectively, not privately and exclusively by the elite (see Chapter 5). Therefore, some advocate that communism should be defined as a socioeconomic system founded on public ownership of the means of production. However, while such ownership is certainly a prerequisite of communism, it does not automatically lead to complete freedom and equality. A prominent example can be found in the former USSR: although the means of production have been publicly owned there, not all citizens have been either equal or free (see Chapter 7). On the other hand, if a society has complete freedom and equality, this would suggest that the means of production are publicly owned. Thus, a satisfactory definition of communism does not require specifying the ownership of the means of production. Keeping this in mind, the distinctions between communism and other socioeconomic systems is visualized in the chart on the following page (Figure 1.1).

In one of their primary works, *The German Ideology*, Marx and Engels proposed that communism will arise as a consequence of the development of productive forces and economy.[2] The economy must be strong enough to produce so much material wealth that people will stop fighting over it. They warned that if the economy is weak and poor, there will not be much to share aside from poverty itself.

Critics believe that communism is impossible because it requires equal sharing of material goods, while the nature of humans is such that they cannot share – they always want to amass as much individual wealth as possible. However, a strong economy that provides a *super*-abundance of material goods can change this mentality, making sharing both easier and possible.

According to Marxism, capitalism will be replaced by communism inevitably, because productive forces and the economy develop and grow

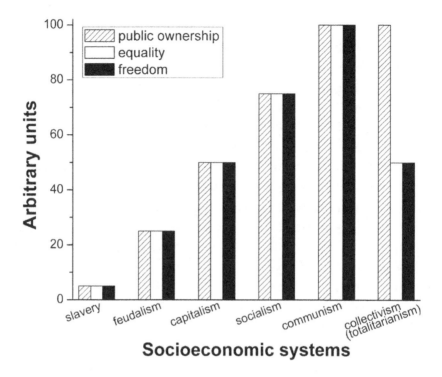

Figure 1.1. Illustration of Communism and Other Systems. Values are set arbitrarily from 0 (minimum) to 100 (maximum); actual numbers cannot be measured because slavery and feudalism are in the past while socialism and communism are still in the future. The graphs are intended for visualization but not quantification. "Public ownership" indicates public/social/collective ownership of the means of production; "equality" indicates equality in distribution of wealth.

It is worth noting that socialism/communism is generally confused with collectivism, authoritarianism and totalitarianism. Despite the inclusion of complete public ownership of the means of production, collectivism has little equality and freedom. The less equality and freedom a collectivist system has, the more likely it is authoritarian and totalitarian.

inevitably. There will be no rich or poor in a communist society. It will be classless, moneyless and stateless. The question then arises: how will this society function and why will people still work? The main stimulus for people to work in any society preceding communism is for their own material needs and wealth. In communist society, material wealth will become so abundant that it will lose its stimulating role. Instead, the driving force behind the economy will be a moral factor: people will work because they enjoy it, they want to achieve something and they want to be useful to others. Thus, the main principal of this society will be "from each according to abilities, to each according to needs."

This should to be distinguished from the main principal of socialism. Some use the words "socialism" and "communism" interchangeably, which is incorrect. Socialism is a transient phase between capitalism and communism, which can also be considered as the first or lower stage of communism. There need be no superabundance of material wealth in socialist society, and a person cannot have as much material wealth as he or she wants. Everybody is paid according to his or her work. The main principal of this society is "from each according to abilities, and to each according to work." At present, even capitalist societies already have socialist elements, as exampled by social programs such as public education, public healthcare, retirement programs, etc. And yet, although socialism and communism are different things, it is important to keep in mind that if we build socialism we also move toward communism, because socialism is the first stage of communism. Communism growth directly out of socialism. Therefore, socialism and communism can be used interchangeably in this context.

Confusion in defining communism goes hand in hand with a misunderstanding of who should be called a communist. One would assume that any person who believes that communist society offers a better future and works to advance this idea is a communist. However, this is not the case. Since 1919, when communist movements split depending on their support of World War I and the Russian Socialist Revolution (see Chapters 2 and 4), only those who believed that capitalism could be transformed into communism through revolution (revolutionary communists) were called communists. Those who believed that communism can be achieved peacefully through reforms were not considered to be communists. Practically, this means that only Marxist-Leninists and Left Communists (see Chapter 4) are currently viewed as communists. Even more misleading, any individual or organization that proclaims to be communist is automatically accepted to be communist.

One of the most significant misunderstandings of communism

comes from confusion regarding its relation to democracy and freedom. Many think that democracy is incompatible with communism because communism is a totalitarian system, in which a government exercises complete control over the state and its citizens. (Surprisingly, some believe that even such a dictatorship as North Korea is a communist country.) Nothing can be further from the truth. As mentioned above, this misconception came directly from the observation of the countries that claimed to be communist, but which were in reality bureaucratic collectivists or even totalitarian states.

First of all, communism is supposed to be a "stateless society." This means that government does not control the state, simply because one cannot control something that does not exist. Second, democracy is indeed incompatible with communism but for an absolutely contradictory reason. They are incompatible because communism is a society of complete freedom, whereas democracy is a system of limited freedom: it only protects the interests of the majority. Since all can vote, it seems that all have equal say in a democracy. However, in a democratic system, the majority wins and everything is decided and ruled by the majority – which can harm individuals in the minority. Thus, individuals representing the minority have no protection against the unlimited power of the majority, so democracy allows the tyranny of the majority over the minority.

Despite this inequality, democracy is required to build communism. It is essential to transform capitalism into communism. Then, when communism has fully arisen, democracy will no longer be necessary, because it will gradually be replaced with complete freedom. The founders of scientific communism expressed it in crystal clarity. In *The Communist Manifesto,* Marx and Engels state that "the first step in the revolution by the working class is to raise the proletariat to the position of ruling class, to win the battle of democracy." [3] In *The State and Revolution,* Lenin wrote that "democracy is of enormous importance to the working class in its struggle against the capitalists for its emancipation." [4]

Ultimately, however, the goal of communism is to replace democracy – freedom for the majority – with freedom for all. As *The Communist Manifesto* states, communism is a system "in which the free development of each is the condition for the free development of all." [3] Complete freedom is one of the main goals of communism that cannot be substituted or replaced, and here is how Marx and Engels viewed this, in words that may seem startling to those who have always associated communism with the USSR: "We are not among those communists who are out to destroy personal liberty, who wish to turn the world into one huge barrack or into a gigantic workhouse. There certainly are some communists who, with an easy conscience, refuse to countenance personal liberty and would like to shuffle it out of the world because they consider that it is a hindrance to complete harmony. But we have no desire to exchange freedom for equality." [5]

Communism may sound like an ideal society to some and a frightening society to others. The idea of great wealth, complete freedom, and working only if one wishes holds a natural appeal for many people. But daunting scenarios have also been painted. For example, some say that personal property and even the family unit will have to disappear, while children and spouses will have to be shared. It is not clear why this would necessarily happen. In truth, communism does not prohibit either personal property or the family structure as we know it.

In *The Communist Manifesto*, Marx and Engels refer to the whole social development before communism as "the prehistory of human society." However, communism is a hypothetical idea, and whether or not such a society will ever be built is unknown. Philosophy suggests that it might be impossible (see Chapter 3), because communism is a perfect, ideal and absolute society. One can move toward an absolute, but can never reach it.

Summary

Communism is a hypothetical socio-economic system in which material distribution is based on need and social relations are based on freely associated individuals. The foundation of communism is a strong economy that provides a superabundance of material goods to all. In modern times, communism is often confused with authoritarian left-wing regimes and even dictatorships. In contrast to autocracy or dictatorship, communism aims to provide complete freedom to all of its members.

Capitalism cannot be transformed into communism suddenly; there must be a transitional phase between capitalism and communism, called socialism, which can also be considered as the first or lower stage of communism.

References

1. Holmes, L. Communism: A Very Short Intoduction, published by Oxford University Press (2009).
2. Marx, K., Engels, F. The German Ideology (1846), published by International Publishers (2007).
3. Marx, K., Engels, F. The Communist Manifesto (1848), published by Verso (1998).
4. Lenin, V. I. The State and Revolution (1917), *Marxists.org web site* (retrieved 2015, July 1).
5. Marx, K., Engels, F. *Communist Journal* (1847, September).

Chapter 2

A Brief History of Communism

The idea of communism can be traced as far back as Ancient Greece. Around 380 BCE, Plato wrote his famous book *The Republic,* in large part to address the question of which society functions better: the just or unjust. He described a society that embraced the idea of something that we know today as communism: a society that limits everything private, from property to families: "... the private and individual is altogether banished from life, and things which are by nature private, such as eyes and ears and hands, have become common, and in some way see and hear and act in common, and all men express praise and blame and feel joy and sorrow on the same occasions ..." [1]

Plato's pupil, Aristotle, questioned whether such a society was possible and if society's problems lay in material possessions. He came to the conclusion that the root of social problems was not in possessions, but rather in the human desire to be equal. This finding is still debated today. However, Karl Marx and Friedrich Engels later stepped around – and perhaps solved – this problem by suggesting that a communist society will have such an abundance of possessions that everybody will have as much as he or she wants; thus, nobody will feel unequal.

The first known movement that is related by some scholars to communism was the revolt of slaves led by Spartacus in the Roman Empire (73 BCE). Although the goal of the revolt was to end slavery, not to build a communist society, it inspired communist movements throughout history and even unto our own time. However, Spartacus's revolt was not a real communist movement, but rather a fight for human rights. Similar clashes took place in many countries without leading to an establishment of socialist or communist governments. The Civil War against slavery in America is a good example.

The first real communist movement took place in 490-520 CE, in territories that comprise present-day Iran. It was organized by a religious activist named Mazdak, for whom the movement was named. Mazdak followed the Zoroastrian religion but believed that it needed to be purified. He wanted to reduce the importance of religious formalities and oppression of the population by the clergy. According to Mazdak, God provided the means for people to exist comfortably if those means were divided equally. However, the strong claimed the means excessively, causing inequality, which resulted in empowering demons: Envy, Vengeance, Wrath, Need and Greed. Therefore, Mazdak believed that in order to prevail over evil and restore order, one must redistribute wealth and make it commonly owned. As one would expect, his followers were mostly urban poor and the peasantry. However, the movement was significantly strengthened when the current ruler, Kavadh I, also became a supporter. For several years, the Mazdakites appeared to be successful: they were able to curtail the privileges of the aristocracy and pass unprecedented social reforms. However, Kavadh I eventually separated from the movement, and it was crushed.

The next significant development in communist ideology did not come until the Renaissance, about one thousand years later, when English statesman and humanist Thomas More (1478-1535) wrote *Utopia*. Printed in 1516, More's book describes the imaginary island of Utopia, where no one is rich or poor. On this island, all people work collectively and receive everything they need free of charge. The author came very close to the communist principle "from each according to abilities, to each according to needs," formulated by Marx and Engels three centuries later. The needs on this imaginary island were very limited, and modest living kept everyone in peace. More's vision is in contrast to Marxism, in which the reason people choose not to fight in a communist society is the presence of a strong economy rather than mere modesty. Naturally, when there is enough of everything for everybody, there is nothing to fight about.

In *Utopia*, More came to the conclusion that complete justice, physical/intellectual development and happiness are impossible in a society wherein the minority takes wealth created by the majority. The narrator of his story says: "…I am quite convinced that you'll never get a fair distribution of goods, or a satisfactory organization of human life, until you abolish private property altogether. So long as it exists, the vast majority of the human race, and the vast superior part of it, will inevitably go on laboring under a burden of poverty, hardship and worry." The principal character of the book sharply criticizes inequality and exploitation of the poor by the rich: "In fact, when I consider any social system that prevails in the modern world, I can't, so help me God, see it as anything but a conspiracy of the rich to advance their own interests under the pretext of organizing society. They think of all sorts of tricks and dodges, first for keeping safe their ill-gotten gains, and then for exploiting the poor by buying their labour as cheaply as possible." Thus, *Utopia* significantly advanced the idea that private ownership must be replaced with common ownership. From that point forward, criticism of private property became a constant reality in different societies.

Soon after the publication of *Utopia*, one of the most serious attempts to establish a communist society took place in Germany. In 1534-1535, the Anabaptists, inspired by the Bible's call for the equality of man in all spheres (including the distribution of wealth), established a theocracy in the city of Münster. They shared all goods but were quickly pushed to starvation, the result of a siege by the army of the Lutheran prince-bishop of Saxony. After one year of resistance, the community was crushed, while the most prominent Anabaptist leaders were captured, tortured and executed.

The idea again resurfaced in 17th century England with a Puritan religious group called "Diggers" who advocated collective ownership of land and a kind of agrarian communism. It again appeared during the Age of Enlightenment (18th century), and since then has maintained a strong presence all the way to our times.

With the Age of Enlightenment, authorities were brought to questioning and communist ideas began to spread. These ideas were developed by French thinkers like Jean Jacques Rousseau (1712-1778), who argued that private property was the reason for inequity, murders and wars. Soon after, during the French Revolution, Sylvain Maréchal wrote *Manifesto of the Equals (1796)*, in which he criticized "the revolting distinction of rich and poor, of great and small, of masters and valets, of governors and governed" and promoted the idea that there "shall be no buying or selling, no fairs nor markets, but the whole earth shall be a common treasury for every man." [2]

Following the French Revolution (1789-1799), communism as a developed theory finally emerged as a political doctrine. French revolutionary Francois-Noël Babeuf (1760-1797) and his supporters (the Babouvists), decided that revolution was the only way to end exploitation and bring equality. The Babouvists believed that such a revolution could be accomplished by a small group of brave conspirators, who would seize power and build a society of equals. They thought that this would require a revolutionary dictatorship – an idea that was further developed by Marx and Engels as something they called "the dictatorship of the proletariat." The very word "communism" also originated around this time, and was coined in 1840 by Goodwyn Barmby in his conversation with the Babouvists.

French intellectuals continued developing communist ideas in the 19th century. Economist Henri de Saint-Simon (1760-1825) originated a related theory that, in order to have a better society that could lift the lower classes from poverty, one must build a stronger economy through industrialization. He foresaw that the key to progress in this goal was science. He also advocated that only the men who were most fit to organize society should rule it. Finally, he believed that a new economy would bring new politics as well as social improvements. This echoes the thoughts of Marx and Engels that the foundation for a communist society is a strong economy.

Another French intellectual, Francois Marie Charles Fourier (1772-1837), was a sharp critic of the capitalist system, which he saw as nothing more than the art of robbing the poor for the benefit of the rich. He became best known for his ideas of a new world order based on harmonious collaboration among people. According to Fourier, the secret to social success was cooperation and unity of action, while the main cause for social problems was poverty. His ideas took root as far away as America, where his followers founded several communities that practiced them. The best-known community was Utopia in Ohio, which was founded in 1844 and lasted about three decades.

In addition to France, the Age of Enlightenment also came to most other European countries, including Germany and Great Britain. In Germany, new philosophical views that became the foundation for Marxism were developed. Georg Hegel (1770-1831) introduced a dialectic understanding of the world, while Ludwig Feuerbach (1804-1872) laid down the groundwork for a materialistic understanding of the world. Together, the dialectic of Hegel and the materialism of Feuerbach gave rise to the dialectic materialism and historical materialism of Marxism (see Chapter 3 for more details).

In Britain, Adam Smith and David Ricardo showed that the economic structure of society is a reason for the existence of classes, while Robert Owen began practicing communist ideas. Adam Smith (1723-1790) laid the foundations of the free market economy and pioneered political economy. His work *An Inquiry into the Nature and Causes of the Wealth of Nations (1776)* became a precursor to the modern economics discipline and Marx's labor theory of value. David Ricardo (1772-1823), was among the first to question the sustainability of the economic system of capitalism. He observed that as the population of Europe grew, land prices also increased. In his book *Principles of Political Economy and Taxation (1817),* he projected that the trend could only continue, which would result in growing inequality and upset the social equilibrium. As a solution, he proposed that governments levy an increasing tax on landlords.

British businessman and social reformer Robert Owen (1771-1858) became one of the first socialists who actively participated in the working class movement. He laid a foundation for social programs that is now accepted in most modern societies, including capitalist nations. Being a co-owner of a large textile factory, he reduced the working day hours from 13-14 to 10.5. He also promoted the adoption of the first law limiting child labor and organized the world's first kindergarten for the children of workers. Welfare programs and labor unions of today owe their existence to Owen and his supporters. Owen believed that caring about employees' welfare was good business practice – an idea that has become more widely accepted in our times. He did not, however, believe that social revolutions were necessary to improve society, but rather that capitalism's problems originated from man's ignorance, and that the system would improve with the enlightenment of the people. Like Fourier's followers, Owen attempted to create a utopian community. In 1825, he founded the New Harmony community in Indiana, in the U.S.; however, it failed after two years.

As one can see, throughout the course of at least two thousand years, there have been many ideas about how to build communism. However, all attempts to do this were short-lived. Why was this? What was wrong with these ideas? Karl Marx (1818-1883) and Friedrich Engels (1820-1895), who were born in Germany but lived out their lives in Great Britain, made a detailed scientific analysis and provided possible answers.* They proposed that the foundation for any society is the economy, and as the economy changed, social relationships and structure would follow. According to them, people must "obtain food and drink, housing and clothing in adequate quality and quantity" before attending to spiritual needs.

They rejected the abstractionist view on human society and developed the theory that man's thinking and actions depend on the environment. People have to meet all of their material needs in order to be happy and live in harmony. Thus, communism is impossible without an advanced economy, and all previous attempts to build communism were simply premature. Marx and Engels described all previous opinions on communism as "utopian," in contrast to their own views, which were later called "scientific" by their followers.

Marx and Engels asserted that since economy always develops and grows, the transformation of capitalism into communism is inevitable. They argued that communism could not be built suddenly at the will of the people, but rather step by step. Before communism, capitalism would enter a "first stage" of communism, in which most productive properties would be commonly owned but class differences were not yet completely erased. Later, Lenin named this first stage "socialism."

Marx and Engels saw communism as the only type of society that allows complete freedom and realization of talents. In *The German Ideo-*

---

* *Marx wrote most of his works in collaboration with Engels. Unfortunately, Engels is usually not credited. When people say "Marx," they usually mean "Marx and Engels." The author will not follow this practice and will credit them both for the work that they have done in collaboration.*

logy (1846), they explained the difference between communism and preceding societies as follows: "As soon as the distribution of labor comes into being, each man has a particular, exclusive sphere of activity, which is forced upon him and from which he cannot escape. He is a hunter, a fisherman, a herdsman, or a critic, and must remain so if he does not want to lose his means of livelihood; while in communist society, where nobody has one exclusive sphere of activity, but each can become accomplished in any branch he wishes, society regulates the general production and thus makes it possible for me to do one thing today and another tomorrow, to hunt in the morning, fish in the afternoon, rear cattle in the evening, criticize after dinner, just as I have a mind, without ever becoming hunter, fisherman, herdsman or critic." More than that, such a complete realization of man's abilities is what would make communism the most productive and prosperous society.

In 1848, Marx and Engels wrote their famous pamphlet *The Communist Manifesto* to popularize the idea of communism. The same year, Europe saw the biggest wave of revolutionary activity in its history: the Year of Revolution. These were essentially bourgeoisie-democratic revolutions aimed at removing the old feudal structure. However, they were suppressed and crushed within a year.

Following the awakening activities of 1848, the first major international organization addressing interests of the working class, the International Workingmen's Association, was founded. In 1864, it united communist, left-wing socialist, trade union, and anarchist organizations and became known as the First International. Marx and Engels soon became leaders of the organization, guiding its activities.

In 1871, the first proletarian revolution took place in France. This revolution attempted to establish a state of the working people, the Paris Commune, but it was defeated within a few months. Marxists have many explanations for the Paris Commune failure: intellectual and organizational immaturity of the working class, lack of contact with the peasants, and others. However, the fundamental reason appears to be the same as the one for all previous failures to establish communism: the attempt was premature, as the economy in France was not sufficiently developed to build communism. The central principle of building communism – a strong economy (see Chapter 3) – had been ignored, and remains ignored in our time.

The communist movement during this period was tightly associated with social democracy, which is no longer considered to be a part of the communist movement. Social democracy originated in Germany, and was based on the views of Ferdinand Lassalle (1825-1864), who advocated a peaceful reformist approach to the transformation of capitalism. Lassalle founded the first major working-class party in Europe: the General German Workers' Association. In 1869, August Bebel and Wilhelm Liebknecht merged this party with other movements to form the Social Democratic Workers' Party of Germany (SDAP). Marx and Engels joined the SDAP, and this party became the first major working-class organization led by Marxists (communists).

Events in Britain reinforced the idea of a peaceful transformation of capitalism into communism through reforms. In 1871, Britain legalized trade (labor) unions, which opened opportunities to improve the living conditions of the working class through parliamentary means. This action prompted Marx to suggest that transformation from capitalism to communism could take place peacefully in some countries. At the Hague Congress in 1872, Marx declared: "We know that the institutions, customs and traditions in the different countries must be taken into account; and we do not deny the existence of countries like America, England, and ... I might add Holland, where the workers may achieve their aims by peaceful means. But this is not true for all countries." [3] Indeed, in 1878, German Chancellor Otto von Bismarck enacted anti-socialist laws, and Germany moved in the opposite direction.

Marxist ideas soon became popular in Russia, where Georgi Plekhanov (1856-1918) became one of the first famous followers of Marx. Consistent with Marxist ideas, Plekhanov asserted that Russia, being less industrialized than other countries in Western Europe, was still a long time away from communist revolution. However, Vladimir Lenin (1870-1924) quickly changed these views. Lenin argued that no teaching was dogma, and that Marx's theories needed further development. But Lenin went even further and changed their very core. Lenin's teachings are now called Marxism-Leninism.

Lenin claimed that Marx was wrong in his belief that revolutions would first take place in the most economically developed countries.

Instead, Lenin suggested that they could first occur in the weakest capitalist countries, such as Russia: the weakest link would break first! In defiance of the core ideas of Marxism, he also claimed that Marx and Engels were wrong about the gradual arrival of communism in most countries in the world at the same time. Instead, he suggested that communism could first be established in Russia alone. Being a talented organizer and leveraging the desperate situation in Russia (which exhibited an enormous gap between the rich and the poor), Lenin managed to lead Russia to a socialist revolution in 1917. The revolution succeeded and quickly expanded to neighboring countries.

In 1919, the communist movement split based on the support of World War I and the Socialist Revolution in Russia. Those who believed that capitalism could be transformed into communism through revolution (revolutionary Marxists) began to consider themselves genuine communists. The rest were classified as reformists and revisionists. Social democracy became the largest reformist movement and predominated in parties affiliated with the Second International. This split caused revolutionary Marxists to break away and form their own organization, the Third International. As a result, although social democrats had their origins in Marxism, they were no longer called communists. Only followers of revolutionary Marxism became regarded as communists. Moreover, after World War II, most social democrats had completely abandoned their adherence to Marxism and became more focused on reforms as a tool for transitioning from capitalism to socialism. Social Democratic parties became popular in Europe and, after World War II, came to power in countries like West Germany, Great Britain (the Labour Party) and Sweden, laying the foundation for modern social welfare programs. They are now an important part of many Western governments.

In 1922, based on Soviet Russia, the Union of Soviet Socialists Republics (the USSR) was created. Following the teachings of Marx and Engels, the revolutionary leadership (Bolsheviks) immediately installed "the dictatorship of the proletariat." Despite the Marxist idea that it should be temporary – just long enough to crush the resistance of the bourgeoisie – the dictatorship never withered away. Lenin's successor, Joseph Stalin (1878-1953), further strengthened this system instead of disassembling it (see more details in Chapter 7).

World War II greatly facilitated the expansion of the Soviet system. Several major battles in this war were fought between the USSR and Nazi Germany. One of them, the Battle of Stalingrad (1942-1943), became the bloodiest battle in human history and the first truly serious loss for the Nazi army. This battle showed that the powerful Nazi army was not invincible, and ultimately became the turning point of the war. Although there is some debate about the exact number of German military losses on different fronts, it is agreed that Soviet forces killed more German military personnel than all other forces combined. This fact is recognized even in America. For example, *The Washington Post* recently reported that "the Germans suffered three-quarters of their wartime losses fighting the Red Army." [4] This victory made the Soviet regime more attractive, and several countries around the world, primarily in Europe, have since joined the Soviet system.

World War II also contributed to the rise of the Communist Party of China, led by Mao Zedong (1893-1976). Following World War II, the Chinese Communists crushed U.S.-backed armies of the Kuomintang and by 1949 had gained control of China, establishing the People's Republic of China. For the next few decades, the Communist Party of China tried to establish new methods of economic and social organization, but to no avail. Its "Great Leap Forward" and "Great Cultural Revolution" failed and became a national disaster (see Chapter 9). After the death of Mao, under the leadership of Deng Xiaoping, China began focusing on its economy, which, according to classical Marxism, is the true foundation of communism. From 1978, Chinese leadership turned to capitalism and allowed a free market economy, which became known as a socialist market economy. This approach was enormously successful and lifted out of poverty the greatest number (hundreds of millions) of people that the world ever saw. China continues to advance its economy, and its path is now successfully emulated by other developing countries like Vietnam.

As stated earlier, the communist idea has been promoted by all the principal religions, spanning thousands of years in history. Strangely, this fact is either ignored or overlooked by both Marxists and anti-Marxists. It is widely acknowledged that religions promote the idea of helping the poor and harshly criticize the human obsession with material wealth. The Christian bible very clearly states that "it is easier for a camel to go through the eye of a needle than for a rich man to enter the kingdom of God." Christianity promotes the directive to share wealth for a common good. For example, verse 44 from the New Testament reads: "Now all who believed were together, and had all things in common." and verse 45 reads: "and sold their possessions and goods, and divided them among all, as anyone had need." [5] The latter verse sounds nearly identical to the Marxist principle of communism: "to each according to need."

Communism strives to be a moneyless society, as everything in such a society would be available for free and nobody would be paid. Saint Paul famously said that "the love of money is the root of all evil," and the love of money – or greed – is widely considered immoral by most religions. Therefore, "the root of all evil," according to most spiritual traditions, will be absent in communist society and should be considered welcome by anyone, no matter what their religion.

Considering how religions and Marxism appear to have shared goals, it is surprising that Marxists completely rejected religion. Marx famously wrote, and Lenin reiterated, that "religion is the opiate of the masses." On the other side of the coin, the overlapping ideology of communism and religion makes the complete rejection of communist ideas by Western governments even more surprising, considering that the Christian religion dominates Western countries. In the most powerful capitalist country, the U.S., 19.6% of the population is unaffiliated with any religion, while 73% identify as Christians, and the Christian phrase "In God We Trust" is printed on all U.S. currency. However, only 20% of the population favors socialist/communist ideas, as found by Rasmussen Reports in 2009. The only possible explanation for this is that communism has been seriously misrepresented and misunderstood. Hopefully, this book will help to correct this.

Summary

The idea of communism has more than 2,000 years of history and is supported by all the great religions. Modern understanding of communism is based largely on Marxism, which suggests that communist societies cannot be created without successful economies already in place. Before Marxism, many attempts to build communism without taking the economy into account had been made and had failed. After Marx and Engels, Marxism has either been distorted or ignored, which has led to even more failed attempts to establish communism.

References

1. Pipes, R. Communism: A History, published by The Modern Library (2001).
2. Graham, G. Anarchism - A Documentary History of Libertarian Ideas, volume 1, published by Black Rose Books (2004).
3. Ishay, M. R. The History of Human Rights: From Ancient Times to the Globalization, published by University of California Press (2008).
4. Tharoor, I. Don't forget how the Soviet Union saved the world from Hitler. *The Washington Post* (2015, May 8).
5. New Testament, acts 2 and 3, chapter 2, published by The Gideons Internationals (1995).

Chapter 3

Philosophy and Communism

A ll philosophical systems must answer one fundamental question: what is the relation of consciousness to being? Depending on the answer, these systems are divided into two: idealism and materialism. Idealism proceeds from the premise that consciousness is primary and being is secondary, while materialism proceeds from the opposite: being is primary and consciousness is secondary. Accordingly, idealists believe that communism can be established at any time depending on the people's wishes, while materialists believe that communism requires certain material conditions, and that once these conditions are met, communism will arise regardless of the people's wishes.

Prior to Marx, idealism dominated in social science. Pre-Marxist philosophers believed that social development was moved only by the ideas of people and by their consciousness. In their view, the course of human actions is determined either by exceptional individuals or by God and spirit.

Marx and Engels contrasted this view with a materialistic interpretation of history, and placed the principle of economic determinism at the heart of the theory of communism. They developed ideas according to which the social being and the production of material values determine social consciousness. They saw that the development of society depends on material causes more than people's ideas, wishes or intentions. Before people can engage in art, philosophy or science, they must obtain food, clothing and shelter, for which they must work to produce this material wealth. Modes of production, the most vital part of which is comprised of tools and instruments, determine social development. One of Marx's best-known descriptions of history is contained in the preface to *A Contribution to the Critique of Political Economy (1859)*: "In the social production of their life, men enter into definite relations that are indispensable and independent of their will, relations of production which correspond to a definite stage of development of their material productive forces. The sum total of these relations of production constitutes the economic structure of society, the real foundation, on which rises a legal and political superstructure and to which correspond definite forms of social consciousness. The mode of production of material life conditions the social, political and intellectual life process in general. It is not the consciousness of men that determines their being, but, on the contrary, their social being that determines their consciousness."

The materialist approach to society is well put in the book *Why Marx Was Right* by Terence Eagleton: Marx "...was aware that the ideas which really grip men and women arise through their routine practice, not through the disclosure of philosophers or debating societies. If you want to see what men and women really believe, look what they do, not what they say." [1] Modern theories of communism connect to Marxism in one way or another and as such, let's analyze the philosophy behind Marxism.

Philosophy of Marxism

Marxist philosophy bases itself on a philosophical system known as dialectical materialism (or materialistic dialectic). It is materialistic because it recognizes that matter/being is primary while spirit/consciousness is secondary. It is dialectical because it sees the material world in constant development from lower to higher. As mentioned in Chapter 2, this philosophy originates from the dialectic views of Georg Hegel (1770-1831) and the materialistic views of Ludwig Feuerbach (1804-1872).

In his most important work, *The Essence of Christianity (1841)*, Feuerbach came to the conclusion that God is nothing but "the outward projection of a human's inward nature." In other words, spirit/consciousness is the product of matter/being. This observation laid the groundwork for Marx's materialism, as well as his belief that being is primary and consciousness is secondary.

Hegel introduced the term "dialectic" to describe a logical process for the stepwise movement of ideas that follows a pattern of laws. As was well articulated in one of the Soviet textbooks, "the term maintains that the world is an endless process of movement, regeneration, the demise of the old and the birth of the new. It maintains that the world is endless ascendancy from the lower to higher. Furthermore, it views the internal contradictions inherent in objects and phenomena as the source of motion and development." [2] In contrast, non-dialectical philosophy interprets development only as a simple repetition of what already exists and as a quantitative increase or decrease. It does not recognize internal contradictions as a source of development and the emergence of the new.

One should note that the term was not Hegel's invention. In ancient Greece, Plato defined dialectic as a logical process that employs argumentation based on thesis and antithesis. In modern philosophy, this process is called the "method of the contrary case."

Dialectical materialism maintains that the source of any development is the conflict of opposites. In the inorganic world, for example, it is the conflict between the opposite forces of attraction and repulsion. It plays a great part in the rise, existence and destruction of atoms and molecules. It is also the most important source of the birth and fall of the universe. One force always prevails over the other. For example, when repulsion predominates, matter and energy disperse and stars die, and when attraction prevails, matter and energy come together, giving rise to new stars.

Opposites do not simply exist side by side, but in a state of constant contradiction and conflict between themselves. Contradictions can be antagonistic and non-antagonistic. The most influential school of communism, Marxism-Leninism, maintains that, in the sphere of social phenomena, antagonistic contradictions are those between classes, whose interests are irreconcilably hostile. Marxist-Leninists believe that the antagonism between the bourgeoisie and the proletariat is a perfect example of such irreconcilable contradictions, and a violent social revolution is the only means to resolve them.

Marx and Engels believed that Hegel had found a general law explaining human history. According to Hegel, the main engine that moves this process is the struggle between nations, which moves nations toward the realization of their spirits. The end of this process is "the absolute idea" and thus a spiritual (metaphysical) phenomenon.

Marx and Engels accepted the study of Hegel about the dialectic, but opposed the notion of "the soul of a nation" and that the struggle between nations is the leading engine of human history. Instead, they developed the theory in which the leading force of history is the struggle between classes, and explained this process in economic rather than spiritual terms. In *The Communist Manifesto*, Marx and Engels declare: "The history of all hitherto existing society is the history of class struggles. Freeman and slave, patrician and plebeian, lord and serf, guild master and journeyman, in a word, oppressor and oppressed, stood in constant opposition to another, carried and interrupted, now hidden, now open fight, that each ended, either in revolutionary reconstitution of society at large, or in the common ruin of the contending classes." [3]

Marx and Engels revealed that dialectical materialism applies not only to nature but also to society, creating the theory of social development called historical materialism (historicism). Of course, this theory did not rise like a sudden revelation. Besides Hegel's dialectic and Feuerbach's materialism, many ideas contributing to historical materialism had already been expressed. For example, French historians (Francois Guizot, Augustin Thierry, and Francois Mignet) pointed to the existence of social classes and their struggle. British economists (Adam Smith and David Ricardo) had shown that economic life is a reason for the existence of classes. Utopian socialists (Francois Fourier and Robert Owen) envisioned and attempted to practice communist society.

According to historical materialism, the history of society is a natural process of the replacement of lower modes of production by higher ones. It is not a spontaneous but rather an objective process that is independent of man's will and consciousness. A popular textbook called *Philosophy Made Simple* provides an excellent description of Marxist views on human history:

> "Everything contains two opposing forces, one is called the thesis, the other is called the antithesis. These two forces destroy

each other, but from the destruction arises a new situation which is called synthesis. Eventually, the synthesis breaks down into its opposites – and we have a new thesis and new antithesis. And then out of these opposing forces arises a new synthesis – and so on. The Marxists, as we shall indicate, make use of this idea in order to demonstrate that communism, as a society, is ethically superior to all previous existing societies.

The historical king-state society, according to Marxists, broke down into its opposites – the king-rulers, on the one hand, and the dispossessed and slaves on the other hand. From the struggle between these opposites, a synthesis was formed, and the feudalism, then, broke down into its opposing forces, the lords and serfs; and this struggle was synthesized and modern capitalism was born. And, now, the Marxists claim that capitalism has broken down into its opposites; the employers, on the one hand, and the employees, on the other hand. The new society, according to the Marxists, will be Marxian socialism. The Marxists argue that each new society is ethically more superior to the society that existed before. Feudalism, they claim, is superior to the king-state; capitalism to feudalism; and communism to capitalistic societies.

...The Marxists claim that they do not create the class struggle; they claim, rather, that they merely show its existence, and then make use of it in order to foster the growth of communism. The additional belief of the Marxists, that each distinctly new society is ethically superior to the old social forms, makes excellent propaganda for Marxism. Undoubtedly, many people become slavishly adherent to communism because they believe that they are working for a world that is better than anything that has ever existed." [4]

Marx and Engels went even further to conclude that although the laws of historical materialism are objective (independent of man's consciousness), they are knowable. Thus, knowing the laws, one can predict the future of human development. This future, according to Marxist philosophy, is communism.

Criticism of Historical Materialism (Historicism)

Of course, not everybody has accepted Marxist theory. The most popular criticism of the theory has been provided in the last century by Karl Popper,[5] who refuted Marx's "historicism" views as follows:

1. The course of human history is strongly influenced by the growth of human knowledge.
2. We cannot predict, by rational or scientific methods, the future growth of our scientific knowledge.
3. We cannot, therefore, predict the future course of human history.
4. This means that we must reject the possibility of a theoretical history, and there can be no scientific theory of historical development serving as a basis for historical prediction.
5. The fundamental aim of historical methods is therefore misconceived; and historicism collapses.

This criticism sounds very logical and scientific, and defenders of capitalism like to refer to Popper's logic. However, this logic is undermined by one word in the very first sentence: "influenced." This word changes the entire outcome. Marx himself would probably agree with the statement "the course of human history is strongly influenced by the growth of human knowledge." Although it is "influenced," it does not mean that it is "determined." Marx demonstrated that while the course of human history is strongly influenced by the growth of human knowledge, it is in fact determined by the growth of the economy. And the growth of the economy is determined by the mode of production and the instruments/machinery employed in the economy.

Thus, since one can predict the future growth of our economy, one can also predict the course of societal development. Naturally, it is neither easy nor straightforward, but it is possible. As a confirmation of this, many economists, institutions and governmental organizations now attempt to forecast economic growth over the next few months, years and even decades. Many major financial institutions, such as Goldman Sachs in the U.S. or the United Bank of Switzerland, periodically publish projections for global economic growth. The World Bank and the International Monetary Fund (IMF) regularly issue global economic outlooks. Most governments have offices to project future economic growth, for example the Congressional Budget Office in the U.S. At this point, it is widely accepted that future economic growth is predictable. Since economic growth determines human history, one can also predict human society's future. Therefore, Popper's logic is misconceived from the very beginning and does not disprove the logic of Marx.

Popper and his followers also ridiculed Marx's theory by saying that it leads to the view that human society should be modeled according to a definite blueprint, and that it demands that we "mold" men and women to fit a new society. Once again, this interpretation arises from the careless use of words. Marx's theories suggest the general direction in which society will develop, but they do not specify dates and events that will necessarily take place during this development. Marxist theory only indicates what will happen eventually, but with no details of when and how. With these unknowns, we should not try to "mold" our society according to a blueprint. Moreover, the core of Marx's analysis is the revelation that the structure of human society is based on the economy and is dictated by economic growth. Thus, quite to the contrary, Marx's theory suggests that human society will undergo certain stages of developments regardless of our wishes or attempts to "mold" anything.

Historical materialism maintains that the leading force in history is the struggle between classes, and this struggle is dictated by economy. Critiques of historical materialism argue that the role of class struggle is overvalued in Marxist analysis while the forces of nationalism and ethnic rivalries are underestimated. If so, then who was right: Marx or Hegel, who advocated that the leading force in human history is the struggle between nations?

Philosophy maintains that practice is the sole criterion of truth: "We can argue as much as we like about the true character of any idea or scientific theory, but this dispute can only be settled by practice, i.e. in economic production, political life or scientific experiment." [2] In his work *Theses on Feuerbach*, Marx himself writes: "Man must prove the truth... of his thinking in practice." So, let's find out what that practice (history) tells us about historical materialism.

History as the Judge of Historical Materialism

As mentioned above, Hegel believed that the main force driving human history is the struggle between nations. Marx and Engels dismissed this belief as idealistic and proposed a materialistic view: the primary force driving human history is the struggle between classes. Let's see what practice (history) tells us about the role of these two forces.

Struggle Between Classes – Marx and Engels believed that the struggle between classes is the driving force of human society. Vladimir Lenin in Russia went further. He claimed that the contradictions between the bourgeoisie and the proletariat in any capitalist society are antagonistic and irreconcilable, which inevitably leads to revolutions, as only revolutions can resolve such contradictions. This claim laid the foundation for the most prevalent interpretation of Marxism, known as Marxism-Leninism (see details in Chapter 4).

If the Marxist-Leninist view is correct, then how many proletarian/communist revolutions have taken place since Lenin claimed this? The answer is: very few, and almost none in West European countries – the most developed capitalist countries that are supposed to be the ripest for revolution. Does this disprove Marxism-Leninism? Or could it be that this contradiction became antagonistic in countries like Russia but non-antagonistic in others?

History shows that this could be the case. Regarding the gap between the rich and poor, the upper and the lower class, Russia stood out among all capitalist countries. For two centuries before the revolution in 1917, the gap was wider in Russia than anywhere else. Since the time of Elizabeth, who became empress in 1741, foreigners were amazed at the sheer luxury of Russian aristocratic life and contrasting poverty of the lower class. Although concrete data on this gap is not available, the picture can be drawn from Russian literature of the time, which often describes the sumptuous formal balls of aristocrats and the misery of the workers. Another facet of the relationship between the upper and lower classes in Russia at this time is even more telling: commonly, members of the aristocracy would despicably refer to the lower class as "chern," which literally translates as "blackness" and means "mob or dirt." This label suggests that the relationship between these two classes in Russia was indeed "hostile."

No gap of this magnitude between the upper and lower classes existed in other developed capitalist countries. Moreover, bourgeoisie around the world offered more and more concessions to the working class, which made the contradictions less antagonistic and less hostile. These included shorter working hours, higher salaries, retirement programs, health care programs, etc. The ability to move from the working class to the aristocracy and vice versa in modern day capitalist countries has increased. In modern times, some workers save money, invest and become rich within years. Some of them have great ideas, open new businesses and become rich within months. Opposite things are also not unusual – it becomes more common for rich individuals to lose their money and drop down to the working class.

Marxist-Leninists claim that the only reason revolutions did not take place in advanced capitalist countries is because these countries colonized the developing world. This expansion allowed them to extract additional wealth, which was used "to bribe" the working class at home, reducing the conditions for revolution. This view could be accepted a century ago, but there are no colonies today. Yes, advanced capitalist nations do business and manufacture goods in developing countries cheaply, and some may argue that this is a source of wealth for them. However, not all advanced capitalist nations do this. Nations like Finland, Denmark, Austria and Norway have no significant manufacturing business in the developing world, yet they are among the richest countries with the most satisfied working class.

Thus, history demonstrates that a Leninist interpretation of Marxism is not quite correct: the contradictions between the bourgeoisie and the proletariat can be reconciled, and they can either be antagonistic (as was the case in Russia) or non-antagonistic (as was true in all major developed capitalist countries). It is up to the bourgeoisie that leads governments to decide their direction. If the upper class abuses its power, then the contradictions may become antagonistic, revolutions will follow, and the upper class will be overthrown.

Struggle Between Nations – Although class struggle is an undeniably important force in history, it appears that the feeling of belonging to a nation can be stronger than the sense of belonging to a class. History illustrates this over and over again. Whenever wars between nations break out, people fight to defend their country and nationality rather than uniting to defend their class regardless of nationality. National loyalties supersede class loyalties. The book *Communism: A History* [6] provides two convincing examples of this.

The first example is illustrated by events preceding World War I. Marxists believed that workers of all countries are brothers, and they have the responsibility to prevent wars unleashed by capitalism. They organized the Second International and unanimously adopted resolutions calling on socialist parliamentarians to vote against war. They also called "to rouse the masses and thereby hasten the downfall of capitalist class rule" in the case of war. "Unfortunately for them, the socialists and their International proved utterly powerless to prevent the general European war that erupted in the summer of 1914. Talk of general strike led nowhere. To make matters worse still, both German Social Democrats and French Socialists, contrary to their solemn pledges, voted for war credits, thereby completely discrediting the notion of international worker solidarity." [6]

The second example came from the war between Poland and Russia in 1920:

> "Poland, eager to forestall the reemergence of a strong and imperialist Russia, had made a common cause with Ukrainian nationalists and invaded the Socialist Ukraine with the aim of detaching it from Russia. The invasion failed to ignite an uprising in the Ukraine, and the Polish armies soon found themselves in full retreat.
>
> As the Red Army approached the borders of ethnic Poland, the Politburo, the directing organ of the Communist Party, had to decide whether to stop or to continue advancing westward. Opinions were divided but Lenin insisted on offensive operations, and as by now was always the case, he had his way. He felt that both Germany and England were ripe for revolution, which the appearance of Communist armed forces on their borders would help to ignite. In the summer of 1920, the Red

Army, accompanied by Soviet commissars of Polish origin, entered Poland. It broadcasted appeals calling on Polish workers and peasants to seize properties of the bourgeois and landlords – slogans that had proved very effective in Russia. But Poles of all classes rallied to defend newly won Polish sovereignty. In the battle for Warsaw, one of the decisive battles of modern history, they repulsed and scattered the Communist army. Lenin could not conceal his bitterness at this outcome. 'In the Red Army the Poles saw enemies, but not brothers and liberators,' he complained." [6]

The more recent collapse of the USSR and Yugoslavia is another confirmation of the significance of the struggle between nations. During the Cold War, the U.S. and its Western allies counted on the Eastern bloc weakening due to national problems. Indeed, the USSR has since been broken down into 15 separate countries, and there is a movement to keep breaking these nations into even more countries: dividing Ukraine into eastern and western parts, bringing a portion of Moldova into Romania and the separation of Chechnya from Russia. Yugoslavia was broken down into six separate nations.

Thus, history shows that the role of the struggle between nations in human history is stronger than the Marxists realized. Could Hegel be right? What is the main engine of history: the struggle between classes or the struggle between nations? Could they be equally important? If so, then could idealists and materialists both be correct, and could their philosophies be two sides of the same coin?

It would appear that the struggles both between classes and between nations have been important in the past. Nations and classes have existed for millennia, beginning from the hunter-gatherer state of humankind. The struggles between classes and between nations have always been present, and their existence will continue as long as classes and nations exist.

The conflict between classes eventually reduces the gap and disparities between them, and the probability of the struggle depends on the size of the gap between classes: the bigger the gap, the higher the probability. In the future, according to Marxism, a gap between classes should become smaller and would completely disappear in communist society, as classes will no longer exist. Consequently, the struggles should also become smaller and would disappear as well. Then what will move human society and its progress? Will development stop?

The same principle applies to the conflicts between nations. Although nations still exist and the struggles between them are still acute, all nations may eventually merge into one and the struggle will disappear. This trend toward a merging of nations is happening today. Western countries are already close to this: their economies are intertwined, and they have similar policies, politics and culture (they listen to the same news, watch the same movies, listen to the same music, etc.). Of course, other nations (Asian, Latin American or Arab nations) may merge and oppose the Western group. However, peacefully or by war, one would expect that the differences between the groups of countries will also be reconciled. Then again, what will move human society and its progress once this reconciliation of differences occurs?

Neither Hegel nor Marx and Engels seriously considered the struggle between religions as the primary engine of human history. However, this fight is essential to the history of people. It led to major religious wars that spanned centuries and even millennia: the Muslim conquests of the 7th-19th centuries, the Crusades of the 11th-13th centuries, the Spanish Reconquista of the 7th-15th centuries and the Ottoman wars in Europe of the 15th -19th centuries, among others. The struggle between religions still plays a dominant role in modern day society, as exampled by the struggle between Jews and Muslims, one group of Muslims (Sunnis) and another (Shiites), etc. Indeed, it is widely accepted that the struggle between Jews and Muslims regarding Israeli statehood is the root of many world problems, and determines policies of the pro-Israel Western bloc on one side and anti-Israel Muslim nations on the other side.

In fact, the struggle between religions can be powerful enough to override the struggle between classes and nations: when religious wars break out, the differences between classes and nations are ignored. Despite this, countries are gradually moving toward more secular societies, in which all religions are accepted and tolerated. This progress diminishes the conflict between religions and, hopefully, all religions will peacefully coexist in the future and such conflicts will disappear. If all of these conditions become the norm worldwide, then what will move human society and maintain its progress?

What is the Driving Force of Communism?

The answer to the question of what will keep society moving after all the struggles between classes, nations and religions disappear depends on whether one believes in capitalism or communism as the final stage of human society. Defenders of capitalism will point out that the most powerful engine of human progress is the desire for wealth and money. They believe that this will always be the case, as man continually seeks more and more wealth. In other words, society advances through the struggle for wealth.

Advocates of communism see it differently. They argue that there are limits to the human desire for wealth: no single person needs more than ten cars, a house with more than ten bedrooms, or more bread than one can eat. In communist society, by Marxists' definition, each and every person will have enough wealth, and thus they will no longer fight over it. Marxists believe that the main reason why people will still choose to work is by virtue of man's nature: the desire to express one's self, to achieve something and to be useful to society. Communism will be possible not solely as a result of a healthy economy and an overabundance of wealth, but also due to a new spirituality of man – a man driven by a desire to be useful rather than a desire to have as much material wealth as possible. Whether humans will ever evolve to this level is debatable and a separate topic (see more details in Chapter 12).

The statement "Man will be driven by spirit instead of materialistic desire" sounds idealistic. Now Marxists sound like idealists. It is important to keep in mind, however, that according to Marxism, people will only be driven by spirit as long as they have an advanced economy and an abundance of material goods; therefore, Marxists put materialism first.

In contrast to and ages before Marxism, Greek philosopher Aristotle (384-322 BCE), suggested that the material needs of everyone could be satisfied if each person consumed modestly. In other words, an abundance of material wealth can be reached through man's modest living rather than by an overabundant economy, which is required by

Marxists. Indeed, if one's needs are fewer, then life appears more abundant. Abundance is not something strictly defined by nature, but rather by our minds. The average person living a millennium or even just a century ago might see the material possessions of today's average living standard as superabundant. For example, the choice and variety of goods in modern supermarkets would be stunning for any human from the past. Many goods that we now have (computers, TVs, phones, cars, airplanes, etc.) were unimaginable in previous eras. How could people from the past need them if they did not even know about their existence?

Of course, one needs to have basic things in order to survive: food, drink, clothing and shelter. But beyond this, how much more does one need? And if one begins to need more, then will there ever be an end to the need? Presently, most members of any developed nation already have the basics to survive. For example, if evenly shared, there is already enough wealth in the U.S. or Switzerland to satisfy the basic needs of every citizen of these countries – so why don't they have communism? Why didn't human society develop accordingly to Aristotle's views? Marxist philosophy, dialectic materialism, suggests that this is because his views are idealistic: they are based on social consciousness (wishes to share material goods) but not social being (excess of material goods).

Summary

Marxism is based on dialectical materialism and, specifically, on the branch that applies to society: historical materialism. Marxists' belief that the struggle between classes is the main engine of human societal development is not supported by history. The conflict between nations and between religions may be at least as much or even more powerful. Thus, we can see that all three forces have similar contributions to human history.

Leninist (Marxist-Leninist) claims that the contradictions between the bourgeoisie and the proletariat are antagonistic and can only be resolved by revolution are not supported by history. The contradictions can either be antagonistic (as was the case in Russia) or non-antagonistic (as in most other capitalist countries). Non-antagonistic contradictions can be peacefully reconciled and do not require a revolution. Thus, the philosophy of Marxism supports either a peaceful or revolutionary path to communism.

References

1.   Eagleton, T. Why Marx Was Right, published by Yale University Press (2011).
2.   Afanasiev, V. G. Marxist Philosophy, published by Progress Publishers (1978).
3.   Marx, K., Engels, F. The Communist Manifesto (1848), published by Verso (1998).
4.   Popkin, R. H., Stroll, A. Philosophy Made Simple, published by Three Rivers Press (1993).
5.   Popper, K. R. The Poverty of Historicism, published by Routledge & Kegan Paul (1957).
6.   Pipes, R. Communism: A History, published by The Modern Library (2001).

Chapter 4

Schools and Currents of Communism

Although the idea of communism can be traced back to more than two thousand years ago, communism did not become a serious force until its analysis by Karl Marx and Friedrich Engels in the 19th century. Their views became popular, and communist movements that adhere to their main ideas are called Marxist.

Marxism holds a worldview that is based on a philosophy of dialectical materialism and analyzes society using a historic materialism approach (see details in Chapter 3). The core idea of Marxist theory is that social consciousness is determined by materialistic environment; in other words, relationships in a society are based on its economy. Relationships and societal changes are dictated by economy rather than human wishes or desires. Thus, views on communism that recognize the supremacy of economy should be classified as Marxist. All other views should be considered non-Marxist.

Traditionally, the single word "communism" refers to the school of Marxism-Leninism. Any school other than the Marxist-Leninist school has its own specific name. This is probably due to the fact that Marxism-Leninism had by far the largest following and influence; for example, leaders of the USSR, China, Vietnam, Cuba and Laos adhered to Marxism-Leninism.

MARXIST SCHOOLS

Different schools of socialism and communism already existed in the time of Marx and Engels. In fact, *The Communist Manifesto*, written by Marx and Engels in 1848, already identified four schools: feudal, petty bourgeois, conservative-bourgeois and abstract intellectual. Marx and Engels believed that these schools utilized socialist phrases but served antisocialist purposes, and called them "false brothers."

All the different followers of Marxism, of course, believe that they got its theories right. Those who believe that Marxism asserted that a transition from capitalism to communism is impossible without armed revolutions consider themselves orthodox Marxists. This school, which is the most proactive, labeled the other schools as revisionist, on the basis that the other schools had revised Marxist theory to show that the transition from capitalism to communism could occur peacefully through parliamentary means. Considering that Marx and Engels were not strong believers in either a peaceful or a violent transition and gave mixed messages (see Chapter 5), this is not surprising, but it can be confusing.

Reformist and revisionist splinter movements later formed Social Democracy. Social Democratic parties became popular in Europe after World War II. They have now completely abandoned Marxism and are not to be considered communist. Social democrats now play an important role in many capitalist Western governments.

Since the deaths of Marx and Engels, different views have multiplied, as many parties have turned to Marxism for theoretical justification of their social and political platforms. Marxist views came to be interpreted in a variety of ways and presently, Marxism includes many different movements. The most popular and historically significant interpretations of Marxism were contributed by Vladimir Lenin, and these views and movements are collectively called Marxist-Leninist.

The most important feature of Lenin's view on communism is that the transformation of capitalism to communism can only be achieved by a revolution that requires a certain organization. Accordingly, communist revolutions cannot succeed if carried out by the working class spontaneously. In order to be successful, they must be led by professional revolutionaries that form a vanguard party. These views of communism that recognize the necessity of the vanguard party over the working class are classified as Marxism-Leninism, or Leninism. All other Marxist views are classified as non-Leninist.

A. Leninist Schools

1) Leninism – Lenin began developing his theories well before the October Revolution in 1917. These theories led to the successful revolution and laid the foundation for socialist Russia and the USSR. Lenin was very pragmatic in his choices regarding achieving and holding political power. Whenever Marxist theories did not fit into the practicalities of the revolution, he changed them on the grounds that no teaching is a dogma. The main elements of Lenin's theories are: a) capitalism cannot be reformed and peacefully transformed into communism because ruling classes will never give up their power voluntarily; and b) the working class cannot carry out a revolution without a professional vanguard leadership, which is the communist party. Lenin was a talented organizer and leader. When he saw that Russians were not happy and were ready for a change, he organized the communist party and led the country in revolt.

The revolution in Russia took place quickly and relatively peacefully, without spilling much blood. This, however, was not an end of the fight. As Marx, Engels and Lenin predicted, the overthrown classes did not simply give up – they began fighting back, which led to civil war. Marx and Engels predicted (and Lenin agreed) that temporary dictatorship of the proletariat would be required to suppress the resistance of the overthrown classes. However, Leninist and Marxist views on the dictatorship of the proletariat were quite different.

Marx and Engels believed that whether peaceful or violent, the revolution had to be democratic, and emancipation of the working class could only be achieved by the working class itself. In fact, *The Communist Manifesto* declares: "Democracy is the first thing that must be established." However, this was only a theory. When revolution actually took place and civil war broke out, Lenin had to deal with the fact that democracy and political freedom were simply not on the menu.

The next step required using any means necessary or the revolution would fail. At this stage, Lenin advocated that the dictatorship be established through the use of force and be unrestricted by law. Moreover, as the proletariat was mainly composed of undereducated workers, the revolution had to be directed by its vanguard: the Communist party, comprised of intellectuals, most of whom were not proletarians. Lenin argued that the socialist revolution would require a highly committed intellectual elite – the Communist party – to exercise the dictatorship. In practice, it placed the Communist party above all classes, including the proletariat itself, whereas *The Communist Manifesto* clearly states that communists "do not constitute themselves a special party over and above other working-class parties." Thus, Leninism introduced an authoritarian element into Marxism.

Lenin's followers see this authoritarian element as an essential contribution to Marxism, while others saw it as a corruption. In practice, Lenin was an obedient follower of Marx and Engels, but when the revolution began, Lenin had to deal with the reality of either following Marxism strictly and risking losing the revolution, or modifying it and winning. Thus, Marxism itself contains the contradictory element that brought Lenin to his actions. As mentioned above, Marx and Engels did not specify whether capitalism would peacefully transform into communism or if a violent revolution would be required. If a violent revolution was required, then fighting was unavoidable, and the dictatorship of the Communist party would direct the fight to victory. If instead capitalism gradually reformed into communism, then no fight and no dictatorship by the Communist party was necessary.

2) Stalinism – Lenin died in January of 1924, less than seven years after the revolution and just over one year after the end of the civil war. He had no opportunity to lead the USSR through a peaceful time of building communism. Stalin, who led the country for the next 30 years, replaced Lenin. However, many historians blame Lenin for what happened after his death and associate him with Stalin. For example, *Encyclopedia Britannica* (2015) states: "Leninism's unrestrained pursuit of the socialist society resulted in the creation of a totalitarian state in the Soviet Union." In a sense, this is like blaming Hitler's predecessor Paul von Hindenburg for the creation of Nazism in Germany and the subsequent atrocities.

In reality, not much suggests that Lenin and his ideas would lead to the creation of the totalitarian state. In fact, Lenin was opposed to having Stalin in the Soviet government and warned against his dictatorial personality. In his last letter, Lenin urged the government to get rid of Stalin. Unfortunately, after Lenin's death, Stalin managed to outmaneuver his comrades and became the leader of the Soviet Union for the next 30 years.

Many believe that that while Lenin contributed to the theoretical basis of communism, Stalin simply followed Lenin's directions and was not a theoretician. This explains the belief that Leninism can only lead to the creation of totalitarian states, such as the USSR. However, this is not quite true. Similarly to Lenin, who "further developed" Marxism, Stalin "further developed" Leninism.

Lenin clearly stated the primary function of the dictatorship: "suppression of the exploiting classes." Stalin agreed, but added to this idea. In his book *Foundations of Leninism* (1924), Stalin declared: "The first aim of the dictatorship is to break the resistance of the defeated exploiters. Next, it must lead the revolution onward to the final victory, to the complete triumph of socialism." [1] From that point forward, the aim of the dictatorship of the proletariat had been changed from the Leninist "to suppress the exploiting classes" to the Stalinist "to complete triumph of socialism." However, the expression "to complete triumph of socialism" is very vague, because it is difficult to pinpoint when socialism is complete and triumphant. For example, when asked how long it would take China to pass the primary stage of socialism, one of the General Secretaries of Communist Party of China, Jiang Zemin, replied: "at least 100 years."

The Stalinist modification of Leninism explains why the USSR became a totalitarian state. It was due to Stalinism, not Leninism, and it was a complete departure from both Marxism and Leninism. Marx and Lenin believed that the dictatorship of the proletariat and even the state itself would "wither away," because conflicts between classes and their struggles would come to an end. Instead of withering away, however, Stalinism led to the increased power of the state apparatus. Therefore, Stalinism was a corruption of Marxism and Leninism, and not a continuation.

3) *Trotskyism* – Leon Trotsky was a prominent Russian Bolshevik*. After the death of Lenin, Trotsky became a fierce opponent of Stalin and formed the Left Opposition. His platform became known as Trotskyism. The most important element of Trotskyism is the theory of "permanent revolution." According to this theory, communism cannot be built in just one individual country because the united forces of capitalism would crush it. This creates the need for a permanent international revolution: socialist revolutions must take place simultaneously in the largest nations, so that the rest of the world cannot stop them. This meant that Trotskyites called on all people to support revolutionaries in order to facilitate socialist change around the world as quickly as possible.

It is widely known that this view was not supported by Stalin, who believed that communism could be built in Russia without global support. However, the concept that communism could be built in one separate country originated with Lenin, and this was one of his key points leading to the Socialist revolution in Russia (see Chapter 7). Thus, classifying Trotskyism as a part of Leninism is misleading.

Trotskyism has a practical rationale. Socialist revolutions in small countries can be squashed by large capitalist nations. A good example of this occurred in Cuba and its neighbor, the United States. When the revolution took place in Cuba, the U.S. bitterly opposed it and attempted to invade Cuba in order to overthrow the new government. The only way that the pro-communist regime of Cuba was able to survive this intervention was through support from the Soviet Union. This new alliance led to the famous Cuban Missile Crisis, in which the Soviets stationed nuclear missiles in Cuba in order to deter future harassments from the U.S. A potential world war was averted by an agreement that the USSR would withdraw its nuclear missiles in exchange for an American promise to never to invade Cuba without a direct provocation. The consequence of this aggression by the mighty capitalist America was

---

* *Member of the majority of the Russian Social-Democratic Workers' Party that seized control of the government of Russia in 1917. The word is derived from Russian "bolshinstvo," which means "majority." Members of the party that lost (those of the minority) were dubbed the Mensheviks.*

that the governments of small nations in Latin America became threatened, and Trotskyism gained more popularity in Latin America than in the rest of the world.

On the other hand, China's experience disproves Trotskyism and demonstrates the opposite: that building socialism and communism in one individual country is actually possible. China is systematically moving toward communism and is succeeding so far (see Chapter 9). Of course, the large size of the country is a strong factor in this progression. Besides using military force, capitalist nations can also crash economies in small communist countries by using isolation and blockades. China, however, is home to about one fifth of Earth's human population and one fifth of the world economy; thus, it has the resources to overcome being isolated by another country or group of countries. Moreover, the world has changed since the time of Trotsky almost a century ago. It is becoming more democratic and socialist, and modern capitalist countries are less likely to attempt to crush another country simply because of that country's change to socialism or communism. A natural consequence of this worldwide trend is that Trotskyism has become irrelevant, with few actual supporters remaining.

4) Maoism – Mao Zedong laid the theoretical groundwork for the communist movement in China, and his theories became collectively known as Maoism. One of the most important elements of Maoism is its reliance on the agrarian peasantry as the key revolutionary force, rather than the working class (proletariat), as suggested by Marx, Engels and Lenin. The working class in pre-revolutionary China was very small and practically non-existent. The whole Chinese economy was undeveloped. Thus, according to Marxism, the material conditions – which are created by the bourgeoisie – for socialist revolution in China did not exist. Mao, however, proposed that the material conditions in poor countries like China would never be built by the bourgeoisie because the character of the bourgeoisie had changed from progressive toward world development, as it was in Marx's time, to regressive. Therefore, the only way for China to transition to communism would be through a socialist revolution that relied on the peasantry. But then, what about the key Marxist theory that the development of human society passes through certain stages determined by the economy rather than by human wishes and ideas?

In order to propose that China could move toward communism regardless of its economic status, Mao had to accept that the principal factor of human history is ideas and consciousness rather than economy. Thus, Mao deviated from the philosophy of Marxism, which is dialectical materialism, and turned to idealism. He directly contradicted the core doctrine of Marxism; therefore, Maoism can hardly be classified as a school of Marxism. Despite this, Mao considered himself a staunch follower of Marx and an anti-revisionist of Marxism-Leninism. His disastrous "Cultural Revolution" came as an attempt to keep Marxism-Leninism in China clean of revisions from a growing number of Chinese communists. In reality, however, Mao himself became the revisionist.

In contrast to Marxism-Leninism, which assigns the working class as the main revolutionary force of socialist revolutions, Mao decided that the working class in developed capitalist countries had been "bought up" by the ruling class, becoming too comfortable and losing its will for revolutions. Therefore, according to Mao, socialist revolutions were more likely to take place in poorer third world countries rather than in economically advanced nations, which contradicts Marxism. On the other hand, this Maoist notion that the working class is "bought up" by the ruling class denies the possibility that the working class in developed countries can peacefully resolve its conflicts with the bourgeoisie and become genuinely free and happy. This leads to rejection of the idea of reformist and peaceful transformation of capitalism to communism, which is in agreement with Leninism but not Marxism. Also, based on the theory that the working class in developed capitalist countries is no longer the main revolutionary force, but that the peasantry in developing countries is, Mao came to the conclusion that China was now to play a crucial role in socialist revolutions worldwide.

A believer that "political power grows out of the barrel of a gun," Mao called upon the peasantry for guerilla warfare and a "people's war." Mao also believed that international capitalism thrives by exploiting the urban-rural division, in which industrial/urban (First and Second World) countries exploit agrarian/rural (Third World) nations such as China. He endorsed national liberation movements as the best way to move toward communism. Nevertheless, in agreement with Marx and Lenin, Mao saw industrialization as a prerequisite for the elimination of inequalities and the establishment of communism.

Similarly to Stalin in his contrast to Marxism, Mao believed that the class struggle would continue even after overthrowing the oppressing class by the workers, because lingering elements of capitalism remain hidden throughout society, including within the Communist Party itself. In fact, Maoists believe that Stalin was the last true socialist in the Soviet Union. Such beliefs led to crackdowns on opponents and excessive use of force in both the Stalinist and Maoist governments.

Currently it is widely accepted that China has abandoned Maoism. Yet, the role of Maoism in China cannot be overvalued. Maoism helped to break China free from its feudal past and moved it quickly through capitalism into socialism. Of course, the cost of this speed of progression should not be ignored. Since Maoism advocates national liberation of Third World countries, it became popular in such countries as India, Nepal, the Philippines and other developing nations.

5) Other Currents – Besides the major schools of Marxism-Leninism described above, other smaller and more short-lived schools emerged around the world: Titoism in the former Yugoslavia, Hoxhaism in Albania, Eurocommunism in several Western European countries and others. Since all of these schools were independent from the policies of the Soviet Union, some analysts classify them as a variety of National Communism. This is not very accurate, however, because many other schools of thought, including Maoism, were also independent of the Soviet ideology and would have to fall into this category as well.

Hoxhaism is a form of anti-revisionist Marxism-Leninism that was named after Albanian socialist leader Enver Hoxha. Similarly to Maoism, Hoxhaism defends Stalinism and sees itself as an anti-revisionist movement of Marxism-Leninism. In 1978, however, the communist party of Albania (the Party of Labor of Albania) split from the policies of China on the grounds that the Communist Party of China had abandoned the principles of proletarian internationalism and aligned itself with imperialism. Hoxhaism won large support from the Maoists and spread around the world, especially in Latin America.

Titoism is a form of Yugoslav Marxism-Leninism that was named after Yugoslav President Josip Broz Tito. The main element of Titoism is that different countries may have different ways of pursuing communism, and the means to attain those goals must be dictated by the specific conditions unique to each country. Practically, it meant that Yugoslavia's policies were formed independent of the Soviet Union or any other country. Therefore, some consider Titoism to be a variant of National Communism. After Tito's death in 1980, Titoism went into rapid decline and no longer attracts an international following.

In the 1970s and 1980s, other communist parties in Europe developed views that collectively became known as Eurocommunism or Neocommunism. The Communist parties of Italy, France and Spain created the most influential movements. Generally speaking, Eurocommunist views were less aligned with Soviet policies and more aligned with Western democracy. A founder of the Italian Communist Party, Antonio Gramsci, made one of the most significant contributions to Eurocommunist theory. In order to become a significant force in government, Gramsci encouraged communists to form alliances with other social movements, and consistently opposed sectarianism. Eurocommunists embraced new social movements such as feminism, the green movement, gay liberation and other movements. Eurocommunist ideas had an important influence on the last Soviet leader, Mikhail Gorbachev, and on his "glasnost" and "perestroika" policies that contributed to the dissolution of the USSR. However, with the dissolution of the USSR, the Eurocommunist movement also lost its significance.

B. Non-Leninist Schools

Non-Leninist forms of Marxism appeared mostly in the West. Their foundation was laid by several intellectuals before Leninism and at the time of its emergence, including Karl Kautsky, Eduard Bernstein, Rosa Luxemburg and others.

Kautsky, who took theoretical leadership of Marxism after Marx and Engels, and who was considered to be an orthodox Marxist, asserted that the working class could achieve political power and realize its communist goals without revolution, but instead peacefully through reforms. In his work *The Economic Doctrines of Karl Marx (1887)*, he presented Marxism as evolutionism, suggesting that society will move toward communism through reforms and evolution rather than revolution. Thus, Marxists-Leninists (communists) labeled him as a reformist.

Bernstein, who became one of the key founding figures of Social Democracy, had noticed that the class struggle was becoming less intense, rather than more intense as projected by Marx and Engels. According to Bernstein, this meant that class conflicts and revolutions might not be required to move toward communism; instead, communism could be built through democratic institutions and cooperation among citizens regardless of class. In his work *Evolutionary Socialism (1899)*, he further advanced this idea that society could move toward communism through evolution rather than revolution. He contended that Marx's economic views, including the labor theory of value, were outdated and needed to be revised; thus, Marxist-Leninists labeled him a revisionist.

Rosa Luxemburg, who favored the revolutionary path, condemned Bernstein's revisions. But she also disagreed with Lenin's idea that the working class must be led by a vanguard, and instead insisted that the entire working class or its majority must be deeply involved in order for a revolution to have success. Later, this view led to the creation of a far-left movement called "council communism." Thus, Luxemburg is considered to be a left communist. In her work *The Accumulation of Capital (1913)*, she took note of a flaw in Marx's theory regarding economic crises of capitalism, in which these crises would become increasingly violent until they ultimately swept capitalism away. She observed that capitalism could actually solve these economic crises by expanding into non-capitalist spheres as well as by finding new markets in colonies and undeveloped countries. Of note, she was right and history confirms her idea (see Chapter 8). In addition, she proposed that capitalism would only reach its limits and collapse after it exploited undeveloped countries and colonies. In contrast to Bernstein, Luxemburg claimed that the contradictions of capitalism would keep growing further as it progressed and continued exploiting colonies. This, she believed, made social revolutions around the world inevitable.

Other schools of socialism and communism began forming before Leninism. One of the earliest examples was social democracy. Social democracy originated in 19th century Germany and was based on the reformist ideas of Ferdinand Lassalle and the revolutionary ideas of Marx and Engels. However, the first official basis of the Social Democratic Workers' Party was Marxism. Thus, social democracy was originally a Marxist school, despite the fact that it is no longer considered to be a school of communism. Later, in Lenin's time, left communism – the opposite of current social democracy – began to form. This development process of the communist idea has continued through modern times, resulting in many other streams of communism. Below is a brief description of the most prominent of these streams.

1) Social Democracy – Currently, social democracy is not considered to be a communist movement. However, it is important to remember that social democracy is rooted in communist ideology and was originally led by Marxists. The detachment of social democracy from Marxism can be traced to the German theorist Eduard Bernstein, who recognized that capitalism does not develop the way Marx projected. Instead, Bernstein saw that capitalism could overcome its major weaknesses, such as the inequality of wealth distribution. He also pointed out that instead of worsening, as projected by Marx and Engels, social conditions in modern capitalist countries were improving. Importantly, capitalist countries were beginning to adopt a universal suffrage system, which could allow the working class to advance toward communism by electing socialist representatives into existing governmental bodies. Therefore, social democrats began advocating a peaceful, evolutionary approach to the transformation from capitalism to communism. They rejected the militant approach advocated by Lenin and totally split from Marxism-Leninism following the Russian October Revolution in 1917. Generally speaking, social democracy rejects both the idea of a totally free market, advocated by bourgeois ideologists, and a fully planned economy, advocated by communists. Instead, it asserts that the economy must be regulated by the state but does not need to be state-owned.

2) Left Communism – This vein of communism emerged in opposition to Leninism and its variants, such as Stalinism, Trotskyism, and Maoism. In general, left communists see their own views as more authentically Marxist. Left communism was largely originated by Rosa Luxemburg, who criticized both Leninists and social democrats. While social democrats claimed that the working class should be organized through governmental institutions, and while Leninists believed that it should be organized by a vanguard party, Luxemburg believed that the workers should be self-organized through councils formed at factories or other work places. This view eventually led to council communism.

Currently active movements of left communism include the International Communist Party, the International Communist Current and the International Communist Tendency.

The International Communist Party (ICP) has a long history. It takes its roots from the Italian Socialist Party, which was established in 1892, with Italy still remaining its strongest base. The ICP does not accept Leninist and Stalinist concepts of building communism in one individual country. Instead, it adheres to the original Marxist view that communism will arise as the result of economic advancements, and thus can only arise simultaneously throughout the world. It accepts the idea that the working class needs a party, but this party is only needed to direct a revolution, not to create it. The ICP stresses the importance of proletarian unity and dismisses any alliances, especially alliances with reformists and labor unions, because they "limit the workers' struggles." It rejects the conclusion that communism or even socialism has ever been built in any country thus far. Rather, it considers the former USSR to have been a centrally controlled state capitalist country and an imperialist bloc, which has countered another imperialist bloc led by the U.S. Moreover, the ICP sees Stalinism as "the most ferocious counterrevolution ever to have overwhelmed the international communist movement."

Nevertheless, the ICP is in conflict with Marxism by rejecting socialism and democracy as tools of the bourgeoisie to "limit the workers' struggles." This does not mean that this party promotes dictatorships. Rather, it chooses to reject any system (including socialism) that compromises complete freedom, preferring to establish communism straight away.

The International Communist Current was founded in 1975. The International Communist Tendency was founded in 1983. The views of these organizations are very similar to those of the ICP.

3) *Council Communism* – This is the most far-left communist school. It opposes the social democratic view that communism should be built through social reforms using existing governmental institutions, as well as the Leninist idea that communism can only be built through revolution led by a vanguard communist party. Instead, council communists believe that the communist movement should be organized by workers' councils that spontaneously arise in municipalities and factories. They emphasize the part of Marxism that proposes that the working class is able to forge its own destiny without a vanguard party. The main principle of council communism is that the government and economy should be managed by delegates of the councils, who are elected by workers and recallable at any time. This school originated in the 1920s from left movements in Germany and the Netherlands.

4) *Other Currents* – Several other currents developed based on left communism views. Some of them have been short-lived and have now dissolved, such as the Situationist International. Others, such as Autonomism, emerged not long ago and are currently extant.

The main concern of the situationists was that modern capitalism forced individual expression into the exchange and consumption of goods, instead of directly lived experiences. It was largely related to Marx's theory of alienation. The situationists called for an awakening and pursuit of real desires instead of those enforced by governments through mainstream media. This school of thought mostly attracted artists and intellectuals, and was active from 1957 to 1972.

Autonomism first emerged in Italy in the 1960s, and was significantly influenced by the situationists. It relates to the Marxist notion that the working class is able to forge its own destiny. The main idea of autonomism is that people should live free (autonomously) of government institutions and political parties; they should form independent social movements that help people navigate everyday life. As such, the autonomists called for independence from either parliamentary democracy or revolutionary communism. Autonomism is still popular in Italy and other European countries.

NON-MARXIST SCHOOLS

Non-Marxist schools of thought began developing before Marxism. The two main schools are anarchist communism (also known as libertarian communism or free communism) and religious communism.

Anarchist Communism – This school of thought takes its roots from radical socialist movements after the French Revolution. It was also significantly influenced by another social anarchist movement, led by Mikhail Bakunin, which was popular at the time. However, it was first clearly formulated by the Italian section of the First International. One of the most important theorists of anarchist communism was Peter Kropotkin (1842-1921). In his book *The Conquest of Bread (1892)*, he was among the first to argue that works and goods produced in communist society must be distributed according to the needs of individuals rather than according to the level of contributed labor. Thus, he replaced the principle of wages with the principle of need. Similarly to Marxist-Leninists, anarcho-communists recognized that the transformation of capitalism into communism was only possible through revolution. However, they rejected the idea of the dictatorship of the proletariat, as well as the intermediate phase of socialism, believing that capitalism should be immediately transformed into communism. Anarchist communists understood that any revolutionary leadership taking control over the transformation of capitalism to communism will never give up its power and will eventually become a new ruling class, instead of "withering away," as suggested by Marxism.

Anarcho-communists confirmed this by pointing to the fact that no self-proclaimed socialist/communist governments have "withered away" so far. This seems like a valid point. However, such a conclusion is premature, since "withering away" may take longer than expected or desired, and is nearly impossible in places where communist countries are surrounded by capitalist nations, as capitalist regimes usually try to destroy them.

Anarcho-communists reject hierarchy in all forms. They reject a state style of organization and believe that people should live in communes, where individuals cooperate with each other for mutual benefit. They believe that state organization should be replaced by associations of communes. Anarcho-communists reject the idea of working for wages, on the grounds that there is no way to measure anyone's contribution fairly, since wealth is a collective product of current and previous generations. They accept the idea of personal property rights but reject any idea of private property, because it would inevitably lead to the unequal accumulation of capital and the reappearance of social classes. They likewise reject the idea of market competition, because it also creates inequities in wealth and power.

Strangely, although anarcho-communists and what are today called communists (Marxist-Leninists) have common roots, they engaged in major fights and wars with each other. The best known attempts to create anarcho-communist societies are the following: a) the Free Territory in Ukraine after the Russian October Revolution of 1917 and b) the anarchist territories (in Catalonia, including most of Aragon, parts of the Levante and parts of Andalusia) during the Spanish Revolution of 1936. Both attempts were crushed by united forces of communist and capitalist regimes.

Although anarcho-communism is currently rejected by major world powers, its elements are present in modern day life. A classic example is a simple gift exchange between people, which helps redistribution of wealth through communities. Another modern day example, facilitated by the Internet, is free databases (such as Wikipedia) and free software. Numerous anarcho-communist organizations are currently active in many countries around the world. The most significant of them is the Anarkismo network that unites about 30 organizations.

Religious communism – Many religions see communism as an ideal social system. Through a long series of religions, there have been many attempts to establish communist societies. The first well-documented attempt to establish a communist society in human history came through the Mazdak movement. It took place in the Persian Empire, led by the followers of the Zoroastrian religion in 490-520 CE (see Chapter 2 for details).

The second well-known example also comes from a religious group: the Anabaptists theocracy (1534-1535) in the city of Münster, Germany (see Chapter 2). More recent examples of communist-like communities include the Diggers, the Shakers, the Harmony society, Hutterites, United Order and others. Nuns and monks from Christianity, Buddhism, Hinduism, Taoism and Jainism have also created communist communities. Many religions advocate the principal communist idea that every person should contribute to society according to ability and receive benefits according to need. Most religions do not have contradictions between their beliefs and the ideas of communism.

Christianity, for example, suggests that Jesus Christ himself promoted communism as the ideal system. The Bible shows that, following the death of Jesus, the Apostles practiced communism and established their own communist society. Verses 44 and 45 of the Bible explicitly state: "Now all who believed were together, and had all things in common. And sold their possessions and goods, and divided them among all, as everyone had need." [2] The Catholic Church also shares these views. On November 26, 2013, in the mission statement for his papacy, Pope Francis criticized the global economic system of capitalism that "prizes profit over people." In 2015, he famously criticized capitalism by stating that unbridled capitalism is the "dung of the devil."

Islam, Buddhism and Judaism also are in close agreement with communist goals and ideas of how society should be modeled. Nevertheless, the American Jewish Committee claimed that "Judaism and communism are utterly incompatible." [3] This, however, appears to be a politically motivated statement, and the facts do not support this claim. For example, Jews were supportive of the October Revolution of 1917 in Russia, and some of the most prominent Bolsheviks, such as Leon Trotsky, Grigory Zinoviev, Moisei Uritsky, Lev Kamenev, Yakov Sverdlov and Grigory Sokolnikov, had Jewish backgrounds. In fact, Kamenev served as the first head of state of Soviet Russia and Trotsky was the founder and the first commander of the Red Army. Many communists of Jewish background became well-known leaders of the USSR, and many city streets, squares and other monuments in the USSR

Flag of the USSR **Symbol of Christian Communism**

Figure 4.1. Flag of the USSR and symbol of Christian communism. The symbol of Christian communism and the symbol displayed on the flag of the USSR have very little difference: the hammer in the symbol of Christian communism is replaced by a Latin cross.

were named after them. One of the most prominent names advocating communism was the known leader of Judaism, Rabbi Yehuda Ashlag, whose work *Talmud Eser Sefirot* is recognized as the most important textbook for students studying Kabbalah. The claims of American Jews were probably driven by fear of prosecution for being associated with communists in the USSR, who were among the main enemies of the U.S. Hopefully, this fear will disappear with a better understanding of communism, and the dissociation of communism from the authoritarian regimes that identified with it.

Quite contrary to the American Jewish Committee's statement, one could argue that Judaism is "utterly incompatible" with capitalism rather than communism. The reason: capitalism operates through loans and interest. In capitalist society, money is lent with only one purpose: receiving it back with interest. On the other hand, the Torah (the central reference of the Judaic religious tradition) and the Talmud (a central text of Rabbinic Judaism) encourage the granting of loans only if no interest is involved. Moreover, the Book of Ezekiel (the third of the major prophets) classifies charging interest as one of the worst sins.

Religious communism and other schools of communism have the same values and goals. For example, communism and religions value justice and compassion while rejecting greed and selfishness. Christian communism aligns with Marx's theory of surplus value and human alienation.

Even the symbol of Christian communism and the symbol of the former USSR displayed on the flag are almost identical (see Figure 4.1). However, for various reasons, religious communism and other schools of communism try to separate themselves from each other. For example, religious communism proposes quite a different means by which communism should be achieved and societies organized. Mostly, it promotes passive resistance and not responding to the wrongdoings of capitalism with violence.

In general, non-religious schools of communism, especially Marxism-Leninism, are not friendly to religions. Marx's famous expression that religion is "the opiate of the masses" sounds quite negative. Many people feel that religion and communism are incompatible because religions believe that positive social development is brought about by supernatural forces (a god), while communists maintain that it is brought about by the people themselves. Taking this into account, along with the fact that some regimes of self-proclaimed communist countries persecuted religious individuals, religious communists have preferred to separate themselves from communism. For example, many Christian communists would rather be called Christian *communalists*.

Nevertheless, it seems that facts about hostilities toward religious communism may be exaggerated. In fact, Marx's attitude towards religion was more sympathetic than it was negative. Before his famous expression that religion is "the opiate of the masses," he also wrote: "Religious suffering is, at one and the same time, the expression of real suffering and a protest against real suffering. Religion is the sigh of the oppressed creature, the heart of a heartless world, and the soul of soulless conditions. It is the opium of the people." [4]

However, there is good reason for the exaggeration of facts associated with the persecution of religions by communists. It would not be surprising if anti-communists intentionally magnify them in order to fight communism, as most people in the world appear to be religious and religion is a very powerful tool.

Lenin did not promote any hostilities against religion either. As he had to turn a theory into a practice, he pragmatically summarized his views as follows: "Unity in this really revolutionary struggle of the oppressed class for the creation of a paradise on earth is more important to us than any unity of proletarian opinion on paradise in heaven." [5] As for the policies of self-proclaimed communist governments toward religion, they were generally discouraging based on the understanding that religion retards social development. However, they were not as hostile as is commonly presented. The only well-documented hostilities took place in China during The Cultural Revolution (1966-1976) and in Democratic Kampuchea (Cambodia) under the Khmer Rouge regime (1975-1979). The policies in other communist societies could be characterized as ranging from discouraging to tolerant.

Currently, the policies of self-proclaimed communist countries toward religion are tolerant. No communist schools or currents have the need to fight religion, as they have the same goal: to create a paradise society. The only difference, as Lenin noted, is that most religions are preparing for paradise in heaven, while communists are working to create a paradise on earth. On the other hand, contrary to the tolerant policies of communists toward religion, some religions have no tolerance toward communists or any non-believers – they assert that the only place for any non-believer is hell. If anything, there is more concern now that religions oppress communists than that communists oppress religions.

Summary

Traditionally, the word "communism" means Marxism-Leninism, while any school other than Marxist-Leninist has a specific label. This is probably due to the fact that Marxism-Leninism has had by far the largest following and influence.

Views on communism that recognize the supremacy of the economy and that communism will arise as a result of a superabundant economy are classified as Marxist. All other views are classified as non-Marxist. Views on communism that recognize the necessity of the vanguard party over the working class are classified as Leninist (also called Marxism-Leninism). All other Marxist views are classified as non-Leninist.

Among the most significant currents within Marxism-Leninism were Stalinism and Maoism. All sub-currents of Marxism-Leninism are presently inactive, with the exception of Maoism, which is still popular in developing countries.

Of the non-Leninist schools of Marxism, left communism and social democracy are considered the most significant. Although social democracy is no longer considered to be a communist movement, it takes its roots from Marxism and the idea that capitalism can be peacefully transformed into communism through reforms.

Anarcho-communism and religious communism are among the most important non-Marxist schools of thought. Religious communism is actually more compatible with communism than is currently believed.

References

1. Stalin, J. Foundations of Leninism, published by International Publishers (1932).

2. New Testament, acts 2 and 3, chapter 2, published by The Gideons Internationals (1995).

3. Diner, H. R. The Jews of the United States, 1654 to 2000, published by University of California Press (2006).

4. Marx, K. A Contribution to the Critique of Hegel's Philosophy of Right. *Deutsch-Französische Jahrbücher* (1844, February 7 & 10).

5. Lenin, V. I. Socialism and Religion. *Novaya Zhizn*, 28 (1905, December 3).

Chapter 5

History as the Judge of Marxism

Before we even begin here, let's straighten up the perception of the Marxist view on capitalism. A widely spread misconception is that Marxism denounces capitalism and calls for its destruction as soon as possible. This is far from the truth. In reality, Marxism praises capitalism for its adaptability and ability to accelerate economic development. For example, in *The Communist Manifesto*, Marx and Engels write: "It has accomplished wonders far surpassing Egyptian pyramids, Roman aqueducts, and Gothic cathedrals; it has conducted expeditions that put in the shade all former Exoduses of nations and crusades." In fact, Marxism praises capitalism for its ability to create communism.

Marx's contribution to the understanding of economics is widely recognized, and even *The New York Times* has acknowledged that his book *Capital* is "the most influential single work of economics ever written." [1] However, Marx's most significant contribution was accomplished with Engels: their discovery that the foundation of and driving force behind any social system (slavery, feudalism, capitalism or communism) is economy. According to them, the development of the economy forces changes in social systems; for example, the transformation of feudalism into capitalism was fueled by developing industry. In Marx's own words: "Men make their own history, but they don't make it as they please." This discovery was made in one of their earliest works, *The German Ideology*, and provided the foundation of Marxism. For clarity, the central idea of Marxism is visualized in the chart below (see Figure 5.1).

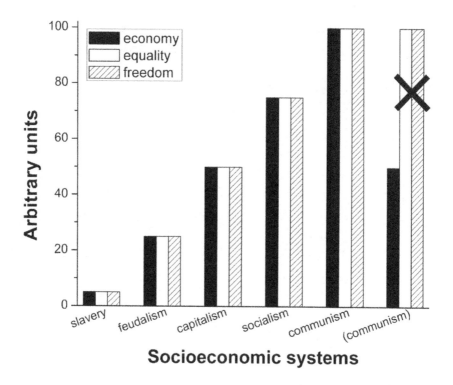

Figure 5.1. Illustration of the Central Idea of Marxism. Values are set arbitrarily from 0 (minimum) to 100 (maximum); actual numbers cannot be measured because slavery and feudalism are already in the past while socialism and communism are still in the future.

It is important to note that communism is only viable in an economically advanced society. If an economy does not provide a sufficient abundance of material goods, complete equality and freedom are impossible, which renders communism impossible as well.

Marx and Engels went even further than this theory. Based on their analyses, they came to the conclusion that the history of any society, including capitalism, is driven by class struggle, and capitalism would not be the last or final social system. They proposed that capitalism would eventually be replaced with other systems like communism, in which classes would no longer exist. Moreover, in *The German Ideology*, Marx and Engels predicted that the transition from capitalism to communism could only be successful in economically advanced countries, as an economy of scarcity would just lead to a socialization of

Table 1. Legatum Prosperity Index
(by Legatum Institute, of 142 countries)

Rank	Year 2012	Year 2011	Year 2010
1	Norway	Norway	Norway
2	Denmark	Denmark	Denmark
3	Sweden	Australia	Finland
4	Australia	New Zealand	Australia
5	New Zealand	Sweden	New Zealand
6	Canada	Canada	Sweden
7	Finland	Finland	Canada
8	Netherlands	Switzerland	Switzerland
9	Switzerland	Netherlands	Netherlands
10	Ireland	United States	United States
11	Luxembourg	Ireland	Ireland
12	United States	Iceland	Iceland
13	United Kingdom	United Kingdom	United Kingdom
14	Germany	Austria	Austria
15	Iceland	Germany	Germany
16	Austria	Singapore	Belgium
17	Belgium	Belgium	Singapore
18	Hong Kong	France	Japan
19	Singapore	Hong Kong	France
20	Taiwan	Taiwan	Hong Kong

The ranking is based on variety of factors including wealth, economic growth and quality of life. The table shows only the top 20 of the most prosperous countries. Rank 1 stands for the highest level of prosperity.

poverty. The socialization of poverty, as Marx put it, leads to "the old crap in new form."

Thus far, history reveals the truth in this prediction. More and more social programs have been introduced into capitalist countries. These programs bring capitalist nations closer and closer to communism. Indeed, the most developed and prosperous countries today have the most extensive social programs. For example, the Nordic countries (Norway, Denmark, Sweden, Finland and Iceland) have all been rated among the top most prosperous countries in the world (see Table 1), and they also have the most generous social programs: free education (including college), free health care, long vacations for workers, shorter working hours, etc. Even the flagship of capitalism, the U.S., is following this trend: working hours through the last century have been continuously shortened and, as of 2014, free healthcare is available to increasing numbers of those who cannot afford it.

Both Marx and Engels thought that the transition from capitalism to communism would happen in one of two ways: in a natural and peaceful process or through a series of violent revolutions, depending on the democratic conditions. Notwithstanding these two paths, those who wanted to accelerate the arrival of communism used Marxism as a basis for armed revolutionary movements. This use resulted in the widespread belief that Marx and Engels only advocated armed revolutions, and left plenty of room for different interpretations (and often wild misrepresentations) of Marxism. The misunderstanding of Marxism has probably generated more terrible consequences than any other theory in human history. So how does Marxism really show the transition from capitalism to communism? The following is an overview of Marx and Engels's theories, and an analysis of whether history confirms these theories.

The Transformation of Capitalism to Communism Can Be Peaceful

Marx definitely saw the value of peaceful reforms for capitalism. In his 1883 letter to the French labor leaders, who rejected the value of peaceful reforms, he accused them of "revolutionary phrase-mongering" and famously wrote: "If that is Marxism, then I am not a Marxist."

Overall, a careful analysis of Marxism suggests that a transition from capitalism to socialism would take place gradually and peacefully, rather than by armed revolution. The very core of Marxist theory – that social relationships are based on economy – clearly points this out. In *The German Ideology*, Marx and Engels wrote: "…in general, people cannot be liberated as long as they are unable to obtain food and drink, housing and clothing in adequate quality and quantity. 'Liberation' is a historical and not a mental act, and it is brought by historical conditions, the development of industry, commerce, agriculture..." [2] An economy must first create such an abundance of products (food, housing, clothing, etc.) that people will stop fighting over them due to no shortage being present. That means that no revolution can deliver communism in poor undeveloped countries. History confirms this: attempts to build communism in insufficiently developed countries (like Russia and Eastern European countries) have all failed.

In his major work, *Capital,* Marx compared the transition from feudalism to capitalism with the transition from capitalism to communism, and came to the conclusion that the latter transition should be easier and more peaceful. This is because in capitalism, an economy requires socialized production, and as capitalism develops, it becomes more and more socialized, creating the foundation for communism: "The transformation of scattered private property, arising from individual labor, into capitalist private property is, naturally, a process, incomparably more protracted, violent, and difficult, than the transformation of capitalistic private property, already practically resting on socialized production, into socialized property." [3] And Marx goes on to provide another argument to support this: "In the former case, we had the expropriation of the mass of the people by a few usurpers; in the latter, we have the expropriation of few usurpers by the mass of people."

Logically, since the basis of communism is a strong economy, and the creation of a strong economy is a gradual process, then the transformation of capitalism to communism can only be a gradual process that takes place simultaneously in all or a majority of the most advanced countries. Both Marx and Engels explicitly expressed that the peaceful transformation of capitalism is possible. For example, in his speech delivered in Holland in 1872, Marx recognized that the workers might achieve their aims by peaceful means in certain countries like England, Holland and the U.S., where the traditions of democracy had already been established. In 1886, in his preface to the first translation of *Capital* into English, Engels wrote: "England is the only country where the inevitable social revolution might be effected entirely by peaceful and legal means."

And yet, despite valuing the peaceful process, many works of Marx and Engels recognize that violent social upheavals and armed revolutions may be unavoidable in the process of transitioning from capitalism to communism. Even in *The German Ideology*, which suggests that only economic development can transform capitalism to communism, they ridicule Georg Kulmann, author of the book *Die Neue Welt: Order das Reich des Geistes auf Erden (1845)* for his adherence to peaceful transformation: "The prophet paints the transition from present social isolation to communal life in truly idyllic colors... [he] proclaims the approach of a terrible social upheaval into a process of comfortable and peaceful conversion, a quiet life which will permit the owners and rulers of the world to slumber on in complete peace of mind." [2]

Ironically, history shows that "the prophet" may have been right, while Marx and Engels were too fast to ridicule him. Such "comfortable and peaceful conversion" is exactly what is happening in many capitalist countries right now (see more details in Chapter 8). So, why would Marx and Engels abandon the idea of peaceful transition?

Transformation of Capitalism to Communism
Can Take Place Either Peacefully or Through Revolution

Marx and Engels were very clear that revolutions could only take place when the organization of society lags behind a progressing economy. Moreover, they believed that this was the core reason for revolutions. Analyzing the French revolution of 1948 in *The Class Struggles in France* Marx wrote: "a revolution is only possible in the periods when both these factors, the modern productive forces and the bourgeoisie productive forms come in collision with each other." [4] But is such a collision unavoidable in a capitalistic society?

First, let's clarify: what are "the productive forces" and what are "the productive forms"? The productive forces include human-powered labor (people) and means of production (equipment, tools, buildings, technologies, materials, etc.). The productive forms include means (economic and political organizations, law, etc.) by which the productive forces are controlled and regulated. In a capitalist society, productive forces are controlled by owners, who appropriate profits. Marx and his followers considered the contradiction between socialized production and private appropriation to be the fundamental problem of capitalism.

Then how did it happen that, more than a century later, the productive forces did not collide with the productive forms, and capitalism is still fine and prosperous? History demonstrates that capitalism appears to be a more flexible and adjustable system than Marx and Engels realized. In modern capitalism, the productive forms are constantly adjusted, preventing their collision with the changing productive forces. Indeed, when Marx performed his analysis, the productive forces were controlled by a few individuals (capitalists), and all profits were going into their pockets. If this condition had continued, one would have had a few capitalists who got richer and richer on one side, and exploited workers who became poorer on the other side, and the workers would revolt. However, what happened in reality is that capitalists were giving more and more of their profits and rights to their workers. Meanwhile, governments have increasingly raised taxes on the profits of the bourgeoisie, directing the collected taxes/money to a variety of social programs: to build public structures (buildings, roads, bridges, parks, etc.), to educate children, to treat the sick, to help the poor, etc. Capitalist governments were in fact taking a part of the profits from capitalists and giving it back to the workers – something that Marx did not foresee. This helped to soften the antagonism between the workers and bourgeoisie.

Of course, a portion of the profits that are taken from capitalists through taxes can and should be regulated. To distribute wealth more evenly, most capitalist governments imposed a progressive tax, meaning that tax was higher for those who made more money. The tax range currently varies from 0% for individuals with very low incomes to as high as 50% or more for higher earners, depending on the country. In a bold move, France recently tried to impose a tax of up to 75% on the rich, defined as those making more than one million euros per year. [5]

Marx realized that "for a popular revolution and the emancipation of a particular class of civil society to coincide, … a particular social sphere must be regarded as the notorious crime of the whole society, so that emancipation from this sphere appears as a general emancipation." [6] But this never happened, nor could it happen, in democratic capitalist countries. Instead, in any democratic country, if a particular sphere begins to be viewed as negative, it is adjusted and reformed before it comes to be viewed as a notorious crime. For example, in the U.S., when slavery began to be viewed as criminal, it was abolished. Another example is the rights of men versus women: when giving more rights to men than to women began to be viewed negatively, women were emancipated.

In democratic countries, most citizens can participate in the decision-making process regarding all policies, as opposed to dictatorships, in which decisions are made by a few (or even single) rulers. In a genuinely democratic country, it is practically impossible to have the situation where a particular social sphere comes to be regarded as the notorious crime of the whole society, thereby leaving no chance for revolutions.

Finally, Marx also noted: "A new revolution is possible only in consequence of a new crisis. It is, however, just as certain as this crisis." [4] Indeed, there have been many crises since Marx wrote this. All major capitalist countries (the U.S., Germany, France, the U.K., Japan, etc.) went through the Great Depression, which was a major crisis, but no revolutions took place. These countries just recently went through another crisis – the Great Recession – and once again, without revolutions: the recession only sparked the Occupy Wall Street movement, which died quickly. Indeed, crises can, but rarely do, lead to revolutions.

Transformation of Capitalism to Communism Can Only Be Done Through Armed Revolution

The position of Marxism on the role of armed battles in the transformation of capitalism to communism is not very clear. It seems to suggest a peaceful process through political fights, but nowhere does it reject armed battles. Today, the popular view is that Marxism leaves no choice but to replace capitalism with communism through violent battles. For example, most forewords to one of the most important works of Marx and Engels, *The Communist Manifesto*, claim that "it is the most influential political call-to-arms written." [7] However, let's read this manuscript and find those "call-to-arms" sentences – and this is easy, because the manuscript is only about 30 pages long.

The first phrase in the manuscript that may sound like a call-to-arms is: "What the bourgeoisie therefore produces, above all, are its own grave-diggers." The word "grave-diggers" sounds like a call-to-arms, but Marx and Engels did not literally call out to kill capitalists and bury them in graves. What they meant was the class struggle: as capitalism develops, it will produce a working class that will eventually grow so powerful that it will take political power from the bourgeoisie into its own hands.

The last paragraph of the manuscript sounds the most militant: "The Communists disdain to conceal their views and aims. They openly declare that their ends can be attained only by forcible overthrow of all existing conditions. Let the ruling class tremble at a communistic revolution." Yes, they use the phrase "forcible overthrow," which sounds like an armed fight. But let's read the next few words – forcible overthrow of what – "forcible overthrow of all existing conditions." It is the conditions that they want to kill, not people!

The next sentence – "Let the ruling class tremble at a communistic revolution" – sounds violent too. But do Marx and Engels mean that the ruling class should tremble because revolution means its execution? Not at all; by revolution they don't necessarily mean armed battles. Fortunately, in the middle of the manuscript, Marx and Engels provide a clue to what they do mean by revolution. In the chapter criticizing bourgeois socialism they write: "A second and more practical, but less systematic, form of this socialism sought to depreciate every revolutionary movement in the eyes of the working class, by showing that no mere political reform, but only a change in the material conditions of existence, in economical relations, could be any advantage of them" (emphasis added). What they mean by "revolutionary movement" is "political reform;" there is no mention of armed battle in the manuscript.

There is, however, one sentence in *The Communist Manifesto* that leaves us unsettled. It criticizes utopian socialists because "they reject all political, and especially all revolutionary, action; they wish to attain their ends by peaceful means..." Just before this, the manuscript elaborates that "revolution" means "political reforms." Now, it criticizes the utopians for their adherence to peaceful means, which could sound like a call to armed conflict.

But is it so important to check each and every sentence that Marx and Engels wrote or said? People change opinions, and sometimes contradict themselves. It is important to understand the theory of Marxism, and to keep in mind that Marxism is based on materialism and its core idea is that the development of society is based on economy, not on people's ideas and wishes. No view can be classified as Marxist if it does not recognize this premise. If we say that capitalism can be transformed to communism by armed uprising any time change is desired, then we say that it can be done at the peoples' wish, which contradicts Marxism. But if we recognize that economy can inevitably transform society no matter what – which is Marxism – then we have to recognize that capitalism can be transformed to communism gradually and peacefully. To say that armed fights may take place during this transformation is not necessarily counter to Marxism. But to say that this transformation is impossible without armed conflict is completely and utterly against Marxism.

So how did Marx and Engels come to be so misunderstood, and why do so many think that they only issued a call-to-arms? Marx and Engels were very passionate and used powerful figurative language at times. Unfortunately, for those (revolutionaries) who have already lost patience and seek armed battles, it is easy be literal and see a "call-to-arms" in their writing. On the other hand, for the majority (the working class) it is hard to understand this writing. This explains why the revolutionaries sometimes ended up in unnecessary armed battles and the working class has followed along.

This is not to say that Marx and Engels were pacifists who called for peaceful resolution of conflicts no matter what. But it is clear that by a fight they often meant a political fight, and by a revolution they often meant revolutionary (large scale) changes through reforms.

One of Marx and Engels's clearest statements in favor of revolutions can be found in one of their earliest works, *The German Ideology*. In this text, they claim that a revolution is necessary because communism will require the transformation of human spirit and morals: "Both for the production on a mass scale of this communist consciousness, and for the success of the cause itself, the alteration of man on a mass scale is necessary, an alteration which can only take place in a practical movement, a revolution; this revolution is necessary, therefore, not only because the ruling class cannot be overthrown in any other way, but also because the class overthrowing it can only in a revolution succeed in ridding itself of all the muck of ages and become fitted to found society anew." [2]

But once again, they talk here about "a revolution," suggesting that this can be any "practical movement," such as a labor union movement. They did not use the words "armed" or "violent," leaving room for a peaceful practical movement. Moreover, suggesting that only armed fighting, and not a peaceful movement, can make man "fit" for communism does not make much sense. Why should humans have to go through armed fights and violence in order to have better morals? Indeed, history does not support this at all. As we know, armed socialist revolutions have happened in several countries, but nothing suggests that these revolutions improved morals, or, in particular, the morals of the class leading these revolutions. Russia and the Soviet Union provide a good example. Instead of an improvement of morals, degradation took place. Uncontrolled corruption and abuse of power became the norm at the highest levels. In the new socialist country, each was supposed to give according to abilities and receive according to work. In reality, each began to receive according to their ability to steal (see more details in Chapter 7). Clearly, attempts to build communism through armed revolution spanning more than 70 years did not produce humans better fit for communism or with better morals.

And yet, Marx's most visible and reasoned projections that the transformation of capitalism to communism may require armed revolutions can be found in his book *Capital*. Although none of these particular projections have been confirmed by history, which disproves them, these projections revealed themselves to be so influential that the arguments behind them deserve a special section, which is below.

Marx's Projections in *Capital*

In his monumental work *Capital*, Marx forecasted the progression of capitalism as follows:

> "Along with the constantly diminishing number of the magnates of capital, who usurp and monopolize all advantages of this process of transformation, grows the mass of misery, oppression, slavery, degradation, exploitation; but with this too grows the revolt of the working class, a class always increasing in numbers, and disciplined, united, organized by the very mechanism of the process of capitalist production itself. ...Centralization of the means of production and socialization of labor at last reach a point where they become incompatible with their capitalist integument." [3]

In other words, Marx projected that capitalist enterprises will constantly merge one with another to form bigger ones, which will lead to a reduction of the number of capitalists – individuals who derive income from profits. On the other hand, he projected that the working class number, organization, oppression and revolt would grow, and that this would inevitably cause social revolutions.

The logic behind his doctrine, called the "law of increasing misery," is as follows: the main goal of a capitalist system is to achieve profits that are as high as possible from its investments. Progress and development of the capitalist economy is based on competition to magnify such profits. However, competition inevitably leads to higher unemployment and lower wages. This is because all owners/capitalists must cut costs in order to win the competition, and since the same machines and technology are available to all owners, the only way to reduce costs is to cut the cost of labor and the salaries of workers. Also, because new technology and machines can reduce the number of employees, unemployment will continue to rise and workers will have no choice but to accept lower and lower wages. In addition, as entrepreneurs compete against each other, some will go out of business and become unemployed as well, making the unemployment problem even worse.

Thus, the capitalists will become richer and the workers will become poorer. Finally, the misery of the workers will exceed its limits and explode in a revolt that will eliminate the (capitalist) system.

A. History Check

Surprisingly, more than a century after Marx wrote this, the capitalist system thrived, and is stronger than ever. Why is this? What went wrong with Marx's hypotheses? Let's check the facts: A) Did the number of magnates diminish? B) Did the working class increase in numbers, unification and organization? C) Did the misery of the working class grow? D) Did the revolt of working class grow? It may be tedious, but for the sake of science and objectivity, let's review all the hypotheses one by one:

A) Did the number of magnates diminish? It is true that capitalist ventures normally grow and merge one with another to form bigger and more profitable enterprises. This was obvious in the 19th century when Marx performed his analysis, and capitalist ventures were just forming and growing. But since the 20th century, it has also become obvious that not all big enterprises remain consistently profitable and survive through the ages. From time to time, some large ventures will go bankrupt and disappear, clearing space for new ones. Small business constantly rises in any developed capitalist (European, American or Asian) country, and this phenomenon is actually considered to be the foundation for a strong capitalist economy. Moreover, governments of developed capitalist countries do everything possible to ensure that small businesses continuously rise and are not suppressed by large corporations.

For example, let's analyze the current situation in the largest capitalist economy, the U.S. According to the American governmental organization the Small Business Administration, small business in the U.S. is constantly growing: "Small businesses provide 55% of all jobs and have provided 66% of all net new jobs since the 1970s. Furthermore, the small business sector is growing rapidly. While corporate America has been 'downsizing,' the rate of small business 'start-ups' has grown, and the rate for small business failures has declined. The number of small businesses in the United States has increased 49% since 1982. Since 1990, as big business eliminated 4 million jobs, small businesses added 8 million new jobs." [8]

European capitalist countries are in a similar situation. An EU press release from February 23, 2011 states the following: "Europe's 2020 strategy and Europe's economy heavily rely on Small and Medium-sized Enterprises (SMEs) achieving their potential. In the EU, some 23 million SMEs employ 67% of the private sector workforce. The Small Business Act (SBA) is the EU policy framework aimed at strengthening SMEs so that they can grow and create employment." [9]

These facts clearly show that the prediction of Marx did not come true: the "constantly diminishing number of the magnates of capital" did not take place. Instead, in order to function well, capitalist countries must strike a balance between large and small business, and a consistently growing small business sector is a necessary foundation for a healthy capitalist economy.

B) Did the working class increase in numbers, unification and organization? In general, the working class includes a majority of the population of industrial countries. Therefore, if the human population keeps growing, the working class will also grow, and that is what has happened so far.

But did unification and organization of the working class grow as well? It did during Marx's life and until World War II, which helped socialist revolutions in Russia and other countries. But unification and organization of the working class in capitalist countries has been statistically on the decline for almost one century now.

Traditionally, the main tool for organization of the working class has been trade unions, which are also called labor unions (American English). The main purpose of these unions is to improve the labor conditions of workers. It seems, however, that the conditions in capitalist countries have been improving so much that the working class has less and less interest in joining the unions. For example, in the world's largest economy, the U.S., the percentage of workers in unions fell to 11.3% in 2012, which is the lowest number in the last 97 years. [10] Similar drops in union membership are happening in other major capitalist economies. In Japan, the second largest capitalist economy, the organization rate, after growing to 55.8% in 1949, had declined to 18.5% by 2010. [11] In Germany, the third largest capitalist economy, the rate had also declined to 18.6% by 2010. [12] Overall, in Organization for Economic Co-operation (OECD) countries, including the main capitalist nations, the rate has declined to 17%. [12] Of course, not every country follows the same course. For example, union membership is still high in the Northern European capitalist countries, where it stands above 50%. However, it is safe to say that worldwide, organization of the working class has not risen.

One of the reasons why the unification and organization of the working class did not increase is that the very substance and composition of the working class have changed dramatically since Marx made his analysis. In Marx's time, the most organized and unified part of the working class, the proletariat, was growing. Proletarian workers were generally employed in large factories, which concentrate worker populations and facilitate interaction, unification and organization. Nowadays, the majority of capitalist countries have entered into a so-called "post-industrial society" stage – a stage wherein the service sector generates more wealth than the manufacturing sector of the economy. The service sector includes many branches of the economy, such as transportation, distribution and sale of goods, entertainment and others. This is now the largest and the fastest growing sector in the Western world. For example, in the United States, the service sector constitutes about 68% of GDP and employs about 70% of the workforce. Thus, the most organized part of the working class, the proletariat, has been diminished, and this trend continues.

However, new technologies are bringing new change to our society. The Internet and social media now make mass connections easier, which can help the organization and unification of the working class once again. It has already facilitated movements like Occupy Wall Street and the Arab Spring revolutions of 2010, demonstrating that the working class can now get organized and unified more quickly than ever before.

C) Did the misery of the working class grow? The best indicator of the growing misery of the working class is its growing poverty. Another good indicator of growing misery is more work and/or longer working days for the same or less money. Mortality rate is also a good indicator, as misery would have a negative impact on health and would increase mortality rates. Let's see if any of these indicators have grown in capitalist nations since Marx wrote *Capital* (around 1850) to the modern time.

Poverty occurs when people lack the means to satisfy their basic needs. It is mostly defined by income, and the World Bank currently defines poverty as living on less than $1.25 (purchasing power parity) per day. Although poverty levels of the working class have gone up and down throughout the last 160 years, overall, they have clearly decreased. This decrease began with the industrial revolution that started around 1760. In fact, improvements to living standards of the working class could already be felt by the time Marx began his analysis. Poverty levels in Western capitalist countries began falling especially quickly after World War II, when a significant redistribution of the national income in favor of the working class took place. As a result, world economic poverty fell from 52.2% in 1981 to 22.4% in 2008, despite the fact that the majority of the human population lives in capitalist countries. According to World Bank data, between 1990 and 2010, about 663 million people moved above the absolute poverty level. [13] Although most countries in the world are ruled by capitalist governments, they have somehow successfully worked toward ending working class misery and continue to do so – quite the opposite to Marxist theories. Continuing in this direction, in 2002, all 191 member states of the United Nations signed the Millennium Declaration to eradicate extreme poverty by 2025.

Of course, the reduction in the rate of poverty does not mean that poverty is no longer a problem. Also, the reduction of working class poverty is just a general trend that fluctuates depending on the time and country. Lately, the trend has reversed and, as of 2015, "the bottom half of the global population owns less than 1 percent of total wealth. In sharp contrast, the richest 10 percent hold 86 percent of the world's wealth, and the top 1 percent alone account for 46 percent of global assets." [14] In the past several years, the overall trend of the rich getting richer while the poor get poorer in capitalist countries has continued and even accelerated (see details in Chapter 8).

Media and governments are paying attention to this negative trend and, hopefully, measures will be taken to stop it. If not, then Marx may be right: working class misery will grow, revolutionary conditions will be created, and the upper class may live to regret appropriating too much of the wealth.

These are just general observations. But let's go into more detail, and analyze the situation in the U.S. as an example. When one reads analyses on poverty in this country, the picture may look bleak. According to a survey by the Associated Press, four out of five U.S. adults struggle with joblessness, near-poverty or reliance on welfare for at least part of their lives. The USDA Economic Research Service states that 14.5% of American households were food-insecure during the year 2012. And this situation seems to be getting worse, not better. Extreme poverty (households living on less than $2 per day before government benefits), doubled from 1996 levels to 1.5 million households in 2011, including 2.8 million children. In 2011, 16.7 million children lived in food-insecure households, about 35% more than 2007 levels.

It does not look like American workers have a good life! Such facts served many ideologists as a basis for the endorsement of Marxism and the bankruptcy of bourgeois theories, suggesting that class distinctions in modern bourgeois society are being eliminated and classes are converging into one huge middle class. For example, the textbook *Marxist Philosophy*, widely used in the former USSR and translated into dozens of languages, uses these facts as evidence for the bankruptcy of bourgeois and opportunistic theories of classes and class struggle. It reasonably points out: "It is true that standard of living of some workers in the US... is high. But we must not forget that far from all American workers enjoy this high standard. In the USA in 1975, an estimated 33.2 million Americans, or 17.3% of the population lived below the official poverty line. At the same time 1% of the population accounted for 25% of the national wealth," [15] and so on.

But then the question arises: why are so many people from all over the world so eager to immigrate to America? Is it because life in this country is relatively comfortable? The reality is that what is considered "poor" in the U.S. could often be considered "rich" in many developing countries. In fact, over 80% of "poor" American households have air conditioning, three quarters own at least one automobile and about 40% own their homes. Most poor people in the U.S. have a refrigerator, stove, microwave, telephone and television. About half have computers and almost half also have internet service.

It should also be noted that the bar for middle class living has risen over time in the U.S. and other capitalist countries, and what was once considered middle class living few decades ago is now considered poor. Thus, being poor in the U.S. today is not as bad as it used to be a century ago, and overall, for the year 2012, the United States ranked 12th on the Legatum Prosperity Index (see Table 1).

Even the most negative outlook on the U.S. does not confirm Marx's theory of growing misery. For example, the documentary film *Inequality for All*, intended to portray a dire situation, finds that the wealth gap in the U.S. is as wide as it was in 1928, when the richest 1% owned more than 35% of the country's wealth, while the poorest 50% owned just 2.5%. Please note that these findings suggest that the situation did not change, which is counter to Marx's prediction that it would worsen.

Let's now check the other indicators of misery: 1) Did workers have longer working days for the same/less money? 2) Did the mortality rate of the working class increase? To both of these questions the answer is very obviously "no." It is now common knowledge that workers in all capitalist counties have much shorter working days (generally limited to eight hours as opposed to more than ten hours previously), more days off and longer vacations than ever before. Overall, work hours declined by about half over the past century. And capitalist countries are the front-runners. For example, in 2011, average weekly work hours in Germany were only 25.6 hours. [16]

At the same time, the wages of the working class have increased instead of decreased, and the quality of life has improved. As a result, the mortality rate of the working class has dramatically decreased, while life expectancy has similarly increased. For example, in early 1800, when Marx was born, life expectancy in Europe and Japan was only about 40 years. Now, in the early 2000s, it has doubled, standing at about 80 years. There are no specific statistics on the life expectancy of the working class, but since society mostly consists of this class, it is safe to say that the life expectancy of the working class has increased. And this trend continues all over the world: about 5.7 billion people (out of about 6 billion total) appear to live in countries where life expectancy has increased between 1980 and 2000.

Overall, contrary to Marx's projection, the life of the working class in capitalist countries got better instead of worse. Employee workdays have shortened, wages have increased and economic security has been strengthened through such fringe benefit programs as pensions and others.

In conclusion, Marx's projections that the misery of the working class would grow did not come true. Why is that? What went wrong with the theory? One reason was Marx's assumption that the only way that capitalists could increase their profits was by cutting the salaries of workers. But reality did not support this. Sometimes, cutting the wages of workers can have the opposite effect. The business practices of some of the world's largest companies and competitors, Wal-Mart and Costco (both American companies), provide a good illustration. As of 2013, Costco paid its workers an average of over $20 per hour, while Wal-Mart averaged just under $13. In spite of this, as reported by CNN, Costco's business was doing better than Wal-Mart's: "Sales at Costco have grown an average of 13% annually since 2009, while profits have risen 15%. Its stock price has more than doubled since 2009. During the same period, discount retailer Wal-Mart's sales grew an average of 4.5% each year, profits rose 7%, and its stock price increased 70%... Research shows that it pays to pay employees well, because satisfied workers are more productive and motivated, according to MIT Sloan School of Management professor Zeynep Ton, who focuses on operation management... The productivity translates into sales." [17]

Some capitalist enterprises and governments took note of this a long time ago, and this contributed to the reduction of working hours that is now observed in many capitalist countries, especially those in Europe. It seems that this reduction does not cause decreased work output, but rather the opposite. This is supported by the fact that in 2011, "... of the 10 countries with the fewest average hours worked, nine have the highest gross domestic product per capita..." [16] For example, the average American worked about 34.5 hours per week and earned only $30 per hour, while the average German worked about 25.6 hours per week and earned over $35 per hour. [16] It seems that Marx ignored or missed an important factor in work productivity: better-rested and more motivated workers can perform better, and that helps produce higher profits.

D) Did the revolt of the working class grow? Although the revolt grew for a few decades after Marx made his projections, nothing suggests that this trend continued during the last half century. One of the most prominent thinkers of the 20th century, Herbert Marcuse, pointed out that the modern working class "shares in large measure the needs and aspirations of the dominant class," [18] which makes it less likely to revolt.

The current situation of the working class in the leading capitalist country, the U.S., is well described in one of the *Outside the Beltway* publications: "In terms of the more fundamental question, middle- and working-class Americans are not overly concerned about the fate of poor or the relative luxury of the rich... For people to demand change, they will have to first come to believe that the game is rigged. Right now, Americans think that they live in the land of opportunity – a country where, to an extent not possible anywhere else in the world, people can climb their way to the top through a combination of talent and hard work. The fact that this is not true and has not been true for quite some time really does not matter; it has not yet altered popular perception." [19] As American writer John Steinbeck famously expressed it: "Socialism never took root in America because the poor see themselves not as an exploited proletariat but as temporarily embarrassed millionaires." This is also probably true for other developed capitalist countries, where the working class is quite content with its life.

Workers' strikes can be used as one of the main measures of revolt, and statistics shows that the number of workers who go on strike in major capitalist countries has been declining over the last century. For example, according to data by the U.S. Labor Department, 2009 saw the fewest major strikes since the agency began tracking such data in 1947 (this despite the country being in a deep recession that year). [20]

Although data regarding labor strikes in many countries is not readily available, overall statistics suggest that the numbers worldwide have also been in decline. This can be extrapolated from labor statistics showing a five-year average in days not worked due to strikes per 1000 employees (1996-2000). In the U.S., where the number of strikes was in decline, the number is 60. [21] In the second largest capitalist economy, Japan, this amount is only one, which is dramatically lower. In the third largest capitalist economy, Germany, this amount is also much lower: only two. These numbers are already so low that they could not have been even lower before 1996. Thus, they suggest that the number of workers going on strike in Japan and Germany has been in decline too, or at least did not grow in recent times. Based on this, it is safe to conclude that the overall number of workers who went on strike in capitalist countries did not increase, which contradicts Marx's projections.

The desire of the working class to revolt, of course, depends upon their living conditions. In the last century, these conditions have been improving overall, and this has led to the decline in revolts. Marx's prediction of the growing misery of the working class did not come true and, as a result, his prediction of growing revolts did not come true either.

Nevertheless, if policymakers make mistakes, this could change. In fact, such mistakes have recently been made, and conditions for many workers over the last few years have been worsening – the rich have been getting richer and the poor have been getting poorer (see Chapter 8 for details). As *The Fiscal Times* publication put it in 2011: "Inequality has been reverted to levels unseen since the Gilded Age, financial regulation has waned, monopoly power has increased, union power has been lost, and much of the disgust with the political process revolves around the feeling that politicians are out of touch with the interests of the working class." [22] This could inevitably lead to the dissatisfaction of the working class, which may have already reached its starting point. For example, "a Gallup poll finds two-thirds of Americans are unhappy with the nation's distribution of wealth." [23] This could reverse the general course of worker satisfaction over the last century very quickly, and a revolt of the working class may grow again.

B. Summary of Marx's Mistakes

So far, history shows that humanity is moving toward a society with more and more social programs, which is socialism – the first stage of communism. Indeed, socialism has taken a strong hold in the most developed capitalist countries like Denmark, Norway, and others. It is even taking hold in countries like the U.S. that fiercely oppose communism. This supports the theory that capitalism will eventually be replaced with socialism and then communism.

However, history does not confirm Marx's projections that the misery and revolt of the working class would grow and lead to armed revolution. Rather the opposite: history demonstrates that the life of the working class has been continuously improving. This indicates that capitalism may peacefully be transformed to communism. What went wrong with Marx's theories? He made the following mistakes:

A) *Ignoring the role of small business in capitalist economy.* Marx assumed that the number of magnates would continuously diminish until finally a small number of them would control the whole wealth of the world. This must be based on his other assumption that once capitalist enterprises were created, they would thrive and exist forever. In reality, it appears that the rise of new enterprises and start-up businesses is an essential part of capitalism. In capitalist economies, new businesses are created, compete against each other and fail constantly. New small businesses are the most vital part of a capitalist economy and therefore, in contrast to Marx's projections, "the number of magnates of capital" did not diminish;

B) *Ignoring the factor of workers' productivity.* Marx assumed that since the same machines and technology were available to all owners, the only way for capitalists to raise profits was to cut labor costs and the salaries of workers. If this was true, then the salaries of workers would continue to decrease and, in order to survive, workers would have no choice but to fight for their lives and revolt. However, history shows that workers' wages have been continuously growing. It appears that capitalists have discovered that well-rested and more motivated workers can do a better job, and better performance means higher profits. This could be one of the reasons why the misery of the working class did not grow, as Marx predicted;

C) *Failing to consider that capitalist governments may change their treatment of the working class and find ways to redistribute wealth.* For many reasons, capitalist governments have increasingly taxed the rich and passed the collected money to the poor through a variety of social programs (see details in Chapter 8). Perhaps Marx did not give enough credit to human nature, and capitalists are kinder people than he thought. Or maybe capitalists became aware of Marx's projections, and decided to keep workers happy in order to prevent revolutions; and

D) *Not foreseeing that the economy could change so drastically that it would change the composition of the working class and its ability to revolt.* It is hard to blame Marx for not foreseeing this. Over a hundred years ago, who could imagine that humanity would enter a post-industrial age, in which the service economy would employ more workers than manufacturing? This change in the working class composition lessened the likelihood of revolt.

Last but not least, Marx's "surplus value" theory, which is a central concept in his political economy, also raises questions and has been criticized. This theory, developed in *Capital*, explains how capitalist society works. It is based on the premise that the labor of workers is one of the sources of economic value, which is added to the value of goods. However, the bourgeoisie pays workers less than the value of their labor. Thus, workers produce a value greater than what it costs to hire them, which creates "surplus value." Mathematically speaking:

value produced by a worker – cost to employ him = surplus value

Capitalists appropriate surplus value as part of their profit. Since a capitalist system is driven by profits, and profits arise from surplus value, it requires that workers are paid as little as possible in order to ensure that profits are as high as possible. This inevitably leads to exploitation, making capitalism immoral society by its very nature.

The theory has been criticized for completely ignoring the value of the services of capitalists as entrepreneurs or managers. It has no recognition that capitalists, through their management, also participate in the creation of "value" and are entitled to at least some profits.

At first, this critique sounds fair and valid. However, it ignores the question: How much profit do capitalists deserve for their services? They certainly deserve something, and perhaps their profits should be higher than the average compensation of workers. But how much higher should it be? Let's try using common sense. In many countries, when a worker does a good job, he or she gets a bonus (typically, one month pay at the end of the year, which means an 8.3% salary increase). When a worker does something exceptional, the salary may even be raised 2-3 times. It is even possible to imagine a worker performing such an exceptional job that his or her salary was raised about 10 times – although such a high raise already sounds alarming and suspicious. However, we can all agree that raising an employee's salary 100 times or higher is outrageous, no matter how incredible the worker is.

Typical capitalists do not apply this thinking to their own labors. They believe their contributions to be so utterly invaluable that their compensation should be unlimited. For example, let's take a look at one of the world's largest companies, Wal-Mart. In 2013, Wal-Mart paid its workers an average of just under $13 per hour, which translates into about $27,000 per year working full time 40 hours a week for 52 weeks. In stark contrast, the net worth of one of the owners, S. Robson Walton (whose father was the founder of the company), was estimated to be $34.2 billion as of 2014. Mr. Walton joined his father's company in 1978, which means that he worked there 36 years and got paid about $1 billion per year. Let's look at the math: $\$1,000,000,000 \div \$27,000 = 37,037$.

Mr. Walton (a capitalist) has been paid over 37,000 times more than the average Wal-Mart employee. This is clearly an affront to common sense and cannot be justified. We can see that capitalists usually take far more profits than they deserve (indeed, as much as they can), which is the problem. Some argue that awarding super-salaries to talented individuals is economically justified because talented managers and executives can dramatically increase productivity. In reality, economic studies disprove this, showing that "the elasticity of executive pay is greater with respect to 'luck'… than with respect to "talent." [24] Thus, real-life examples don't justify high pay of owners/executives and do confirm Marx's theory of surplus value.

Governments can – and do – regulate such abnormally high profits through taxes. This is especially evident in European countries, where higher incomes are taxed at higher rates. After collecting excess profits, governments can return them to workers through a variety of programs. However, this is the measure of socialism. The more the government redistributes the wealth, the more socialist it becomes. When all the wealth is distributed equally, a country becomes communist.

The role of governments in the economy has been continuously increasing in almost every country in the world. Collected taxes are the base for government spending and, in 1850, the average share of government spending in relation to the GDP of capitalist economies was only 5%. However, this increased to 30% by 1950, and today it averages around 40%. This is a clear indication that governments are collecting and redistributing wealth more and more, and the world is becoming more and more socialist, just as Marx predicted.

Summary

Marxism makes the claim that capitalism will inevitably be replaced with communism. So far, history confirms a definite trend in this direction. The main reason for this is the continuous advancement of world economies rather than people's wishes. Marx and Engels suggested that the transformation of capitalism to communism could only be accomplished by "a revolution," which has been widely interpreted as an "armed revolution." However, by "a revolution" they meant either peaceful or armed revolution, depending on the political conditions.

The primary cause of an armed revolution, according to Marx, would be the growing contradiction between productive forces (centralized means of production) and productive forms (socialized labor). He projected that working class misery, oppression, slavery, degradation and exploitation would grow, and that these factors would plant the seeds of revolt. He also projected that the size, discipline, unification and organization of the working class would constantly grow. But we can see that none of these projections came true, which minimized the possibility of armed and violent revolutions. Instead, history has demonstrated that capitalism can be peacefully transformed into communism. In fact, capitalist countries continue introducing more and more socialist measures, and this is the secret to the survival and success of capitalism.

References

1. Das Kapital. *New York Times* (1967, September 16).

2. Marx, K., Engels, F. The German Ideology (1846), published by International Publishers (2007).

3. Marx, K. Capital (1867), published by Penguin Classics (1992).

4. Marx, K. The Class Struggles in France, 1848 to 1850 (1850). *Marxists.org website* (retrieved 2013, February 05).

5. Shan, L. French Court Approves New 'Millionaire Tax' on the Wealthy. *Los Angeles Times* (2013, December 30).

6. Marx, K. Contribution to the Critique of Hegel's Philosophy of Right: Introduction (1844), in Karl Marx: Early Writings, published by Mcgraw-Hill (1963).

7. Marx, K., Engels, F. The Communist Manifesto (1848), published by Verso (1998).

8. Small Business Trends (2014). *U.S. Small Business Administration website (retrieved 2014, April 10)*.

9. Europe's Small Business Act Strengthens Small Businesses and Drives Growth. *European Commission Press Release* (2011, February 23).

10. Greenhouse, S. Share of the Work Force in a Union Falls to a 97-Year Low, 11.3%. *New York Times* (2013, January 23).

11. Labor Situation in Japan and Analysis (2010). *Japan Institute for Labor Policy and Training website (retrieved 2013, December 12).*

12. Trade Union Density (2010). *OECD StatExtracts website (retrieved 2013, December 12).*

13. The World Bank. World Bank Sees Progress Against Extreme Poverty, but Flags Vulnerabilities. *Press Release* (2012, February 29).

14. Kersley, R., O'Sullivan, M. Global Wealth Reaches New All-Time High. *Credit Swiss Group web site, News and Experise* (2013, October 9).

15. Afanasiev, V. G. Marxist Philosophy, published by Progress Publishers (1978).

16. Sauter, M. B., Hess, A.E.M., Nelson L.A. Countries Where People Work Least. *NBC News* (2012, July 29).

17. Fox, E. J. Worker Wages: Wendy's vs. Wal-Mart vs. Costco. *CNN* (2013, August 06).

18. Ferrier, J., Boetsch, J., Giroud, F. Marcuse Defines His New Left Line. *New York Times* (1968, October 27).

19. Joyner, J. Why Doesn't the Middle Class Revolt? *Outside the Beltway* (2012, June 6).

20. Daneman, M. Fewer Workers Go on Strike as Organized Labor Shrinks. *USA Today* (2010, July 6).

21. Strike Statistics - Countries Compared (2010). *Nation Master website* (retrieved December 19, 2013.

22. Thoma, M. Why a Working-Class Revolt Might Not Be Unthinkable. *The Fiscal Times* (2011, September 13).

23. Rugaber, C. S. Wealth Gap: A Guide to What It Is and Why It Matters. *Associated Press* (2014, January 27).

24. Piketty, T. Capital in the Twenty-First Century, published by Belknap Press of Harvard University Press (2014).

Chapter 6

The World of Communism Today

By definition, there are no communist countries in the world at the present time. Indeed, this may be far off in the future. However, socialism is the early first stage of communism, and elements of socialism are already present in most countries. These elements include public property, a public sector economy and a variety of social programs (public education, public healthcare, retirement programs, etc.). Overall, the presence of these elements reduces inequality and creates more balanced societies. To judge how much communism is present in a particular country, one has to evaluate the presence of these elements and to estimate the degree of equality among its citizens.

Socialism has several important characteristics: 1) regarding the structure of the economy, socialism means that the public owns the means of production and therefore, controls the economy. This is in contrast to capitalism, where the means of production are privately owned; 2) regarding class structure, socialism requires that an economy is socialized in such a way that it equally benefits all working members of society, which means income fairness. This is in contrast to capitalism, where most of the money disproportionally ends up in the pockets of a small group of people (capitalists), leading to income inequality. To clarify, socialism does not mean that all society members have absolutely equal incomes – this would be communism. In socialist society, everyone is paid according to his or her work.

It is also important to remember that socialism means democracy and freedom (see Chapter 1), and some define socialism as a maximally egalitarian/democratic society. Others define it as a society ruled by the

**Table 2. Self-Proclaimed Socialist/Communist Countries
(as of 2015)**

Number	Name	Year of Inception
	Marxist-Leninist Orientation	
1	People's Republic of China	1949
2	Republic of Cuba	1959
3	Lao People's Democratic Republic (Laos)	1975
4	Socialist Republic of Vietnam	1976
	Non-Marxist-Leninist Orientation	
5	Democratic People's Republic of Korea (North Korea)	1948
6	United Republic of Tanzania	1964
7	Cooperative Republic of Guyana	1970
8	People's Republic of Bangladesh	1971
9	Democratic Socialist Republic of Sri Lanka	1972

working class. However, both of these definitions mean the same thing: if a society is democratic, then it is ruled by the working class because the working class constitutes the majority in any society. Thus, socialism can be defined either as a maximally egalitarian/democratic society or a society ruled by the working class.

Some also define socialism as a planned economy in which production for profits has been replaced with production for needs. Socialism, however, does not require a planned economy. In fact, neither Marx nor Engels nor Lenin ever suggested that the economy must be planned in a socialist society.

Currently, several countries claim to be socialist. As of 2015, there were nine self-proclaimed socialist countries in the world (Table 2). However, the list is constantly changing. Some analysts now add several other countries to it: India, Portugal, Nepal, Nicaragua, et. al. North Korea's situation is not completely clear; in 2009, all references to communism were removed from the country's constitution.

Nevertheless, this country still describes itself as a "Korean-style" socialist republic.

Please note that the simple self-proclamation of being socialist does not mean that those countries already have socialism, let alone communism. What it means is that those countries desire and aim to build socialism. So why don't they have it? Because they can't afford it, they don't have sufficient wealth to share, and their economies are simply not there yet. Such countries may have initiated socialism and may already be in the primary stage of socialism, but developed socialism is still a distant future. For instance, when asked how long it would take China to build socialism, former leader Jiang Zemin replied, "At least 100 years." Indeed, simple analysis shows that self-proclaimed socialist countries in today's world are not very socialist at all, while some capitalist countries are quite socialist already.

One of the most important indicators of the existence of socialism or communism is freedom. However, currently, there are no objective data evaluating this factor in different countries around the world. The second most important indicator is equality – how equally or unequally income is distributed across the population. This is currently measured by a Gini index, where a value of 0 indicates absolute equality, while a value of 100 stands for absolute inequality. The index is published by several organizations like the World Bank and the U.S. Central Intelligence Agency (CIA). Current analysis shows that the top countries with the greatest equality are classified as developed capitalist countries, mostly in Europe (Table 3). On the other hand, China, which is classified as a socialist country, is near the bottom of this list, ranking 29th among countries with the greatest inequality.

The other important indicator of socialism and communism is the presence of a public sector in the economy or the nationalized economy. The basis of a capitalist economy is private ownership, and a higher presence of a public sector indicates a more socialist/communist economic nature. Once again, developed capitalist countries are at the top of the list (Table 3), while not even one self-proclaimed socialist country is in the top 30.

Ideally, a well-developed public sector (nationalized) economy should facilitate a more even distribution of incomes. What is produced

Table 3. Countries with Socialist Features (as of 2011)

Countries with the greatest equality [1]			Countries with the greatest public sector revenue [2]		
Rank	Name	Gini index	Rank	Name	GDP,%
1	Sweden	23.0	1	Kuwait	67.1
2	Slovenia	23.8	2	Norway	49.5
3	Montenegro	24.3	3	Hungary	48.2
4	Hungary	24.7	4	France	42.7
5	Denmark	24.8	5	Belgium	41.2
6	Norway	25.0	6	Greece	41.0
7	Luxembourg	26.0	7	Algeria	40.6
8	Slovakia	26.0	8	Denmark	40.5
9	Austria	26.3	9	Portugal	39.9
10	Finland	26.8	10	Macao, China	39.9
11	Germany	27.0	11	Bosnia & Herz.	39.7
12	Belarus	27.2	12	Luxembourg	39.5
13	Malta	27.4	13	Oman	39.3
14	Iceland	28.0	14	Finland	38.4
15	Belgium	28.0	15	Italy	37.6
16	Serbia	28.2	16	Serbia	37.6
17	Ukraine	28.2	17	Malta	37.2
18	Kazakhstan	28.9	18	Slovenia	36.9
19	Cyprus	29.0	19	Austria	36.3
20	Switzerland	29.6	20	The U.K.	36.3

[1] Data from *The World Factbook* published by the U.S. Central Intelligence Agency (CIA); [2] The World Bank data.

Countries with both the greatest equality and public sector revenue (underlined) can be considered to be the most socialist. The top ten socialist countries are (alphabetically): Austria, Denmark, Belgium, Finland, Hungary, Luxembourg, Malta, Norway, Serbia and Slovenia.

through common means should be distributed equally among all citizens. However, this is rarely the case. As Michael Harrington pointed out in his 1989 book, nationalization cannot be seen as the sovereign socialist remedy because "the nationalized industry also has to be socialized." [1]

Kuwait is a good example. Public sector revenue in this country is among the greatest compared to other countries (Table 3). However, this country is not even on the top 30 list of countries with the greatest equality. The most obvious explanation for this is that the common economy was used to enrich one part of the population at the expense of the other. In other words, the country may be corrupt. Indeed, in 2011, Kuwait was ranked 54th (from the lowest to highest) in the corruption perceptions index published by Transparency International, which includes 182 countries. This suggests medium levels of corruption and explains why this country is not at the top of the list of countries with the greatest equality, despite the high presence of the public sector in the economy. It is clear that corruption is a major obstacle in the process of building socialism, and eventually communism.

Ironically, many self-proclaimed socialist countries are among the most corrupt countries, while highly developed capitalist countries are among the least corrupt (Table 4). Most mixed socialist-capitalist economies (e.g., the Scandinavian countries) are less corrupt than those that are decidedly more capitalist, suggesting a positive role in the infusion of socialism into capitalism. Countries with the greatest degree of equality can be considered to be the most socialist. However, the way wealth is produced is a factor, even if it is distributed equally. If wealth is created by private enterprises but distributed equally among all, the owners may feel robbed, while individuals who receive part of the wealth may feel indebted to the producers. This can create all kinds of problems for society: moral, economic and political.

Therefore, creating wealth through public enterprises may make the situation more agreeable for both sides. Countries with the greatest degree of equality and the strongest public sector could be considered the most socialist. Following from Table 3, the top ten most socialist countries are as follows: Austria, Denmark, Belgium, Finland, Hungary, Luxembourg, Malta, Norway, Serbia and Slovenia. They are simply listed alphabetically because socialist ranking needs to take into account

Table 4. Rating of Corruption (as of 2011)

Self-proclaimed socialist countries		Non-proclaimed socialist countries	
Name	Rank*	Name	Rank*
Cuba	61	Denmark	2
China	75	Finland	2
Sri Lanka	86	Norway	6
Tanzania	100	Luxembourg	11
Bangladesh	120	Austria	16
Vietnam	112	Belgium	19
Guyana	134	Slovenia	35
Laos	154	Malta	39
North Korea	182	Hungary	54
		Serbia	86

* According to the corruption perceptions index published by Transparency International. Rank 1 stands for the lowest corruption; 182 indicates the highest corruption.

several factors; thus, it is difficult to determine. Such ranking would require an entirely separate study. What is remarkable here is that these countries are also among the most economically advanced and prosperous countries in the world (Table 5). For example, Norway and Denmark have been rated as the most prosperous nations in the world for the last few years. Since socialism is the first stage of communism, this situation is a reflection of Marxist central idea that the most economically advanced countries will approach the standard of communism first.

Clearly, the self-proclaimed communist countries are neither among the most prosperous, nor are they the most socialist. The fact that these countries are not prosperous is not proof that communism hurts prosperity. What does hurt prosperity is the self-proclamation of communism – because history shows that capitalist countries are simply not willing to accept a world in which some countries choose to identify

Table 5. Prosperity Ranking, by Legatum Institute (as of 2011)

Self-proclaimed socialist countries		Non-proclaimed socialist countries	
Name	Rank*	Name	Rank*
Cuba	n/a	Denmark	2
China	52	Finland	7
Sri Lanka	63	Norway	1
Tanzania	96	Luxembourg	n/a
Bangladesh	95	Austria	14
Vietnam	62	Belgium	17
Guyana	n/a	Slovenia	22
Laos	n/a	Malta	n/a
North Korea	n/a	Hungary	36
		Serbia	n/a

* Rank 1 stands for the highest prosperity, while 110 indicates the lowest prosperity; n/a – data is not available. The ranking is based on a variety of factors including wealth, economic growth and quality of life.

as communist. For example, when Vietnam turned to communism, the U.S. bombed it. When communists took over power in Cuba, the U.S. tried to invade and overthrow the government, and when this did not work, it blockaded Cuba. Having great economic power, the West generally suppresses the economic development of countries with communist identification. This makes it difficult to predict how successful these countries would be if they were given equal chances for development and not economically suppressed. However, some data suggests that countries that choose a communist direction develop faster. Here is a comparison of the democratic capitalist country of Nicaragua and communist Vietnam, seen in the magazine *Foreign Affairs:*

"Both are poor countries with primarily agricultural economies. Both have suffered from long periods of conflict. And both have benefited from substantial foreign aid. But only Vietnam has reduced poverty dramatically and enjoyed steady economic growth (five percent per capita since 1988). Nicaragua has floundered economically, with per capita growth too modest to make a real dent in the number of poor people.

Vietnam faced a U.S. embargo until 1994, and it is still not a member of the World Trade Organization (WTO). Despite these obstacles, it has found markets for its growing exports of coffee and other agricultural products and has successfully begun diversifying into manufacturing as well, especially of textiles. Nicaragua, on the other hand, benefits from preferential access to the lucrative U.S. market and had several billion dollars of its official debt written off in the 1990s. Yet its coffee and clothing export industries have not been able to compete with Vietnam's.

Why has Vietnam outpaced Nicaragua? The answers are internal: history and economic and political institutions have trumped other factors in determining economic success. Access to the U.S. market and the largesse of Western donors have not been powerful enough to overcome Nicaragua's history of social and economic inequality: land and power there have long been concentrated in the hands of a few elites, and the government has failed to invest enough in infrastructure and public welfare." [2]

As a result of these government policies, people in Vietnam live a better life than in Nicaragua: in the list of the 2014 Prosperity Legatum Index, Vietnam has been ranked 56th while Nicaragua is only 76th.

It is ironic how large the gap is between reality and the common perceptions of the most socialist countries. The situation is quite often reversed: countries that are perceived to be successfully capitalist tend to be among the most socialist (Denmark, Norway, etc.), while countries that are perceived to be socialist (e.g. China) are among the most capitalist in practice. Thus, some capitalist nations had no plan to build socialism (the first stage of communism), but that's what they did. On the other hand, self-proclaimed socialist countries planned to build socialism and eventually communism, but they could not achieve it. This is a clear confirmation of Marxist theory, which states that society develops based on the economy, regardless of our wishes.

Then how does one classify self-proclaimed socialist countries as socialist if they do not have socialism? Indeed, it is not easy to classify them as either capitalist or socialist. But if these countries are not capitalist and not socialist, then what are they? As far back as the 1920s, Russian Bolshevik revolutionary Nikolai Bukharin defined them as "bureaucratic collectivist." American thinker and socialist Michael Harrington describes them as follows: "They are collectivist, but not socialist. The means of production are indeed nationalized, but the people have no control over the economy they theoretically own. The state that possesses those means of production is virtually the private property of bureaucracy that manages them in the name of people. Power is thus determined by the position of an individual, or a class, in the dictatorial political structure rather than, as under capitalism, in the economic and social structure. I call this system bureaucratic collectivism and argue that it is neither capitalist nor socialist." [1]

An illustration of communism around the world can be drawn by looking at how taxes are allocated. Most of the resources collected through taxes are funneled into two social spheres, which are key elements of socialism and communism: 1) public health and education, providing equality of access for everyone regardless of income; and 2) replacement incomes (pensions and unemployment compensations) and transfer payments (guaranteed income and family allowances). Recent analysis by Piketty [3] demonstrates that tax revenues have continuously increased over the past century in all rich capitalist countries: they went from a ratio in which less than 10% of their national income was consumed by taxes to a ratio of 30-50%. And what effect did growing taxes have on capitalist states? It enabled them to broaden social programs, which consume between 30% and 50% of national income, depending on the country. In fact, there is currently no serious political movement in any Western country that promotes a return to the old system, in which only 10% of national income was collected through taxes. The world of capitalism has clearly moved closer to communism.

In general, as economies develop and countries become richer, they raise taxes to improve social services. For example, in 1970-1980, governments of the poorest countries (India, South Asia and Sub-Saharan Africa) collected about 10-15% of national income through taxes, while governments of intermediately developed countries (China, Latin America and North Africa) – 15-20% of national income, and rich countries (the West) – 35-40% of national income. [3] Some countries like China and Vietnam make no secret that their socialist programs depend on economy and income: they don't have certain socialist programs simply because they cannot afford it, and will only have them as their economy advances, providing the necessary money and resources. Thus, trends in taxation show that as countries become wealthier, they get closer and closer to communism – which is again well in agreement with Marxist theory that communism will rise as the result of advances in the economy.

Surprisingly, in the past few years, the capitalist world began sliding back toward more inequality (see Chapter 8 for details). This is especially pronounced in the U.S. and the U.K. However, not all nations have moved in this direction. Countries with deeper roots in socialism, e.g., Scandinavian countries, have not experienced this move back toward more inequality. Democracy and socialism have become so permeated in these societies that the development toward communism seems irreversible.

Summary

There is a large gap between reality and common perceptions regarding which countries are the most socialist in the modern world. Self-proclaimed socialist countries are in fact not very socialist, while some capitalist countries are quite socialist already. Ironically, some capitalist nations had no plan to build socialism (the first stage of communism) but ended up becoming socialist anyway. On the other hand, most self-proclaimed socialist countries did plan to build socialist societies, but failed. This is a clear confirmation of Marxist theory that society develops (into communism) based on economy, regardless of our wishes. Also, the data shows that socialism and prosperity are closely related, with the top ten socialist countries being among the most economically advanced and prosperous countries in the world. This is perfectly in line with the core idea of Marxism that the most economically advanced countries will reach communism the soonest.

References

1. Harrington, M. Socialism: Past and Future, published by Arcade Publishing (1989).
2. Birdsall, N., Rodrik, D., Subramanian, A. How to Help Poor Countries. *Foreign Affairs* (2005, July/August).
3. Piketty, T. Capital in the Twenty-First Century, published by Belknap Press of Harvard University Press (2014).

Chapter 7

What Happened
in Russia and the USSR:
The Anatomy of Failure

M any people around the world believe that the Great October Revolution, which took place in Russia in 1917, was the first large-scale test of Marxist theories in practice. As we know by now, it was not successful. Was it a real test? Did it happen according to the theories of Marxism?

Before the Revolution

According to Marxist theory, Russia was not ready for communism in the first place, because the basis for communism should be a strong economy – and this was not the case. Before the revolution, Russia was less economically developed than most other capitalist nations. If anything, more industrialized countries such as the Netherlands, Great Britain, France, Germany and others should have begun moving toward communism first. And the best known advocates of Marxism at this time warned against a communist revolution in Russia. For example, before Lenin, the first prominent Russian Marxist, Georgi Plekhanov, asserted that Russia, being less industrialized than other countries, was still a long time away from a communist revolution. Karl Kautsky, who was called by some the "Pope of Marxism," was an outspoken critic of the Bolshevik Revolution. He saw the Bolsheviks as conspirators who led the way to a revolution for which there was no economic rationale in Russia. As a result, the revolution brought nothing but a bureaucracy-dominated society, the defects of which outweighed the problems of Western capitalism.

However, the revolution moved forward, and went through two stages: the Democratic Bourgeois Revolution in February of 1917, and then the Socialist Revolution in October of 1917.

Lenin managed to neutralize the crucial Marxist theory that communism is based on economy rather than peoples' wishes, and convinced the masses that Russia was ready to build communism. How was this possible? A combination of three special circumstances contributed to this: a) the brutal abuses by the Czarist regime in Russia, b) the international situation at the time (World War I), and c) the organizational genius of Lenin.

The abuses of the Russian regime at this time were obvious. Although there is no official data, it seems clear that the gap between rich and poor in Russia was one of the widest of any capitalist country. This is well documented in rich Russian literature of the pre-revolutionary time period. While most workers could barely survive, the luxuries of the Russian aristocracy amazed the world. The gap was huge both economically and socially. Just one example is very revealing: the aristocracy referred to workers using the derogatory term "chern," which means mob/dirt. Understandably, World War I made the life of Russian workers even tougher. Most people did not want this war and preferred to exit the conflict. And that is where Lenin came in. His platform to oppose the war and give land to peasants was exactly what most Russians wanted, and it received huge support. More than that, Lenin managed to convince most Marxists that Russia was ready and needed a revolution.

Leninism

Based on Marxism, Lenin developed theories that became known as Leninism. One of the core ideas of Leninism is that capitalism cannot peacefully transform to communism – the transformation can only take place through armed revolution.

In "The Disarmament Slogan" essay (1916), Lenin develops his argument for the revolution as follows: "We cannot forget, unless we become bourgeois pacifists or opportunists, that we are living in a class society, that there is no way out, and there can be none, except by means of the struggle and the overthrow of the power of the ruling class. In every class society, whether it is based on slavery, selfdom or, as at present, on wage labor, the oppressing class is armed. The modern standing army, and even modern militia – even in the most democratic bourgeois republics, Switzerland, for example – represents the bourgeoisie armed against the proletariat. This is such an elementary truth that it is hardly necessary to dwell on it. It is sufficient to recall the use of troops (including the republican-democratic militia) against strikers, which occurs in all capitalist countries without exception." In other words, the revolution and violence cannot be avoided because the ruling class will never negotiate, will never give up its privileges, and will never allow more freedom or wealth to the workers without a fight.

Lenin was familiar with statements by Marx and Engels on the possibility of peaceful transition from capitalism to socialism in countries such as England and the U.S. (see Chapter 5). In his essay "The State and Revolution" (1917), however, he declared that this is no longer true: "This was natural in 1871, when England was still the pattern of a purely capitalist country, without a military machine and, in large measure, without a bureaucracy... Today in 1917, in the epoch of the first imperialist war, this distinction of Marx becomes unreal, and England and America, the greatest and last representatives of Anglo-Saxon 'liberty' in the sense of the absence of militarism and bureaucracy, have today completely rolled down into the dirty, bloody morass of military-bureaucratic institutions common to all Europe, subordinating all else to themselves, crushing all else under themselves."

Another Lenin's important idea was that revolutions cannot succeed spontaneously without appropriate leadership. In his essay "What Is to Be Done" (1902), Lenin wrote that a revolution must be led by a "vanguard" (communist) party – an elite composed of well organized, disciplined and educated intellectuals. Moreover, Lenin claimed that workers are unable recognize their own interests and cannot be trusted to govern themselves. Indeed, the socialist revolution in Russia would probably not have succeeded without Lenin's leadership.

He claimed that no teaching, including Marxism, is a dogma, and any theory has to be further developed. He then proceeded to completely change Marxist theories to justify the revolution. Later, Soviet textbooks claimed that Lenin actually "enriched" Marxism. One of them reads: "A key element of the theory of socialist revolution is Lenin's thesis that socialism can triumph initially in one country taken separately," [1] which is contrary to Marxist theory that socialism and then communism will simultaneously arise in the most economically developed countries. In his essay "The Military Program of the Proletarian Revolution," (1917) Lenin justified it as follows: "The development of capitalism proceeds very unevenly in the various countries. It cannot be otherwise under the commodity production system. From this it inevitably follows that socialism cannot be victorious simultaneously in all countries. It will be victorious first in one, or several countries, while others will for some time remain bourgeois or pre-bourgeois." [2] Further, Lenin proposed that it would first happen in the weakest capitalist countries like Russia: "The weakest link in the chain of capitalism will break first!" This catchy phrase was sufficient to convince many – despite its clear contradiction with Marxist theories.

Lenin proposed that the times had changed since Marx and Engels: capitalism had entered the stage of imperialism, and this dictated that Marxism now had to be changed. In the book *Imperialism, the Highest Stage of Capitalism (1916)*, Lenin suggested that social revolutions would not first begin in advanced capitalist countries as suggested by Marx and Engels, because the working class in these countries had become comfortable and oriented toward gradual reforms, instead of upset and revolutionary. Revolutions, he suggested, would start taking place in either colonial countries brutally exploited by imperialism, or in backward countries like Russia, where such brutal exploitation still persisted. History confirms his prediction: indeed, revolutions took place in Russia and colonial countries but not in advanced capitalist nations.

Remarkably, Lenin had already begun to notice that workers in advanced capitalist countries preferred to achieve their goals through reforms. Somehow, little by little, the upper classes in all developed nations were giving up a bit of their privileges while sharing some of the wealth, to the point that the workers were becoming sufficiently satisfied with their lives. It appeared that contradictions between the upper and lower classes were reconcilable after all. Why they looked irreconcilable one hundred years ago but have become reconcilable now is a good question. It may very well be because workers did fight. It may very well be that, without Lenin and the revolution, they would still look irreconcilable. Thus, as much as one may dislike the thought, the West may owe some thanks to Lenin (and other revolutionaries) for its comfortable life today.

Lenin thought that some theories of Marx and Engels could not be applied to capitalism any longer, as capitalism had changed. Capitalism gave birth to monopolies and became imperialism – a society ruled by a few large companies in which free competition is no longer possible. As Soviet textbooks put it: "During the transition from pre-monopoly capitalism to imperialism the capitalist economy underwent important change: free competition gave way to monopoly." [1] As we now know, this is not true. Lenin did not recognize the flexibility of capitalist systems, and did not foresee that capitalism could undergo yet another "important change." Today, it is so easy to see that free competition continues to drive capitalism that one does not even need to dwell on it. In fact, competition and small business serve as the foundation for a healthy capitalist economy.

Lenin modified theories of Marx and Engels so dramatically that his views were no longer called Marxism, but rather Leninism or Marxism-Leninism. From then on, the revolutionary movement in Russia and life after the revolution was organized under Leninism. Russia and then the USSR adopted it as "Marxism of the new historical epoch, the epoch of imperialism and proletarian revolutions." [1] Lenin's followers praised him for fighting consistently against revisionism and dogmatism. But little did they notice that he revised and changed Marxism's very core.

The Revolution

Although the political and economic reasons for a revolution in Russia had been ripening, the participation of Russia in World War I was the main event leading to its success. Two revolutions took place in Russia in 1917: first, the bourgeois-democratic in March (February, according to the old Russian calendar) and then the socialist in November (October, according to the old Russian calendar).

The war exacerbated the misery of the working class. It took a heavy toll on soldiers and peasants alike. Riots broke out in several cities. The protests and clashes, known as the February revolution, were confined to the capital, Petrograd. The February revolution lasted less than one week. Revolutionaries first clashed with police, but then managed to get the support of the army and won. This led to the abdication of Czar Nikolas II and the end of the Russian monarchy.

Revolutionaries established the Provisional Government led by a moderate socialist, Alexander Kerensky. The government was dominated by liberals and moderate socialists who wanted to reform Russia and create democracy. However, Lenin, who was at this time in exile in Switzerland, called to extend the revolution into a socialist one. In his "April Theses," he condemned the Provisional Government as bourgeois and urged no one to support it. He also called on citizens to dissociate from Social Democracy, which according to him betrayed the socialist movement, and to form the Communist Party. This later led to the separation of Social Democracy and Communism into separate movements.

Luckily for Lenin, at this time, Russia was a part of the Triple Entente* fighting against Germany in World War I. Kerensky's government remained committed to this war. Thus, Germany assisted Lenin and the revolutionary movement in Russia, hoping that this would lead to Russian withdrawal from the war. When Lenin was arrested for his revolutionary activities in Poland, German allies facilitated his release into Switzerland. Germany also helped other revolutionaries, providing them with about 45 million marks in funds. When the Provisional Government declared that Russia would stay in the war, Germany organized Lenin's return to Russia. He was placed in a special security train to cross Germany, and from there he went by boat to Sweden and continued by train to Petrograd (now St. Petersburg).

The events flew by so fast that Lenin barely made it from his Swiss exile to Russia in time for the October revolution. He arrived in Petrograd on April 9, 1917 and quickly mobilized Russian revolutiona-

---

* *The alliance between Russia, France and Great Britain*

ries to carry out the October Revolution.

Just before the revolution, Lenin formulated his principle of "All Power to the Soviets!" right when the majority in the Soviets (councils) was held by his opponents. However, Lenin managed to take it away from them by making some popular calls: 1) to oppose Russian participation in World War I, and 2) to give land to the peasants, who comprised the majority of the Russian population at this time. His slogan "Peace, Bread, and Land" performed miraculously. Thanks to Lenin's political talents and organizational skills, the Bolsheviks quickly won full control of the Provisional Government. Thus, by the time the October Revolution commenced, the revolutionary forces already controlled the capital and the revolution had been relatively peaceful.

After the Revolution

The Bolsheviks were the first "communists" to confront reality. They had to reorganize the government and the entire economy according to their principles. This was accomplished through the Soviets.

The word *Soviet* can be translated from Russian as "council" or "advice." Although this word is now associated with the USSR and its authoritarian regime, the concept of a Soviet system is very democratic. A Soviet is a form of political and economic organization in which an entity, such as a factory, farm, school, city, etc. is controlled by workers through delegates. In this system, workers democratically elect temporary/revocable delegates who make decisions on behalf of the workers' needs and agenda. Delegates elected to make decisions concerning the affairs of an institution form an Institutional Soviet; affairs of a city, a City Soviet; concerning a region, a Regional Soviet; and concerning a country, a Country or Supreme Soviet.

The revolution was not the end of troubles for Russia, but rather a new beginning. The revolution was relatively peaceful and the real violence came shortly thereafter. The new Soviet Government tried to avoid blood at any cost. It ended its participation in the war without secret diplomacy and "no annexations, no indemnities." It gave away Russian territories that are now known as Ukraine, Poland, Belarus, Moldova, Lithuania, Latvia, Estonia and Finland. Encyclopedia

Britannica (2015) cites: "In the Treaty of Brest-Litovsk the Bolshevik regime turned to Germany 34 percent of Russia's population, 32 percent of Russia's farmland, 54 percent of Russia's industrial plant, 89 percent Russia's coal mines, and virtually all of its cotton and oil." (Of note, part of these territories had been returned to Russia by the agreements of the Paris Peace Conference in 1919.)

But this was not the end. The Bolsheviks now had to reorganize the country and rebuild the economy. And before they could begin this process, the Bolsheviks' Red Army had to get through a bloody civil war with their opponents – the Mensheviks, who had formed the White Army and received help from capitalist powers. British, French and U.S. military forces joined the Mensheviks through the northern city of Arkhangelsk. Separate French forces joined them through the southern city of Odessa. And Japanese and U.S. troops invaded the far east city of Vladivostok. Despite these efforts, in 1923, the Red Army prevailed and the civil war finally ended.

Contrary to the popular view that the Bolsheviks brought nothing but dictatorship and misery, they administrated more freedom than Russia had ever known before, and more than the main capitalist powers had at the time. The Communist Party effectively legalized homosexuality, no-fault divorce, abortion and other civil liberties. Before Stalin took control in the 1930s, the Soviet Union was one of the most welcoming countries for gay people and other minorities. Socialist Russia right after the revolution had more freedom in some ways than capitalist Russia now, one century later.

As the Bolsheviks separated state from religion, religious minorities became less oppressed, and the Jewish community was one of the most welcoming to the revolution, and the most hopeful about it. There is a widespread belief that religion came to be abolished and prohibited in the USSR, which was not the case at all: religion was discouraged and teaching of religion was forbidden at schools but not in private. In fact, during World War II, Radio Moscow began broadcasting a religious hour, and Stalin held a meeting with the Orthodox Church leader in 1943.

In 1919, a member of the foreign ministry of Soviet Russia, Lev Karakhan, issued a manifesto offering to relinquish all special rights acquired by the Czarist regime in China. This was the first unilateral offer of respect and equality from any foreign country. The new Soviet government led by Lenin was a firm supporter of the rights of nations for self-determination. Such policies made new Russia more attractive to other nations and helped to form the Soviet Union, unifying Russia, Byelorussia (Belarus), Ukraine and the Transcaucasian (Georgia, Armenia and Azerbaijan) republics.

The next few years after the revolution were a period of hope and enthusiasm for many. Lenin was working to replace the traditional rule of state with self-ruling Soviets. However, reality was a sobering reminder that the revolution had come up against core Marxist theories. As Harrington explains in his book:

"Lenin, in the period leading up to and right after the October Revolution, was dead serious about his utopian plan to begin the 'withering away of the state' immediately. That strategy was based on a euphoric attempt to make the dynamic – and very democratic – energy of the Soviets at the heights of the revolutionary upheaval a principle of everyday life.

These utopian hopes were quickly and rudely shattered. The socialization of poverty, as the young Marx put it pungently in German ideology, leads to 'the old crap in new form'. ... Russian bourgeoisie was too weak and dependent on foreign capital to take the leadership of the transformation; the peasants were dispersed and disorganized; and the workers, although a small minority, were concentrated in huge factories, militant, and therefore, possessed a social and political weight disproportionate to their numbers...

Lenin and the Bolsheviks had assumed that the European revolution would quickly save the Soviets from the contradictions that made a socialist revolution possible in a country not yet ready for socialism. So Lenin wrote in 1920, 'Soon after the victory of the proletarian revolution in at least one of the advanced countries, a sharp change will probably come about: Russia will cease to be the model and will once again become a backward country (in the 'Soviet' and the socialist sense).' But the European revolution did not come, and

Lenin was now reduced to maneuvering within constraints that damaged his basic purposes." [3]

It had become clear that the revolution might not survive and there would be no communism without a strong economy. And once again, Lenin's talent and vision came forth to save the situation. He correctly envisioned that electrification was the key to advancing the economy, and the government developed the GOELRO plan for total electrification of the country. Lenin understood that revolution does not mean the breaking and discarding of all things – he directed people to save and use whatever was good and positive from Czarist Russia. He even promoted the development of the movie industry, stating: "out of all arts, the most important is cinema," which is still true today, one century later.

Lenin understood early on that confiscating and nationalizing industry during the revolution was easy, but getting real control of its operation and socializing it was something much more complex. Indeed, the USSR could never fully accomplish this. The West did a much better job in this respect, and this was one of the main reasons why the revolution and the USSR eventually failed.

The Bolsheviks, guided by Lenin, did an admirable job of adjusting to new conditions and trying new things. When it became obvious that a socialist society must rest on a strong industrial base, Lenin took a step back and introduced New Economic Policies (NEP), which permitted markets operated under state control. It also became known as a system of state capitalism, in which means of production are owned by the state but the organization of enterprises is profit-seeking and commercial. This was clearly a step in the right direction. Employment of similar policies (markets under state control) in modern China dramatically stimulated its own economy and produced excellent results. This example has been very successfully followed by other self-proclaimed socialist countries, such as Vietnam and Laos. However, in Russia, these policies would soon be shuttered by Stalin.

Stalinism

Lenin did not lead Russia for long – he died in 1924, and Stalin took over his position. Although Lenin created precedents that led to Stalin's rule, by no means did he have very much in common with him. In fact, Lenin was the opposite of Stalin, and warned against his danger. Before death, in his letter to the Soviet Congress (also known as Lenin's Testament), Lenin wrote: "Comrade Stalin, having become Secretary-General, has unlimited authority concentrated in his hands, and I am not sure whether he will always be capable of using that authority with sufficient caution."

Moreover, he suggested removing Stalin from his position as a leader (General Secretary of the Russian Communist Party's Central Committee): "I suggest the comrades think about a way of removing Stalin from that post and appointing another man in his stead who in all other respects differs from Comrade Stalin in having only one advantage, namely, that of being more tolerant, more loyal, more polite, and more considerate to the comrades…"

Although extremely important, this piece of history remains little known. First, not surprisingly, Stalin and his new government did everything possible to hide it. The West found it convenient not to advertise this information either. The West was politically motivated to simply keep the picture black and white: all Soviet leaders were dictators, and that is the inevitable result of communist revolutions. Not mentioned is that the West itself was partially responsible for buttressing Stalinism by fighting the Soviets in any possible way, including military interventions.

Imagine Russia after the revolution: it is chaos, and the economy and governance must be reorganized. Then the civil war (between the Reds and the Whites) breaks out. Many thousands are killed (over 300,000 altogether) and the foreign powers (mainly Britain, the U.S. and France) contribute to the misery by sending their troops to help the Whites. How would any other country react to a situation like this within its borders? For example, how would the U.S. react if Russia and China had sent their troops to assist in the Los Angeles riots in 1992? We know how the U.S. reacted after the September 11 attack: even though it was relatively small on a global scale, with about 3,000 dead, the U.S. still invaded several countries, causing hundreds of thousands of deaths in response to the attack. The U.S. government also began attacking its own civil liberties and began to spy on its citizens, violating its constitution. It even began using interrogation techniques that included torture, going against the

Geneva Convention and its own laws. Stalin's government reacted during the civil war in nearly the same way.

The terrible situation in Russia, combined with Stalin's brutal personality, led to dictatorship. Many intellectuals opposed Stalin's dictatorship. However, being in the minority, they either had to flee abroad into exile or end up in jail. The security machine became increasingly suspicious, jailing and executing many innocent citizens. It is estimated that during 1937-1938, at the height of the Great Terror, Soviet security detained for alleged "anti-Soviet activities" about 1,575,000 people, of whom 1,345,000 received some sort of sentence and 681,692 were executed. [4]

Stalin also turned the country from NEP (state capitalism) to total collectivization and planned economy. Collectivization (forcing private farms to merge into large collective farms) began in 1929, lasted for three years and was especially dramatic. It brought starvation and terror. It met resistance not only from intellectuals but also from peasants. In 1930, nearly 2.5 million peasants took part in about 14,000 revolts, riots, and mass demonstrations against the regime. [4] And then came the great famine in 1932-1933, one of the darkest periods in Soviet history. An estimated six million people died from starvation in 1933. [4] As Stalin later confessed to Churchill, collectivization had been more stressful than World War II.

By 1928, the economy had begun to be planned for the next five years (called 'pyatiletka') and the market economy was totally dismissed. Anyone who disagreed with Stalin's policies was exiled, jailed, or shot. One of the most influential Bolsheviks, Leon Trotsky, did not think that a planned economy was a beneficial idea. In his book *The Revolution Betrayed*, Trotsky reasonably criticized advocates of planned economy: "The professors forgot to explain how you can 'guide' a price without knowing real costs, and how you can estimate real costs if all prices express the will of the bureaucracy and not the amount of social labor expended." Eventually, he was exiled and then assassinated by Stalin's order.

In the end, the Stalinist planned economy performed terribly. By 1933, real earnings of workers went down to only about 10% of what they had been in 1927, just before Stalin abolished NEP and introduced planned economy. However, Stalin never gave up on his policies, despite how unsuccessful they were.

The Dictatorship of the Proletariat

Stalin's leadership came as a result of the theory of the dictatorship of the proletariat. According to Marx and Engels, the dictatorship of the proletariat will be required if the development toward communism takes place through armed revolutions. It will have to be temporarily established in order to suppress the resistance of the bourgeoisie and win a revolution. Lenin agreed with this and clearly defined the main function of the dictatorship: "suppression of the exploiting classes."

Following this theory, such dictatorships were established in Russia and other self-proclaimed socialist countries. However, as time went on, it became impossible to get rid of them. It did not quite happen as intended: instead of being a short, transient phase between capitalism and socialism, the dictatorships became permanent. Moreover, the role of the dictatorship of the proletariat was so misunderstood in the last century that some analysts even claimed that "the real and ultimate objective and true goal of Communist strategy is… to install a proletarian dictatorship under the hegemony of Moscow in every nation." [5]

The theory of the dictatorship of the proletariat has been criticized since the time that Marx and Engels came up with it. Russian revolutionary anarchist and founder of collectivist anarchism Mikhail Bakunin was especially critical of this idea. In his work *Statism and Anarchy (1873)*, he dismissed the idea that the dictatorship of the proletariat and the state would wither away after it had served its purpose of suppressing counterrevolutionary activity from the bourgeoisie. He warned that no state had ever given up its power and no state ever would. And he was correct, at least in the case of the USSR.

Why was the dictatorship not dissolved soon after the revolutionary victory? This was Stalin's justification: "The first aim of the dictatorship is to break the resistance of the defeated exploiters. Next, it must lead the revolution onward to the final victory, to the complete triumph of socialism." [6] From that point forward, the view of the main function of the dictatorship of the proletariat was changed from the Leninist "to suppress the exploiting classes" to the Stalinist "to build socialism."

Really? Building democracy and socialism through dictatorship? Soviet scholars probably felt that something was very wrong here. To mask this nonsense, their textbooks claimed that they were building "a new type of democracy." What is that, "a new type of democracy"? Would "a new type of democracy" still be a democracy? Then they came up with "different forms of the dictatorship of the proletariat." However, a dictatorship is a dictatorship, period!

Practically speaking, the dictatorship of the proletariat meant that the proletariat (factory workers) in the USSR had been lifted above all other classes: peasants (collective farmers), service workers, professionals and intellectuals. Salaries of factory workers were kept above the salaries of professionals (doctors, teachers, scientists, etc.) and several multiples above the salaries of peasants. Ridiculously, leaders had to be selected from among factory workers rather than intellectuals. Obviously, this system did not encourage education or intellect, and could only lead to dysfunction.

In 1978, one of the most prominent text books in the USSR prematurely wrote: "it is due to the dictatorship of the proletariat that socialism scored complete and final victory in the Soviet Union." [1] This statement raises a logical question: since it had already accomplished its function ("socialist victory"), even according to Stalin's definition, why was the dictatorship not removed after 1978? As we now know, the USSR soon collapsed, and the word "victory" would be replaced with "failure."

Since the dictatorship of the proletariat in the USSR had never been fully dismantled, can anyone say that socialism had really been established there? The answer is a definite "no." Socialism is the first stage of communism, and communism is supposed to be a stateless society in which the role of government will slowly diminish and be replaced by local and global agencies (see more details in Chapter 12).

According to Marx, Engels and Lenin, the state will "wither away" as communism arrives. In complete contradiction of this concept, the state power in the USSR showed no signs of withering away. State control spread to all spheres of Soviet life. Everyone's personal life became a target of state control. Instead of allowing freedom of expression and cherishing diversity, Soviet leaders tried to control the kinds of movies people could watch and the music the young generation could listen to. It would be no exaggeration to say that, in fact, dictatorship was the main reason for the collapse of the USSR. The lack of freedom led to decreased economic competitiveness, and the country fell further and further behind in competition with the West. Could socialism have been built successfully in the USSR if the dictatorship of the proletariat ended shortly after revolution, as suggested by Marx, Engels and Lenin? We don't know, but it is possible.

Lenin versus Stalin

Although Lenin and Stalin were associated with each other by the revolution, they had very little in common. Clearly, Stalin did not have an advanced vision of the world and his own country's development. This is in striking contrast to Lenin, who had a great vision and a fast reaction to changing conditions. Stalin was a dictator, whereas Lenin was a democrat; at least inasmuch as the conditions allowed him to be. After the revolution, in the early 1920s, Russia under Lenin's leadership became one of the most progressive and liberal countries in the world. When the economy faltered, Lenin reversed the policies from nationalization and collectivization to state capitalism (NEP). He also predicted that total electrification of the nation was the key to advancing the Russian economy.

Stalin had none of Lenin's foresight. Stalin was often surprisingly blind and backwards. Reversing Lenin's NEP, he introduced and enforced a five-year planned economy, which put the brakes on progress and was one of the main reasons for the collapse of the USSR. And yet, despite his well-known dictatorship and despotism, many still credit Stalin for his contributions to World War II and the victory over fascism.

While it is true that the Soviet Union was the decisive force in World War II, facts suggest that the victory may have come despite Stalin, rather than due to his leadership. First, he did not make sure that the Soviet army was properly equipped, trained and ready for the war. Second, he refused to recognize that Nazi Germany was preparing to attack the Soviet Union. Any information suggesting this was taken by

Stalin as a provocation. Intelligence agents who informed him of German plans to invade the USSR were repressed.

By no means was Stalin a good leader. It is obvious that the USSR led by Lenin would have been better off. However, this does not fully justify Lenin's revolution. A country should not be at the mercy of one individual. A system that performs and functions well regardless of its current leadership is a superior system, as opposed to the system created by Lenin. As Churchill observed after Lenin's death, "The Russian people were left floundering in the bog. Their worst misfortune was his birth: their next worst his death." [7] One cannot say this about Stalin, whose death was probably the best possible outcome for the Soviet people. Lenin's ruthlessness was of desperate necessity, where Stalin's was that of a twisted man.

Unlike Stalin, Lenin was one of the greatest men who ever lived. Probably no man changed the world so profoundly. Although his actions eventually led to Stalinism and many difficulties for the country, they also brought about some profound changes. The revolution in Russia helped shake the world of the degrading type of capitalism. It pushed the West toward democratic reforms that helped to reconcile contradictions between capitalists and the working class, making life in the West better. Despite all of its hatred, the West owes a debt of gratitude to Lenin for its comfortable life today.

The Czarist regime, which made life in Russia miserable, was more responsible than Lenin for inciting the revolution. And let's not forget Lenin's letters urging the Soviet government to get rid of Stalin. One cannot describe the legacy of Lenin better than the Chinese premier at the time, Sun Yat-Sen, who said: "Through the ages of world history, thousands of leaders and scholars appeared who spoke eloquent words, but these remained words. You, Lenin, were an exception. You not only spoke and taught us, but translated your words into deeds." [8]

The Real Face of the Soviet System

It is hard to judge the performance of the Soviet system from its beginning in 1917 to the 1950s because this was a special period: a period of wars, destruction and rebuilding. First, there was the revolution, then the civil war, and then – even worse – World War II, which claimed the lives of 27 million Soviets. After these difficult periods had been passed, the system finally had a chance to show its capabilities.

A few years after the revolution, when Stalin took the reins of power, Trotsky argued that if the working class did not take power back from the Stalinist bureaucracy, the bureaucracy would restore capitalism in order to enrich itself. In some ways, Trotsky was right. The materialization of his prediction became apparent soon after World War II.

By 1952, bourgeois ideologues had already noticed that "there is abundant evidence that in present-day Soviet Russia a doctrinal aristocracy of communist elite has replaced the former feudal landholders and capitalists who constituted the exploiting classes in the Czarist period." [9] This arrangement continued until the collapse of the Soviet Union, when the communist elite (also called the nomenklatura*) "numbered some 750,000 members – with their families around 3 million persons, or 1,5% of the population, approximately the proportion of service nobles under the czarism in the eighteen century." [10] And as the communist elite abused the system, the working class followed their lead by ignoring work ethics and standards. After Stalin's death, with the fear of punishment gone, workers were left with very little incentive to work. A popular saying among workers during this time illustrated the problem: "They pretend to pay us and we pretend to work."

As Marx, Engels and Lenin established, in order for socialism to work and advance communism, people have to achieve a certain level of consciousness. The Soviets even invented "the moral code of the builder of communism," which included qualities such as "conscientious labor for the good of society" and "concern of everyone for the preservation and growth of public wealth." However, the Soviet communist leaders were the biggest violators of their own code. This was painfully obvious and was made public before the Soviet Union collapsed.

Leaders used every excuse to take advantage of the system for their

---

* *A system in which appointments to specified posts in government and administration were made by the communist elite.*

own materialistic desires. Corruption and systemic abuse of power was getting out of control. The book *The Strange Death of the Soviet Empire* gives the following examples: "Nikolai Schelokov, the Minister of Interior, stole 700,000 rubles from state funds, and the most luxurious trappings he could lay hands on for himself and his family. When his Ministry took delivery of nine German cars, he appropriated five of them for himself, his wife, his son, daughter and daughter-in-law. In Georgia, the First Secretary Vasily Mzhavanadze auctioned jobs, and pocketed the bids."[11]

Also, it is well known now that the selection of consumer goods in the USSR was poor, and one had to wait in line in order to obtain items like high quality meat products and any Western brand goods. Communist leaders found a way around this inconvenience: they opened special stores filled with such products, where only the privileged elite and their family members were allowed to shop. Eventually, the public discovered these secret benefits. The leaders justified this abuse of power with statements like: "We are too busy, and our time is too valuable for society to be wasted by staying in lines." The public did not accept this.

Instead of achieving a higher level of consciousness, as prescribed by Marxism, the level was progressively dropping. When it came to state property, no morals were attached at all. "State property" became equal to "nobody's property," and stealing it became the norm. A popular saying of this time sadly illustrates this reality: "If you don't steal from the government, you are stealing from your family." The book *The Strange Death of the Soviet Empire* also made this connection: "In an inversion of Marxism, each was receiving not according to his needs but according to his ability to take." [11]

Let's remember here that the main principle of socialism (not to be confused with communism) is: "From each according to abilities, to each according to work." This principle has not been followed and, therefore, the political system in the former USSR can by no means be qualified as socialism, nor was it anywhere close to communism. What was built there was bureaucratic collectivism (under Stalin) that increasingly shifted toward anarchy by the end of the Soviet Union. Socialism was never present in either Russia or the USSR.

This situation did not remain unnoticed by the leaders. As early as

1970, the Soviet leader at the time, Leonid Brezhnev, had to admit: "We have entered a stage of development that no longer allows us to work in the old ways but calls for new methods and new solutions." In 1978, he reported the existence of "uninstalled equipment worth several billion rubles unused in warehouses." One year later, a number of reforms were administered, but to no avail.

In the 1970s, the country began to decline in many respects, including morally and economically. To create the impression that the Soviet system was working just fine, the communist elite tried to suppress any information showing Western successes. However, these actions only diminished the trust of the people in the system. Also, isolating the country from the West only meant that the USSR could not participate in the world economy and the advances in information technology. The regulation of entertainment made everyday life boring; this, combined with a general lack of motivation for workers to exert themselves, led to epidemic levels of drunkenness. The Soviet Union had one of the highest alcohol consumption rates in the world and the highest rate of death from alcohol. Finally, as the West was overtaking the USSR in more and more fields of endeavor, the Soviets lost faith in their country's ideology.

Although Soviets understood that democracy needed to be an integral part of socialism, only a false display of democracy had been created. People were forced to vote for unknown leaders. How was this done? Everyone was told to vote on a certain election day, and organizers would have a high target level of participation. If anyone refused to vote, they were classified as a person with a lack of social consciousness and education, thus not deserving of a decent job or career promotion. Therefore, very few dared refuse to vote. Candidates were pre-selected by the communist party elite, and everyone was required to vote openly, so that officials could see who voted for whom. Open voting was justified by the idea that "Soviet people have nothing to be afraid of or hide," as opposed to voters in capitalist nations, who afraid to reveal their selections. This manipulation and fictitious appearance of democracy was readily apparent even to the least educated of citizens.

Meanwhile, the overall situation continued to deteriorate. The book *The Strange Death of the Soviet Empire* provides with the following example. One of the most important Soviet newspapers, *Izvestia*, on October 3, 1991 revealed that "over the last three years the Government, with the approval of Gorbachev, has deflected for some unknown purposes gold worth $25 to $30 billion. In any normal country, the article went on, the President and his Prime Minister would have to account for such a fantastic embezzlement... They [officials] picked the flesh off the bones of the Soviet Union, as their predecessors with Tsarist Russia." [11]

In the final years of the Soviet Union, Mikhail Gorbachev undertook the most dramatic attempt to change the degrading system and to introduce elements of market economy, as directed by Lenin long ago. This was supposed to be the period of 'glasnost' (meaning openness/publicity) and 'perestroika' (meaning rebuilding/change). Unfortunately, not much change happened in the USSR. While many talked of rebuilding, very few acted on it, which was typical of the apathy already rooted in Soviet culture. Gorbachev tried to turn the country in the right direction, but he was unable to gather sufficient support. He did not side with the nomenklatura, nor did he connect with the people – that was the reason he lost reelection and the country.

The USSR was dissolved in 1991. The new government, led by Boris Yeltsin, proclaimed democracy, a free market and a return to capitalism. But it was not that simple, and public opinion was split on which direction Russia should develop: communism or capitalism. The former communist elite, the nomenklatura, still had the power to push events in any direction. However, behind the backs of the workers, it had already appropriated or stolen a great deal of state property, enabling some of the biggest communists to instantly transform into the biggest capitalists. Yeltsin then decided that a restoration of communism was the worst of all evils and, to win against communists, made a deal with the nomenklatura: they could keep everything they had stolen in exchange for their support.

Russia after the USSR

After the dissolution of the Soviet Union, Russia implemented probably the largest and fastest privatization of all time. Owing to the speed and scale, this privatization was dubbed the "big bang." The former communist elite wanted to appropriate state property as quickly as possible before workers could realize what was happening. Not surprisingly, such privatization was perceived by the average Russian as nothing more than theft. "By late 1995, Russia has privatized over 122,000 state enterprises, or more than half the total, but virtually gave them away free – principally via credits to managers, access to foreign exchange at a fraction of the legal rates, and comparable mechanisms." [12]

Not surprisingly, this was a morally degrading process. According to Yeltsin himself, an estimated "40 per cent of businessmen and two-thirds of commercial organizations were involved in bribery and illegal transactions... Western sources estimate that slightly over half the 86 billion that Russia received in one form or another has found its way illegally into private accounts in Western banks." [11] In other words, it had been stolen.

The theft and abuse of power crossed all lines. A mafia grown from government insiders was selling everything that it could freely acquire: "Grenades, rifles, Kalashnikovs, fuel and radio sets and tanks found their way to market... Eventually the director of something called the Ukrainian-Siberian Commodities Exchange was to offer for sale the newest jet fighters... *The Sunday Times* in 1993 was to report that 'oil barons' had emerged from the Nomenklatura and the KGB. They appeared to earn fifty dollars a month but somehow possessed houses in Geneva." [11]

This was the situation that the next president, Vladimir Putin, inherited. Some of the former communists had now become super-rich "oligarchs" with the power to buy everything, including politics. In 2004, Putin "decided the oligarchs' political influence through their vast funding and control over the media had to end and began prosecution of one of the most blatant giant firms, which he accused of avoiding taxes, laundering money, and even murdering rivals. But oligarchs cut their local investments and precipitated an economic crisis, and by early 2005 Putin was compelled to reverse his course, assuring the oligarchs that the existing privatization would stand and that they could keep their empires." [12]

In a matter of a few years, Russia had transformed from a country on the quest toward communism to a capitalist country — with some of the worst flaws of capitalism. "In 2004, the Russian edition of Forbes reported that the 100 richest business people had personal fortunes equal to one-quarter of the entire GDP – in the United States billionaires control only 6 percent." [12] Today, Russia is the leader among European countries with the most unequal incomes. [13]

Despite this change, the communist party in Russia did not disappear. It still remains and attracts many followers. In fact, it is currently one of the largest political parties in Russia and represents the strongest opposition party in the government (State Duma). Nevertheless, its ideology has changed, and it is now more reformist than revolutionary. Although its immediate goal is the nationalization of most industry, it allows for the development of small and medium private enterprises.

Why the Revolutionary Experiment Did Not Work?

The main impetus leading to the end of the Soviet Union was its economic underperformance, and its increasing public awareness of this. Piece by piece, this awareness was brought home by Soviets traveling abroad, mass media, entertainment, etc. Movies, through which the Soviets could compare their lifestyle with the lifestyle in developed capitalist countries, especially contributed to this awareness. As Lenin stated: "Out of all arts, the most important is cinema." It became increasingly apparent that people in developed capitalist countries had more comfortable and interesting lives than the average Soviet. The Soviets wanted to wear those Western clothes, drive those big American cars and drink those sodas from shiny cans – and no Soviet propaganda could do anything about this. It reached the point where many Soviets began to believe that life in capitalist countries was a paradise – just as it was portrayed in some Hollywood movies – where everyone was rich, healthy and gorgeous. And the Soviets wanted it too. They wanted it immediately, and they thought that it would come right after a switch to capitalism. The leader of the USSR at that time, Mikhail Gorbachev, had repeatedly warned: "There will be no miracle!" But who wanted to hear this? The people were excited and desperate to integrate into what they believed was a capitalist paradise. (The author of this book included.)

Of course, many other reasons that contributed to the Soviet Union dissolution have also been named, and as the saying goes: history is written by the victors. Since the main force opposing the USSR was the U.S., the obvious victor was the White House. Many in the U.S. decided that they had won and gave credit for the victory to the American administration that was led by President Ronald Reagan. They correctly recognized that the Soviet Union collapsed due to its underperforming economy. However, wishfully, they claimed that the economy had underperformed not due to the internal problems of the Soviet system, but rather due to the wise policies of the Reagan administration.

This claim suggests that, if the Reagan administration had not derailed it, the economy of the USSR would be just fine and the country would still exist. It does not make much sense, because it contradicts the very mainstream official view by the U.S. that the Soviet Union had a dysfunctional political and economic system.

Indeed, the Reagan administration may have contributed to the Soviet economy weakening. It began an unprecedented arms race, hoping that the Soviets would not be able to afford both weapons and a good life (bread and butter). The Reagan administration also pressed Saudi Arabia, its ally and the world's largest oil producer, to lower the price of oil so that the Soviets, whose main export was oil, would earn less profit. These actions definitely did not make life in the Soviet Union easier. What was even more financially damaging was that the USSR got dragged into a war in Afghanistan, which took a large toll on resources. And again, the Reagan administration contributed to these difficulties by arming anti-Soviet fighters and training them (Osama Bin Laden being the most famous one). Nonetheless, one cannot claim that all of this crippled the Soviet economy and caused its collapse. Facts about the state of the economy of the USSR before its dissolution contradict this view.

Although statistics on the Soviet economy are unreliable and vary significantly from source to source, all sources point out that the economy was still growing, rather than shrinking as suggested by some Western ideologues. For example, according to the Soviet official data, Gross Domestic Product (GDP) rose 3-4% each year during the 1980s. Wikipedia states that, between 1960 and 1989, the growth rate per capita income in the Soviet Union was even slightly above world average. Even the Central Intelligence Agency of the U.S. (CIA) confirmed significant growth of the Soviet GDP, from \$0.9 trillion to \$1.5 trillion, in the last five years of the USSR. [14] Indeed, people who lived in the Soviet Union during this time were seeing more choices of goods and higher standards of living. And the author of this book, who also lived there during this time, can confirm this as well.

Nonetheless, the economic growth in the USSR was still insufficient to offset its lagging behind developed capitalist countries. And the real reason for this was the very structure of the Soviet economy and its leaders' mistakes, rather than decisions made by some wise men in Washington. The Soviet economy was planned for years in advance, which created too much rigidity and not enough freedom to adjust to changing conditions. Every five years, the communist party was making plans and projections that had to be followed.

This could work centuries ago when the economy did not move or change quickly. However, in modern times, when it is hard to predict which technology will be developed even a year in advance, planning five years ahead puts a brake on progress. The bureaucratic administration was simply not capable of a fast and flexible response to innovations. This inability to adjust to changes slowed down the Soviet economy, and was the main cause of the Soviet Union's collapse. In other words, the country had rotted from within, rather than being destroyed by outside forces.

Subsequent events confirmed the fact that Washington's policies and falling oil prices were not a decisive factor in the USSR's dissolution. Recently, a new experiment tested this hypothesis. When a new cold war broke out between the U.S. and Russia in 2014, Washington decided to go to work on changing the Russian government and removing president Putin from power. As history has shown, crippling the Russian economy would be the best instrument to achieve this goal. So the U.S. president, Barack Obama, traveled to Saudi Arabia on a mysterious mission – presumably, to arrange the oversupply of oil in order to cripple its price.[15]

No matter the official reason, a few months later the price of oil tumbled. In addition, the whole Western Bloc added to this problem with economic and political sanctions against Russia. The value of the Russian ruble plunged twice and the Russian economy fell into recession. To make matters worse, oil and gas accounted for over 60% of Russian exports at this point, whereas previously they had accounted for only 40% of exports in the former USSR. If the USSR collapsed due to falling oil prices, then the Russian government would have to collapse too. But instead, the government gained strength and Putin's approval rating shot up above 80%. None of the Western presidents had ever had such a high approval rating.

This demonstrated that citizens could trust their governments despite economic hardships. There were no approval rating surveys for leaders in the former USSR, but if there were, they probably would have been around 10%, and never higher than 50%. On the other hand, the data clearly shows that, in the 1990s, when the Soviet Union collapsed, about 80% of its population had a positive view of the U.S., demonstrating that people admired the Western social system. In 2014, the viewpoint had reversed, and 74% of the Russian people had a negative view of the U.S.[16] Therefore, this recent economically challenging event confirms that the real reason for the USSR's dissolution was not oil price manipulation and economic undercutting by foreign powers, but the people's distrust in their own social system and government.

Moreover, if the world functioned as the ideologues in Washington believed, then none of the self-proclaimed socialist or communist countries would exist. After decades of Western blockades, embargos and sanctions, Cuba would have turned capitalist a long time ago. Continuing with this logic, Iran (as well as North Korea) would also have changed their governments, due to strong international sanctions caused by their nuclear programs. But history shows that societies simply don't operate this way, and if anything, external pressure creates the opposite effect.

As discussed in Chapter 3, contradictions between classes, between nations and between religions are the most powerful and dangerous forces in human society. Lenin and early Soviet leaders were well aware of this, and paid close attention to them. However, later Soviets leaders wishfully thought that all of these contradictions would become neatly resolved in the USSR: classes almost disappeared, most people became atheists and nationalities just merged into one happy entity. This nearly became the case with classes and religion. However, this was not the case with nationalities. In his time, Lenin could foresee rising national problems and warned against the danger of "the Great Russian Nationalism," but this warning was all but ignored until the end of the USSR. Soviet textbooks even claimed: "For the Soviet nation communism is its immediate future, and already today the close-knit family of people of the USSR is making practical efforts to build it." [1] This was false. Ironically, the very anthem of the USSR tells it all. The anthem began as follows: "Inviolable union of free republics, great Russia rallied for ages." This basically meant that Russia was a big brother while the other nations of the union didn't really matter as much, which was offensive to the other nations of the union.

Baltic and Transcaucasian Republics were especially unhappy in this union and waited to break away for decades. The readiness and happiness with which most republics detached from each other when the USSR collapsed quickly became apparent. Soon after the USSR's dissolution, national tensions revealed themselves and millions of people had to move, escaping national discrimination or prosecution; for example, Russians and Armenians had to flee Azerbaijan. Several bloody national conflicts ensued. The Nagorno-Karabakh War between Armenia and Azerbaijan and the Chechen War in Russia are the best-known examples.

Legacy of the Revolution

Socialist revolution took place in Russia in 1917. The USSR was created in 1922 and dissolved in 1991. After about 70 years, self-proclaimed socialism failed and lost its competition with capitalism. Despite this failure, one cannot say that this system was completely terrible and backward. Why? To begin, Russia and the other 14 republics comprising the Soviet Union had never been the most advanced or rich countries. Moreover, in these 70 years, the USSR went through both a civil war and World War II, which brought more destruction to this country than to most others. In World War II, over 20 million Soviet lives were lost and most of the country was left in ruins.

By comparison, the U.S. lost less than half a million lives, and no destruction on its soil. Yet only 15 years later, the Soviets beat the Americans in the space race by sending the first satellite and then the first man into space. When Americans created a nuclear bomb, Soviets responded only a few years later with even more nuclear bombs than the U.S. Also, no one was left starving in the USSR after World War II, and life continued to improve. Of course, one cannot ignore the human cost and suffering through which the Soviet system put many of its citizens in these years. However, this country also experienced some real successes that should not be ignored.

Many in the West see the former USSR as it is described in the book *Social Democracy versus Communism* by Karl Kautsky: "Foreign tourists in Russia stand in silent amazement before the gigantic enterprises created there, as they stand before the pyramids, for example. Only seldom does the thought occur to them what enslavement, what lowering of human self-esteem was connected with the construction of those gigantic establishments."

However, suggesting that this country was created through huge sacrifices and enslavement is a gross exaggeration. Life indeed was not as pleasant in Russia compared to the West. But most Russians (or Soviets) did not live in labor camps where they were forced to work and starve to death. The life of the average Soviet after the war was not too bad: there was no homelessness or even the threat of losing one's home, there was no unemployment or threat of job loss, working hours were reasonable (40 hours per week), mothers had three years of paid maternity leave in order to take care of their newborn children, paid vacations were long (one month minimum per year) and retirement was early (55 for women and 60 for men). Not surprisingly, many in the former countries of the USSR miss this system and want it back. In 2013, an opinion poll shown that "about 60 percent of Russians believe there were more positive than negative aspects to life in the former USSR." [17]

Yes, the selection of material goods was limited, but after the post-revolutionary reorganization of the economy and the wars (civil war in the 1920s and then the Second World War in the 1940s), nobody was starving or lacking clothing to wear or a roof over their heads. Remarkably, the USSR implemented universal health care in 1937, becoming the first country in the world to provide free health care to all of its citizens regardless of income.

Could Russia have achieved these successes if it had remained capitalist? Assuming that dictators (czars) had continued to rule, it is very unlikely. However, the system still failed, and the main reason for its failure was the weakness of the economy. This only confirms the Marxist principle that the foundation of communism is a strong advanced economy, and this confirmation is one of the legacies of the revolution. However, the main legacy is that this revolution was the first practical test of Marxist theories. If not tested, how could one be sure whether these theories were correct? There would always be a temptation to see if such a revolution could be successful. If not in Russia, a similar revolution would eventually take place in another country – Russia spared the others from this well-intentioned but ultimately misguided path.

Summary

The revolution in Russia took place in conflict with Marxist theories, because Russia did not have an advanced economy. The political system built in Russia and the USSR after the revolution did not qualify as socialist, and not even close to communist, because it was not sufficiently democratic. Instead, properly identified, it was a system of "bureaucratic collectivism." This system of bureaucratic administration and five year planning was incapable of quick or flexible responses to innovation. As opposed to a free-market economy, it brought too much rigidity and limited freedom to be able to adjust to changing technologies. The overall lack of freedom led to decreased economic competitiveness, and the country fell further and further behind in competition with the West. This led to Soviet citizens losing their trust and faith in the system and the eventual dissolution of the USSR. Overall, the Soviet experience confirms the Marxist idea that communism cannot succeed without a strong and advanced economy.

References

1. Afanasiev, V. G. Marxist Philosophy, published by Progress Publishers (1978).

2. Lenin, V. I. The Military Programme of the Proletarian Revolution, in Collected Works, published by International Publishers, volume XIX, p.363-364 (1942).

3. Harrington, M. Socialism: Past and Future, published by Arcade Publishing (1989).

4. Werth, N. A. State Against Its People, in The Black Book of Communism, published by Harvard University Press (1999).

5. Pontificia Academia Romana di S. Tommaso d'Aquino e di Religione Cattolica. The Philosophy of Communism, published by Fordham University Press (1952).

6. Stalin, J. Foundations of Leninism, published by International Publishers (1932).

7. Roberts, E. M. Lenin and the Downfall of Tsarist Russia, published by Methuen (1966).

8. Gorin, V. Lenin: A Biography, published by Progress Publishers (1983).

9. Fisher, M. J. Communist Doctrine and the Free World, published by Syracuse University Press (1952).

10. Pipes, R. Communism: A History, published by Modern Library (2001).

11. Pryce-Jones, D. The Strange Death of the Soviet Empire, published by Metropolitan Books (1995).

12. Kolko, G. After Socialism, published by Routledge & Francis Group (2006).

13. Sergeev, M. The First in Europe - on Mortality and Inequality. *Independent Newspaper (In Russian)* (2011, December 14).

14. CIA. The World Fact Book (1990), *CIA.org web site* (retrieved August 15, 2012).

15. Lyulko, L. Obama Wants Saudi Arabia to Destroy Russian Economy. *Pravda* (2014, April 03).

16. Klikushin, M. Russians Rage Against America. *New York Observer* (2014, December 29).

17. Interfax. About 60 Percent of Russians See Communism as Good System - Poll. *Russia Beyond the Hedlines* (2013, October 12).

Chapter 8

What is Happening in the West: The Anatomy of Success

The economic and social system of the Western countries is based on capitalism. One cannot separate the success of the West from the success of capitalism – a system based on economic organization in which the means of production are privately owned and operated for profit.

In its modern form, capitalism originated in 18th century Europe, and it did not easily bring the comfortable life that the West enjoys today. In France, a labor law prohibiting factories from hiring children younger than eight was not passed until 1841. The following year, Britain passed a law prohibiting mining labor for children under the age of ten. This meant that children above these ages were still employed in dangerous conditions after passing these laws, which is atrocious by modern standards.

In the U.S., millions of workers have either been injured or killed due to poor working conditions. For example, more than 35,000 workers died and more than 700,000 workers were injured from industrial accidents in 1913 alone. Employees of mining companies, who rented equipment and homes from their employers, had six-day workweeks and 12- to 16-hour workdays – only to find out at the end of the month that they owed more money than they had earned. At the turn of the 20th century, paid vacations did not exist, working hours were long, and the average life expectancy was short: 32.5 years for black males, 46.6 years for white males, 33.5 for black females and 48.7 for white females.

As industry kept growing, the industrial working class (the proletariat) was growing with it. And as the proletariat expanded, it acquired more power, and began fighting for its rights and a better life. Slowly, workers' movements began to yield positive results and helped to transform the capitalist system. In Marx's time, the capitalist West did not even have universal suffrage (equal rights to vote). In the 20th century, such a voting system was adopted and a few instances of social legislation were enacted: maximum working hours and minimum wages, unemployment and old age insurance, progressive income taxes and other improvements. Since then, programs of a communist nature designed to help the working class, such as free basic education and socialized health care, have been initiated. The idea that the state must intervene to control cyclical recessions and the depressions of capitalism has been accepted. Such state interventions through taxation and credits, stimulus investments, planned public projects and others have become routine.

Contrary to the predictions of Marx, Engels and Lenin, in the search for higher profits, capitalism slowly became a more humane society. This humanization was initiated by labor unions as well as by socialist and communist movements. Interestingly, even capitalists such as Henry Ford greatly contributed to this process with new ideas and practices.

After World War I and the Socialist Revolution in Russia, the West enjoyed a period of prosperity. However, after several years of a booming economy, capitalism entered its first big crisis – the Great Depression. This period forced capitalism toward social reforms, more equality and socialism.

After searching for better methods of business, the West adopted the Keynesian model: capitalism regulated by governments in order to prevent monopolization and to soften the effects of boom and bust cycles. The Keynesian model of capitalism worked successfully from the 1930s until the 1970s, when global capitalism again entered a stage of stagnation. This after-Keynesian stage was broken in the 1980s by monetarism or marketized capitalism, which was mainly promoted by Ronald Reagan in the U.S. and Margaret Thatcher in the U.K. This new capitalism turned back from a Keynesian to a free market model, and operated on the assumption that the market could fix all the problems, and that governmental regulations were not that necessary after all. Finally, in 2007, after unrestricted freedom, capitalism got itself into trouble again: the Great Recession demonstrated that, if unregulated, an economy inevitably runs into crises.

Before the Great Depression

Two centuries ago, as the Western economies were becoming more industrialized, the life of the working class was changing for the worse – exactly as Marx and Engels predicted. Capitalist governments advocated *laissez-faire** capitalism and squarely stood behind the interests of big business. Labor unions were illegal and individuals who tried to organize them were treated as criminals.

As the life of the working class was worsening, communists and their ideas were becoming more popular. Strikes and protests of workers became more frequent and workers began organizing into political parties. The last few decades of the 19th century marked the beginning of the labor union movement. According to Lenin's observations, this process was the most prominent in Germany. Lenin wrote that during 1871-1914 the Social Democrats of Germany "were able to achieve far more than other countries in the way of 'utilizing legality,' and organized a larger proportion of the workers into a political party than anywhere in the world." [1] And yet, even this movement was still weak, and Lenin evaluated it as follows: "What is this largest proportion of politically conscious and active wage slaves that has so far been recorded in capitalist society? One million members of the Social-Democratic Party – out of 15,000,000 wage-workers! Three million organized in trade unions – out of 15,000,000!" [1]

Capitalism was just in its first stage of development when Marx and Engels analyzed it. But even then, they could see that capitalism was a very dynamic and adaptable system. In *The Communist Manifesto* they wrote: "All other rulers wanted tomorrow to be like yesterday. But

---

The phrase "laissez-faire" comes from the French and implies "let capitalists do as they will," drawn from the literal translation of the phrase, "let things be." In general, it means a policy that allows businesses to operate with very little control and interference from the government.

capitalism, the most dynamic mode of production ever, has had to constantly change in order to conserve itself." [2] But capitalism revealed itself to be even more dynamic than Marx and Engels could imagine. Since then, capitalism has undergone several developmental stages and transformations. In fact, the system has proved itself to be so adaptable that in order to survive, it began incorporating elements of communism.

Although capitalist systems are not centrally planned, they are also not chaotic. In general, they are self-regulated by supply and demand as well as markets. Prior to the 20th century, under the *laissez-faire* system, capitalism was hit by frequent periodic crises. With minimal governmental regulations, capitalism was regularly hit with recessions due to over- and under-production as well as a misbalance of supply and demand. However, capitalists soon realized that some regulations and governmental interventions could soften crises and improve the system. Moreover, new technologies as well as new corporate organization forced its socialization. All of this had positive consequences: it benefited both capitalists and workers, turning capitalism into a more balanced system.

Although socialists, communists and labor movements helped to turn capitalism into a better system, the capitalists themselves were no less important in this process. Fordism, the movement named after Henry Ford, was one of the crucial elements in the initiation of this process. In his book, Michael Harrington gave this evaluation:

> "The socialists, the Fabians as well as Marx and Engels, had seen this trend earlier than anyone else. But, oddly, it was a capitalist genius and crank, Henry Ford, who came to very similar conclusions in the first decades of the twentieth century... Mass production, Ford understood, could not exist unless there was mass consumption... So Ford decided before World War I to pay the incredible wage of five dollars a day and to help buyers finance the purchase of his cars, in order to deal with the new challenges of both production and consumption. More than that, Ford tried to persuade his fellow industrialists that, in their self-interest, they should increase the pay – and the buying power – of their 'hands' just as he had done... Antonio Gramsci was one of the first to realize how momentous this

development was. Fordism, he thought, might mark a 'passive revolution,' that is, a historic transformation in which the popular energies do not explode from below, as in France in 1789, but are absorbed and tamed by a modern reformism." [3]

Although capitalism began turning more toward socialism in the beginning of the 20th century, and regimes that included socialists became more popular, the bourgeoisie still held a tight grip on power, and unrestrained capitalism continued to rule. *Laissez-faire* capitalism seemed to function fine. The rich were getting richer and the system seemed to work economic miracles. In the U.S., the stock market was booming and going up "to heaven" – until the Great Depression undid everything.

From the Great Depression to Prosperity

When the crash came in 1929, the population was suddenly unable to buy the work of their own hands. Businesses shrank and unemployment rose quickly. In the U.S., unemployment reached 25% and workers grew increasingly unhappy, making communist movements more popular. Labor unions and socialist and communist parties began to grow, raising the possibility of a social revolution and a repeat of the Russian scenario.

The U.S. president, Franklin Roosevelt, understood this and approached oligarchs with the following proposal: to either share some of their wealth, or risk losing it all. He became a staunch fighter for the rights of workers. His speech in 1932 is reminiscent of *The Communist Manifesto* itself. Roosevelt realized that workers had a bad deal in wealth sharing, demanded a new deal, and openly issued a call to arms: "Throughout the nation men and women, forgotten in the political philosophy of the Government, look to us here for guidance and for more equitable opportunity to share in the distribution of national wealth... I pledge myself to a new deal for the American people. This is more than a political campaign. It is a call to arms." [4] The bourgeoisie labeled him as a "traitor of his class." However, the majority supported him and the U.S. moved toward reforms and socialism. Ironically, while Stalin was turning the USSR into a dictatorship, Roosevelt was turning the U.S. toward communism.

Astoundingly, in the midst of the depression, the social security system was created in the U.S.: individuals over 65 years old got pensions, unemployment assistance was created, and a minimum wage level was established. To alleviate unemployment, public employment programs were created. From 1934 to 1941, this program created about 15 million new jobs. All of this required a huge amount of funding, the money for which was raised by increasing taxes on the rich. The tax rate for individuals making over $25,000 per year (equivalent to about $390,000 in 2015) reached 94%. For comparison, the rate was down to 37% in 2017.

Similar situations were observed in the capitalist nations of Europe. Economic difficulties were further exacerbated by World War II, which required all possible resources and led to the maximization of tax on the rich. Right after the war, social democrats took power in several countries of Western Europe, laying down the foundation for social welfare programs. This included the largest countries, such as West Germany and Great Britain. As a result, wealth in the capitalist West was more equally distributed, governments became more involved in business regulation and society achieved more balance. All of a sudden, the capitalist West left the depression behind and entered three decades of prosperity.

The understanding of governmental regulation benefits came largely due to the ideas of British economist John Maynard Keynes, who demonstrated that state intervention is necessary to moderate the "boom and bust" cycles of a capitalist economy. To mitigate the adverse effects of these cycles, he advocated using fiscal and monetary tools available to governments. In his book *The General Theory of Employment, Interest and Money (1936)*, he proposed that in times of economic crisis, governments should lower interest rates for money borrowing and increase spending, which would increase demand for products and encourage businesses to borrow and invest.

World War II and the consequent destruction forced governments to follow the Keynesian model. Governments had no choice but to spend huge sums, first to build up their militaries for war and then to rebuild whole cities and countries afterward, even if that meant going into debt. When the Great Depression ended, capitalist economies began to grow and prosper. The Keynesian model under liberals in the U.S. and social democrats in Europe shaped Western capitalism up until around 1975. It functioned well and generated so much growth that the lives of the masses could be improved without further redistribution of wealth.

Transitional programs to help the poor were created and welfare programs expanded. Capitalist nations in Europe began implementing universal health coverage for all their citizens – a model that was previously available only in the USSR. The public sector grew, and between one fifth and one third of all household income came from public revenue during this time. Although this number does not reveal anything about the distribution of this publicly generated income, it is obvious that all classes (lower, middle and upper) benefited.

In his last book, Michael Harrington described the social and political situation at the time as follows:

"After WWII, the socialists all settled for a situation in which they would regulate and tax capitalism but not challenge it in any fundamental way. The capitalists, in turn, had to concede legitimacy to forms of government intervention that they had denounced as Bolshevism in the not-too-distant past... The 'Fordist' strategy providing a mass-consumption basis for mass production through a range of public programs worked. As a result, a 'virtuous circle' was set in motion: increasing investment led to high productivity; higher productivity generated economic growth, which made it possible to have a simultaneous rise in real wages, profits, and social outlays; the expansion of buying power that resulted led to bigger markets, and higher profits; the higher profits made still more investment and productivity possible; and on and on, for more than a quarter of century... And even the Reagans and Thatchers were only able to attack the margins of social decency... It would have been political suicide to have attempted a head-on assault against the post-war welfare state." [3]

Additionally, as more wealth ended up in the hands of workers, it became easier for them to become capitalists. This was illustrated by the ownership of stocks. In 1952, an important trend had been reported: "A study of the stockholders of most large American corporations reveals not the concentration of stock in the hands of a few capitalist owners, but rather diffusion of stock ownership among many different kinds of people. The middle class, lower middle class, white collar workers, and even industrial workers and farmers in increasing numbers are owners of a few shares of stock, thereby broadening the base of the capitalist system." [5]

This period became known as the time of the Great Prosperity. It prompted some political theorists to speculate that capitalism may be a perfect ultimate society. A prominent economist of the time, Simon Kuznets, noticed a reduction in inequality and came up with a new idea about the nature of capitalism: although income inequality rises in the first stages of capitalism, it automatically decreases with industrialization in advanced phases. Also, a new philosophical view was born: economic growth is like a rising tide that lifts all boats (rich and poor alike).

One of the most prominent philosophers and theorists of the time, Herbert Marcuse, argued at a West Berlin conference in 1967 that contemporary capitalism "functions extraordinary well... We struggle in a society that has succeeded in eliminating poverty and suffering to a degree that the previous stages of capitalism never attained." The only problem now, according to Marcuse, was that society had become "one-dimensional" and humans had become slaves to material goods. People were victimized by technology and manipulated by false needs, becoming programmed and visionless. However, according to Marcuse, intellectuals from the various classes (upper class, educated working class, students, hippies, etc.) would rebel against the repression of the human soul, and would eventually liberate us.

It is true that the period of 1945-1975 in the capitalist West was the time of the "Great Prosperity." But caution should be used regarding the reasons behind this. Let's not forget that the same period was also a time of prosperity in the socialist East (the USSR and East European countries). This inevitably raises questions: how much did this prosperity have to do with capitalism, and were there any other reasons for it? Indeed, the prosperity of 1945-1975 around the world may have had little to do with capitalism or socialism. Before 1945, the world had just gone through the Depression and then, even worse, was ruined by World War II. The economic situation could hardly get any worse than it was already. From this point, there was no other direction for the world economy to go but up. Both the capitalist and socialist worlds were rebuilt quickly and functioned much better than they had a few decades earlier.

In addition, these significant economic improvements could be attributed to new technologies and innovations that began to develop during this time. TVs, radios, refrigerators, washing machines, etc. – everybody wanted to have them at home, and people bought them by the millions, pushing economies to new heights. Indeed, if more equality and social programs were the driving force behind the prosperity, then why did the process stop in the 1970s?

From Prosperity to the Great Recession

In the mid-1970s, inflation surged, capitalist economies began to slow down and the Keynesian system came under scrutiny. Domestic consumption in the West reached its limits and the growth of work productivity almost stopped. Between 1945 and 1965, productivity averaged an annual 3.5% gain. This drew higher profits and facilitated hiring new workers. As a result, unemployment was going down and governments had money left over for social programs. Then, for not-quite-understood reasons, labor productivity sharply went down in all major economies. For example, in the U.S., it fell from 2.44% in 1950-1973 to 0.80% in 1973-1979. A part of the reason could be the shift in Western economies from the manufacturing of goods to service jobs, which were mostly low skill and low pay. However, since the seventies, this trend has evolved: service sector employees, who had been low-skilled workers in previous times – receptionists, hairdressers, etc. – now became mostly comprised of skilled workers employed in high-tech sectors – analysts, scientists, etc. – and paid more than workers in manufacturing.

When the Keynesian model stopped working, the West did not know how to fix it and initiate economic growth again. One of the most significant attempts to fix the system took place in France. In 1981, after their victorious elections, socialists tried a radical version of the Keynesian strategy. They decided to stimulate their economy through spending programs that would further redistribute wealth from the rich to the poor. This strategy did not work. To avoid high taxes, the wealthiest French diverted their capital to countries with lower taxes. On the other hand and for the same reason, big money stopped coming to France. Within a year, the government had to put its programs on hold and introduce austerity measures aimed at reducing trade deficits, in order to gain the approval of its policies from international financial organizations. Meanwhile, money and jobs streamed into Germany, the U.K. and other countries at the expense of France. There were two lessons to be learned from this experience: 1) the welfare state works well when it is based on the growth of the economy – but not on simple redistribution of wealth; and 2) the financial system has become so globalized that money supply can no longer be manipulated by a single national government or bank.

By the 1970s, when the domestic consumption of goods began reaching its limits, the Western nations looked outward to resolve this problem. They began deregulating the national finance systems that stood in the way. Production and manufacturing industries began moving to developing countries with cheaper labor. On the other hand, jobs in the West began to shift from manufacturing goods to service and technology sectors, which required high-level skills. For example, the manufacturing sector in the U.S. employed 34% of the population in 1950 but only 18% in 2012; contrarily, the service sector employed 50% in 1950 but rose to a staggering 80% in 2012. [6] This trend was observed in other major capitalist economies as well. Thus, the class structure of Western society began to change, increasing the proportion of skilled workers while reducing the rate of unskilled ones, which represented the classical Marxian proletariat.

Globalization could provide the West with cheaper labor, additional markets and new opportunities. Clearly, governmental regulations and the Keynesian model stood in the way of these new opportunities and were now out of favor. Instead, a new economic model, monetarism, favored by right-wing, free-market-oriented politicians, began to replace it. Monetarists pointed out that the reason for high inflation was the increased supply of money from states and central banks. They proposed that governments should cease interfering with the economy and pumping more money into it, and let free-market forces solve economic problems. Since the Keynesian model was no longer working, Western governments had no choice but to switch to monetarism and the free-market system.

Reagan in the U.S. and Thatcher in the U.K. pushed their countries especially hard toward free markets and limited state intervention. A few years later, in the 1980s, economic growth picked up again. However, this increase was largely facilitated by the accumulation of debts (public, individual and corporate) and by enormous military spending directed against the USSR. The public debt of the U.S. rose from 26% of GDP in 1980 to 41% in 1988, and the military budget increased a whopping 43%. Moreover, this growth was internationally financed, confirming that the new capitalist model could no longer function within one nation. For example, the U.S. international balance went from equilibrium to over $100 billion of deficit per year. The total federal deficit rose from 2.65% of GDP in 1980 to 3.04% in 1988. The country began fixing its economic problems by borrowing from foreign countries and future generations. Encyclopedia Britannica (2015) describes the situation as follows: "Because the 'Reagan Revolution' in foreign and domestic policy was purchased through limits in new taxes even as military and domestic spending increased, the result was annual federal deficits measured in hundreds of billions of dollars financed only by influx of foreign capital. Once the world's creditor, the United States became the world's biggest debtor." Beginning in 1985, the U.S. began to own a lot fewer foreign assets and, presently, it owns about 4% less in foreign assets than the world owns in the U.S. [6]

The expansion of the West was also facilitated by reducing poverty in the Third World. Just as Henry Ford understood decades earlier, mass production cannot exist unless there is mass consumption, and mass consumption cannot exist where there is poverty. Unintentionally, Reagan and Thatcher's policies played a huge role in the struggle against global poverty. To encourage investments, they did not hesitate to use tax policy to redistribute income from the working people to the rich. This naturally made the rich even richer at the expense of the poor. For example, the share of income growth for the bottom 90% of earners under the presidency of Reagan (1981-1989) dropped more than twice as

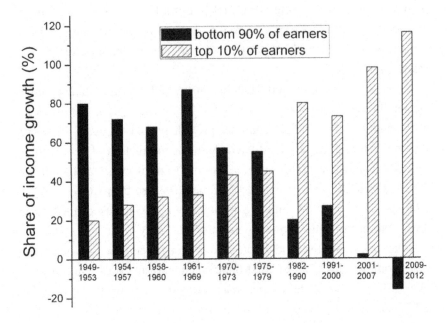

Figure 8.1. Distribution of Average Income Growth in the U.S. During Expansions. Based on numbers (Pavlina R. Tcherneva calculations based on data from Thomas Piketty, Emmanuel Saez and N.B.E.R.) published by *The New York Times*, [7] in the postwar era, inequality has increased with each expansion, especially since 1981 when Reagan took the presidency. Finally, in 2009-2012, while the share of income growth of the top 10% more than doubled, the share of the bottom 90% began declining instead of rising as in previous decades.

much as the decade before (see Figure 8.1).

But this also meant that the rich ended up with surplus capital that they had to invest profitably. And investments were more profitable in poor nations where workers could be hired at much lower wages than in developed countries. Money began flowing from the West to the East, where it facilitated a fast reduction of poverty in countries like China. Socialists and communists themselves would not have been able to accomplish what capitalists did! The other (socialist) possibility for reducing global poverty would have been to ask the Western voters whether they were willing to send more help to the poor in the Third World, which would have been very unlikely. Most voters would prefer to spend their money on themselves and would likely reject such a proposal.

Of course, the international movement of capital and business also brought some problems: developing countries ended up with huge debts. However, the rapid development and growth of these nations represented the greatest opportunities for Western capital expansion. Global financial institutions like the World Bank bought up those debts and continued with these policies, allowing the process of internationalization and globalization to proceed unabated.

This internationalization of the financial system, combined with monetarism that relied on a free market, created the perfect conditions for speculative investing. Capitalism became a "casino society," in which the word "investing" no longer meant using money to create wealth-producing assets. It now meant multiplying money regardless of the method. Americans no longer worked to make something, but rather to make money. In this new reality, interventions of governments and public international organizations became even more urgent in order to make sure that money was used to actually produce something instead of mere speculation.

Many believed that markets were capable of self-regulation and able to function best without government regulations. Even socialists, such as Michael Harrington, believed that in a society based on equal rights and opportunities (an egalitarian society), markets didn't need regulation: "They would function as a decentralized and instantaneous device for registering the needs of people as determined by people themselves…The new socialist can and should argue that their policies would lead to the liberation of markets from the conscious manipulation to which they are subject under capitalism… People, if they are not systematically misinformed, are quite capable of making intelligent decisions for themselves." [3] To illustrate this, Harrington described the situation leading to the ban of cigarette smoking: "Prior to the banning of cigarette commercials on television, there was a period in the United States when the anti-smoking lobby was given free television time for public-service announcements, computed as a percentage of time of the paid advertisements. Those television spots were some of the most effective instruments of public-health education." [3]

Unfortunately, this practical example actually contradicts the suggestion that society is better off with unregulated markets. Who gave the antismoking lobby free television time to educate the public about the harm of smoking: markets or government? It was government. Corporations continued advertising that smoking was attractive, trendy and healthy. But delivering the message that smoking was harmful required organizations sponsored by the government and the public. Thus, if anything, the antismoking campaign illustrated that governmental intervention in markets is necessary to navigate society in the right direction. Markets are driven by profits – not by public interests – regardless of whether they operate in an egalitarian society or not.

Free-market policies appeared to perform well for a few decades, and business was booming. In the U.S., the policy of giving more freedom to markets seemed successful and continued to be praised. This policy was extended with each new American president and the boom in business kept on going. It seemed that the markets could fix all of the problems, and that business did best when government left it alone. Politicians and analysts alike began praising free markets and capitalist greed as an ideal system that could run forever.

But then, in 2007, as usual, the unregulated capitalist paradise went into a crisis. There was a sudden realization that its wealth was overvalued and that it had become a bubble inflated by overpriced real estate: people who didn't have money were buying homes, while banks that didn't have money financed those homes. Home prices were going up and up — to make an analogy with the stock market before the Great Depression — "to Heaven." The mainstream opinion was that home prices would never go down; thus, it was safe to buy homes and it was safe to lend money to purchase them. In the U.S., many began using their homes as ATMs: banks were lending money to those whose homes had risen in value, which at the time included nearly anyone who possessed a home. Some people quit their jobs and made fortunes by flipping (buying and selling) homes. Life was getting better and better.

Even government officials of the U.S., the country that writes "In God We Trust" on its dollar bills, began claiming that greed was good after all. This reckless expansion continued until one of the large financial firms involved in the housing business, Lehman Brothers, was forced to show the money that it guaranteed — but it had only paper promises. Most of the other financial businesses found the same thing: the money that they were manipulating was just imaginary! Suddenly, "the music stopped playing." Later, the chairman of the U.S. Federal Reserve, Alan Greenspan, admitted that he had put too much faith in the self-correcting ability of free markets: "Those of us who have looked to the self-interest of lending institutions to protect shareholders' equity, myself included, are in a state of shocked disbelief." [8]

The bubble burst in 2007, and all of the major capitalist nations entered the Great Recession. And it did not take long before capitalism reverted to the Keynesian model. Britain's Prime Minister, Gordon Brown, immediately called to pump money into the economy through higher government lending combined with lower interest rates, and most major nations have followed Britain's example, despite the risk of inflation and sharply rising government debts.

Contemporary Capitalism

Keynesianism, to which Western capitalism reluctantly returned with the Great Recession, does not work well in a global economy. In order for a Keynesian model to work, governments would have to cooperate and coordinate their policies, which the West has begun to practice. For example, before raising or lowering interest rates or corporate taxes, national governments now have to consider tax policies in other countries. If a nation imposes a high tax, then its businesses may move to nations with lower taxes. Monetary authorities (central banks or reserve banks) of different nations also have to coordinate their interest rates; otherwise money will flow from countries with low rates to countries with higher rates. For example, the U.S. Federal Reserve and the European Central Bank constantly coordinate these rates with each other.

Today, the capitalist West relies on a social-market economy, which is a free-market economy where the state provides significant services in the area of social security but keeps its intervention in markets to a minimum. Regardless of how much freedom the markets have, the West still enforces minimum safety standards and minimum wage laws. It also enforces laws promoting competition and prohibiting the formation of monopolies. It has achieved a successful system with little class struggle.

This success, however, is not granted forever. It does not mean that the West cannot slide back and become a backward society. And the signs of this possibility have been revealing themselves over the last few years. Most Western societies have recently reversed their course of becoming balanced societies: the rich are once again getting richer while the poor are getting poorer, especially in the U.S. (see Figure 8.1). As the rich get richer, they also gain more and more power and influence in government. In the U.S. 2012 election campaign, it took only forty-six hundred rich donors to match eight million small ones. Outside groups contributed about 2.5 billion dollars to campaigns, for the first time outspending political party committees.

Of course, political spending does not directly translate into buying desired elections and governmental policies. However, money can influence the opinions of voters, especially considering how sophisticated the media has become in manipulating public opinion. Smoking policies are a good example. First, in the early 1900s, the media created the perception that smoking was trendy and cool, encouraging more people to smoke. Then, in the late 1900s, advertising of cigarettes was halted, and public service announcements were placed on TV and in magazines advertising the harms of smoking, pressuring people not to start or to quit smoking. It is easy to imagine that, if given the chance, the media could reverse this.

Capitalists believe in whatever profits them most. In good times, they believe in unlimited freedom and the power of markets, but they are the first to call for government interventions and help in times of fiscal crisis. The recession that began in 2007 is a perfect example of this. As soon as troubles came, the very hawks defending market freedom and capitalism were the first to call for government intervention, financial assistance and a return to the Keynesian model. In the U.S., taxpayers had to contribute about $4 trillion to rescue reckless lenders, of which $1.2 trillion was never paid back. Where did the money go? It clearly ended up in the pockets of the rich: while the income of the bottom 90% began declining, income gains of the top 10% accelerated even more (see Figure 8.1). This disproves the so-called trickle-down theory of wealth, which claims that when wealth pours into the pockets of the rich, it inevitably spills into the pockets of the poor.

Inflation data also confirms that the money pumped into the economy by governments to alleviate the recession ended up creating even more profit for the rich. Today, in 2016, many ask: how is it possible that inflation did not rise with so much money (trillions of dollars) pouring into the Western economies? The answer is simple: if money had found its way into the hands of workers (the poor and middle class) – it would inevitably have led to inflation, because workers would spend it on things that they needed and wanted, driving up prices. But since the money actually ended up back in the hands of the rich, it did not lead to inflation, because the rich don't need more money to buy things that they need and want – they have all these things already.

Where does capitalist economy stand today, several years after the recession began? Mainstream Western media is making the impression that everything is fine, the recession is over and the economy is booming again. However, many economists believe that the economy is now in the worst shape of their lifetimes: it is stagnating and stays afloat by continuing to print money and borrowing from the next generation. Despite the fact that work productivity has been increasing every year, the wages of American workers have not increased since the 1970s, when the "time of prosperity" ended. Not surprisingly, the reversal in income distribution was followed by a reversal of social progress and democracy: some experts consider the U.S. to have slid from a democracy to an oligarchy. [9]

Interestingly, although workers' real wages have stayed flat since the 1970s, workers still saw their lives improve. This was due to the fact that money borrowing became easier, and workers began borrowing against their future, creating a temporary illusion of wealth. It is clear that this cannot go on forever; borrowed money will have to be returned somehow.

As one can see, over and over, the West bounces between monetarism and a Keynesian model. When things go well, capitalists don't like government because they have to support it by paying taxes. When things go badly, capitalists like government because it rescues them at the expense of the working class. And yet, regardless of how bad things get, capitalists manage to make money. Moreover, the recent

Great Recession demonstrates that having economic crises still works in their favor. In times of crisis, capitalists have managed to swindle money and enrich themselves like never before. Losses of capital have been socialized and its gains have been privatized. If policies are left unchanged, this model of bouncing between the free market and governmental interventions will continue to repeat, and will become the best way for the rich to consistently profit. Such a model, however, is unlikely to survive for long and may backfire, as workers won't remain silent forever.

Class Changes

In the 20th century, as business was becoming increasingly transnational, the class structure of the West began to change. As mentioned above, the service industry in the West grew quickly, while primary (agriculture, fishing and extraction industry) and secondary (manufacturing) sectors moved to developing countries and shrank. For example, in the U.S., the service sector (government, entertainment, healthcare, mass media, information technology, financial services, hospitality, etc.) constituted about 79.4% of GDP as of 2013, [10] leaving a much smaller role to manufacturing. Thus, Marx, Engels and Lenin's predictions about the working class simply did not materialize, and its structure changed more than they could ever have imagined. Nevertheless, the proletariat (the industrial working class) did not disappear; it just became smaller and lost its ability to be a major driving force.

The founders of Marxism believed that the proletariat would be the decisive force in the building of communism because it was concentrated in huge factories, making it more organized and dynamic than dispersed peasants. And as Marx projected, the proletariat grew in the West until around 1950. But then, instead of further growth and concentration, it began to differentiate into different types of workers. First, rising incomes permitted workers to spend more money on entertainment, travel, etc.; this stimulated the service sector and created a new kind of working class. Then developing technology and an increased demand for highly skilled workers made college-educated technicians a necessity, and they emerged as an intermediate stratum. These changes in the structure led to changes in social movements, and new movements other than the working class were born: the women's movement, the environmental movement, minority movements and many others. At the same time, a large number of the working class separated from the communist movement to create social democratic parties.

These changes did not mean that social classes disappeared and became irrelevant. Millions of workers were still employed in manufacturing, despite the decline of their numbers in the West, as this type of work was being outsourced to developing countries. Also, at present, as manufacturing costs in developing countries begin to rise, there is a tendency to return some of these jobs to the West.

Nevertheless, due to technological advances in manufacturing and production, the classic blue-collar working class will continue to shrink throughout the world, giving way to a new white-collar working class (clerks, technicians, analysts, scientists, etc.). But this does not necessary mean that the new working class will become less organized and its role in bringing about socialist change will diminish. It is true that it is becoming harder for the new working class to get organized in a face-to-face way because it is no longer concentrated in huge factories. But new communication technology and social media can easily reverse this trend. The organization and mobilization of the working class can happen faster and more easily than ever before.

As of the mid-2010s, the working class in the West was politically inert, content with its station and having no hunger for communist revolts. One of the main reasons, as mentioned, is that communist movements have been discredited by self-proclaimed communist regimes, which turned out to be bureaucratic collectivist or totalitarian regimes (see Chapter 6). And although dramatically rising inequality in the West creates conditions for revolts, Western governments have become more skilled in preventing them. To counter the ability of the working class to mobilize using new communication technologies, governments have acquired new tools and methods to deal with revolts, especially in the U.S. As recent NSA (National Security Agency) scandals have revealed, governments now have the capacity to monitor each and every citizen: they can hear all conversations, they can read all letters and messages, and they can track the location of anyone at any time. This puts the prospects of a working class movement or revolution under a big question mark.

Inequality

Inequalities, hierarchies and classes have existed since the beginning of human history. Before capitalism, however, orders and hierarchies were primarily determined by heredity. Peasants were born and died as peasants while nobles were born and died as nobles. Capitalism created something completely new: a fluid society based on wealth rather than classes determined by heredity. In older societies, a penniless aristocrat remained an aristocrat; in the new one, a bankrupt aristocrat/capitalist is declassed and becomes the worker. The opposite is also true: a worker who accumulates money becomes a capitalist. Such fluidity gives people a feeling of living in a fairer society and alleviates conflict between classes. This reduces the chances of violent protests and revolutions in the contemporary West. As for the inheritance of wealth, its importance has not changed since the 18th century, and an end to inherited wealth is just an illusion. In his acclaimed book *Capital in the Twenty-First Century*, Thomas Piketty comes to the following conclusion: "Only its form has changed: capital was mainly land but is now industrial, financial, and real estate." [6]

Regardless of fluctuations, inequality remains one of the main characteristics of capitalism, and it cannot be otherwise. If the population of any capitalist society becomes equal, then such a society would have to be reclassified as socialist or communist. In Marx's time, inequality was growing and pushing the working class toward more misery. Marx projected that this trend would continue and make life in the working class so miserable that it would revolt, leading to socialist revolutions and overthrowing the bourgeoisie (see Chapter 5). But it did not happen as Marx thought it would.

For a few decades after Marx's projections, the West did see growing inequality followed by the growing misery and revolt of the working class. Comprehensive analysis of inequality in the West made in Piketty's book concludes: "What we see in the period of 1870-1914 is at best stabilization of inequality at an extremely high level, and in certain respects an endless inegalitarian spiral, marked in particular by increasing concentration of wealth." [6] In the 1880s, the labor union movement began. At the turn of the 20th century, all major capitalist countries saw increased numbers of strikes and protests. This culminated in 1917 with the socialist revolution in Russia and the formation of the USSR. Then the frightened bourgeoisie began yielding to the demands of workers: working hours began to shorten, salaries began to increase and many social programs were introduced. This led to the reduction of inequality, a better life for workers and fewer revolts. A decrease in income inequality was especially noticeable in the period between the 1940s and 1970s.

In the last several decades, inequality has been growing once again. Its levels are rising within most nations of the Organization for Economic Cooperation and Development (OECD). [11] Remarkably, income inequality in the U.S. is now estimated to be higher than it was in the 1900s. [6] Data presented in the book *Capital in the Twenty-First Century* shows that, although less marked in comparison to the U.S, this trend was observed in all other major capitalist nations: France, Britain, Germany and Japan.

Inequality in the U.S. has become especially pronounced. Quantitatively, the top 10% currently own about 72% of America's wealth, while the bottom 50% claim just 2%. [6] Inequality of total income (labor and capital) in the U.S. as of 2010 was as high as in old Europe in 1910. [6] All of this disproves the theory that although income inequality rises in the first stages of capitalism, it automatically decreases with industrialization in advanced phases.

Remarkably, the increase of wealth inequality is substantively confirmed by growing inequities in other spheres of human life: for example, in health and longevity. Wealthy individuals generally have better health care and are living increasingly longer. In the U.S., a 50-year-old man earning in the top 20% could expect to live five years longer than a 50-year-old man from the lower 80% income group in 1980. Over the course of just 30 years, by 2010, the gap between these two groups had shot up from five years to almost 13 years. This doesn't even begin to touch the fact that wealthy individuals will now receive even more at the expense of the rest of population by collecting social benefits and pensions in these extra 13 years of living.

Why is inequality on the rise again? There are many explanations for this phenomenon. The above-cited book, *Capital in the Twenty-First Century*, argues that the period of decreasing inequality in the West is not a general trend but rather the result of special circumstances: the two World Wars and the Great Depression.

These events caused inflation and bankruptcies, which destroyed much wealth originated from capital ownership, thus diminishing the importance of old money and inherited wealth. On the other side, wars required a lot of resources, which forced capitalist governments to raise taxes. Since most of the resources were in hands of the rich, they were the first targets of increased taxation. Nevertheless, after the 1970s, capitalist governments reversed this course of taxation. This resulted in the rate of return on capital becoming greater than the rate of economic growth, leading to a concentration of wealth in the hands of a tiny minority and more inequality.

Indeed, the reversal of taxation policies in the West is nothing short of spectacular. In general, about one century ago, Western countries adopted progressive income tax systems, in which higher tax rates applied to higher incomes. However, with the spread of Reaganism and Thatcherism, taxes for the top income earners became regressive instead of progressive. For example, in 2010, middle-income earners in France paid tax at about a 50% rate while the top 0.1% earners paid only 35%. [6] In the U.S., the tax rate for the top earners dropped from 70% in 1980 to only 28% in 1988. [6]

Although this explanation for growing inequality is completely plausible, not everyone agrees. Most economists see globalization and advances in technology as the reason for the recent reversal to inequality. Indeed, both the first (1870-1914) and the second (1970-present) wave of globalization coincide with periods of growing inequality. Globalization opened the door for the West to invest in poor developing countries, where the cost of labor is many times cheaper than in its own countries. For example, the cost of labor in China from the 1970s until around 2000 has been below one tenth of the cost of labor in most Western countries. Thus, globalization has facilitated much higher returns on invested capital.

Technology also facilitates a quick and profitable return on investment, because most technology companies are valued not based on the profit that they make, but rather on their potential to grow and making money in the future. This enriches founders, chief executive officers (CEOs) and other executives of the technology sector very quickly. For example, the founder of Facebook went from being a college student to a billionaire in only eight years. More than that, technology enterprises don't even have to make profits in order to be highly valued. For example, in 2015, Sprint was valued at $20 billion but was expected to lose a staggering $2 billion in the same year and $1.2 billion the year after. Twitter has lost more than $2 billion since its launch in 2006, but continued to operate with a value of $10 billion in 2016. And these losses do not reflect the rate of compensation for executives and managers. For example, despite heavy losses at a dying company, the CEO of BlackBerry was still paid about $1 million annually.

This shows that the old capitalist model, wherein one has to make a profit in order to be paid, no longer applies. Founders and executives of newly launched companies are now among the wealthiest people despite the fact that the companies often don't make a profit for years, if at all. This has generated a new phenomenon of the past two decades: the rise of super-salaries leading to a rapid increase in wage inequality. In the U.S., the share of national income for the top 1% rose from 9% in 1970 to 20% by 2010, "of which roughly half went to the 0.1 percent" (those making more than 1.5 million a year). Furthermore, "the higher one climbs in the income hierarchy, the more spectacular the raises." [6] Of course, other sources, such as income from capital (dividends and capital gains), contributed to the rising inequality. However, analysis shows that the vast majority of the top income earners in 2000-2010 consisted of executives/top managers.

Other economists point out that wealth and the rate of return is increasing due to the steep rise in land prices. Those who acquired land one or more decades ago can now sell it for prices several times higher than what they paid, thus dramatically increasing the rate of return on capital. However, the data doesn't support this theory, at least in the U.S. For example, out of the 400 wealthiest Americans in 1982, only 36 (less than 10%) remained on the list in 2012. [12] If those 400 wealthiest had been real estate owners, then they would be even wealthier now, which is not the case. This means that the vast majority (more than 90%) of the wealthiest individuals did not increase their rate of return due to the increased price of real estate.

Strangely, no one has proposed that the shrinking inequality in the last century and its current reversal may also be due to political forces, such as the communist movement or its current repudiation. One of the major conclusions of *Capital in the Twenty-First Century* is that political factors are very important in wealth distribution: "The history of distribution of wealth has always been deeply political, and it cannot be reduced to purely economic mechanisms. In particular, the reduction of inequality that took place in most developed countries between 1910 and 1950 was above all a consequence of war and policies adopted to cope with the shocks of the war. Similarly, the resurgence of inequality after 1980 is due largely to political shifts of the past several decades, especially in regard to taxation and finance." [6] However, the book does not go far enough to question what makes governments change their policies – and the possible role of communist forces in this process.

It is entirely possible that capitalist governments may improve their policies largely due to the threat of communist movements to overthrow them if they do not. In fact, there is a consistent correlation between the activity of communist movements and inequality: activation of the movements is associated with a decrease in inequality, while its reduced activity is associated with the rise of inequality. Indeed, the communist movement became activated by the works of Marx and Engels at the end of the 19th century. It culminated in the socialist revolution in Russia and the creation of the USSR in 1922.

Another peak of communist momentum was observed shortly after World War II, when communist parties took power in a number of Eastern European countries and in China (1945-1949). Thus, communist momentum reached its peak of power in 1922-1949. This was followed by the rapid decrease of inequality in the capitalist West in 1930-1975. On the other hand, the least active period of the communist movement began with the fall of the USSR in 1991 and continues to the present time.

Clearly, the fall of the USSR diminished the appeal and power of communism all over the world. Western ideologues wrote books associating communism with terror and declared that communism was dead. Most of the West just disposed of the idea as a social hazard. This period was followed by the rapid rise of inequality that we see today. Of note, there is about a ten-year delay between the reduced activity of communist movements and inequality changes. But this is expected and logical: it takes some time for governments to change their policies (taxation and social programs), and then it takes a few more years for policies to have a visible effect on equality.

Of course, this is just an association and not direct proof that the communist movement was one of the reasons for the reduction of inequality in the capitalist West. Nevertheless, the consistent parallel of the rise and fall of communist movements with the rise and fall of equality in capitalist societies is more than a simple coincidence. It is difficult to imagine that communist movements had no effect on the ruling class in the West. There is no way they ignored groundbreaking events such as a) the analysis of Marx and Engels predicting the fall of capitalism, b) the Russian revolution and the rise of the USSR, c) the turning of Eastern Europe and China toward communism, and d) the increase in labor movements and revolts in the West itself. There is no doubt, the communist movement pushed the capitalist West toward reforms and more equality. How much it pushed is a different question.

Most likely, several factors contributed to the reduction in inequality and then to its current rise. First, the two World Wars and the Great Depression facilitated more equality by uniting citizens to rebuild their countries. After the recovery from these events, globalization and technological progress facilitated a return to inequality. Inequality can be regulated by governments through systems of taxation and social programs. However, capitalist governments, being mostly comprised of and influenced by rich elites, tend to distribute wealth in their favor, unless they are forced to act otherwise. Threats of communist movements to overthrow capitalist governments push them to distribute wealth more equally, while in the absence of such threats, wealth is redirected into the pockets of the elite. Thus, the communist movement improves capitalist systems and they cannot function well without it.

Capitalism and Public Property

The capitalist system is based on private property and market competition. This is in contrast to socialism, which is based on social ownership and refers to state ownership, common ownership, cooperative enterprises, etc. Nevertheless, the capitalist system has increasingly included elements of public (also called social or collective) ownership, and has benefited from this. This goes back to the beginning of capitalism and applies to all countries.

Analysis by Gabriel Kolko in his book *After Socialism* demonstrates that social property is much more common in the West than most people realize. For example, the U.S. South saw more than half of the capital for railroad construction prior to 1861 coming from public sources. Prior to 1848, nearly half of the funding for railroad construction in France came from the government. Similar situations were observed in Canada, Australia and other capitalist countries. Recent estimates demonstrate that in the U.S., even "ignoring immense military and defense expenditures entirely, from 1925 to 1988 the stock of public capital amounted to 46 percent of the value of private capital." Naturally, "states and regions that had greater publicly funded infrastructure grew more quickly than those that did not." [13] In America's huge military industry, the government subsidizes most large military contractors directly or indirectly.

Furthermore, the book demonstrates that the agricultural business in the West is especially socialized. "From 1918 to 1964, the richest one fifth of U.S. farmers were receiving – at the very least – 51 percent of the total income from governmental subsidies... The U.S. exports its wheat, corn, rice, and cotton at far less than the cost of production... Still, the U.S. spends less on farm subsidies than the European Union and others. Combined, the OECD nations spent $257 billion in subsidies in 2003... About one fifth of gross American farm receipts came in the form of subsidies in 2003, and about 40% in the EU... Nowhere is there a free market in agriculture or industry in the developed nations." [13]

A story of rivalry between two Western commercial aircraft makers, Boeing and Airbus, is a good illustration of the mixing of private and social funds in the West. In 2005, the U.S. accused European governments of unfair competition caused by their financial support of the Airbus consortium and filed a case against the EU with the World Trade Organization. In response, the European Commission showed that the American government was doing the same: it subsidized Boeing at an estimated cost to Airbus of $45 billion. These mutual accusations have gone on for many years now without any verdict. What is clear, however, is that both sides use public money to advance their business sectors.

Overall, the public sector in the capitalist West is as important as private business. In conflict with ideological rhetoric, public sector spending in the U.S. was almost one third of the GDP in 1998. Still, this number is lower proportionally than in most other capitalist nations. Why is there such contradiction between ideology and practice? This is simply because capitalism is driven by opportunities to make money, and profits are always prioritized over ideology and principles in capitalist societies. When a law is written in these countries, a profit possibility is always kept in mind. When laws get in the way of making profits, they are simply changed.

As such capitalist behavior becomes more visible and understood, different societies begin to see the value of governmental regulations and social programs. Of course, it varies among countries. For example, compared to the EU, there are fewer regulations in the U.S., where money and business have more power. But overall, the West regularly moves two steps toward socialism and then one step back toward capitalism. Thus, it moves inexorably closer to communism.

The U.S. Model

Among the largest countries, the U.S. is currently the world's richest and thus considered by many to be the most successful Western country. As described above, socialization makes capitalism a more balanced and successful system, and the West is slowly making progress toward communism. America, however, is one of the least socialized Western countries, in apparent contradiction to the notion that socialization makes societies more successful. For example, while most Western nations have socialized education and health care systems, the U.S. has no completely free public education system and its socialized health care system was initiated only recently, in 2014.

Surely, the U.S. has an efficient economic system; however, its wealth is not solely attributed to its social system and governance. The success of this country owes much to special circumstances and its position after World War II. The main advantage was its geographic location, far from Europe and Japan, which spared the U.S. from the devastation of the war on its land and cities.

After the war, all of the major economic powers of the time (Europe, the USSR and Japan) were in ruins — all except the U.S. So the world economy was reorganized mostly under American leadership and currency, and the U.S. was highly motivated to fulfill this role. American involvement in the rebuilding of Europe and Japan was in its best political interest, because this helped its fight against the communist movement. But even more so, it was in its best economic interest. All that Europe and Japan lacked at this time was capital. Compared to other countries, they already had skilled workers and managers ready for work. The U.S. investments paid back handsomely, and its economy after the war grew faster than other Western economies. As Michael Harrington stated in his book, "Though the United States profited from its own generosity – the subsidized loans and grants to foreigners returned almost immediately as payments for American goods... Between 1946 and 1959 the purchases financed by American generosity and new world economic organization created a balance-of-payment surplus of $58 billion and generated about two million new jobs within the U.S." [3]

As most international economic operations were handled using the U.S. dollar, this currency became the world's dominant reserve currency. This meant that the world began to store its wealth in U.S. dollars. In turn, this meant that the U.S. acquired the ability to borrow unlimited amounts of money without ever going bankrupt, because it could print as much money as it needed. The only danger of printing too much money for the U.S. was making the dollar less valuable. This made it safe for foreign countries to lend money to the U.S. And indeed, the world's wealth pours into this country. For example, in May of 2012, the U.S. Treasury owed $5.29 trillion to foreign entities, [14] which was about 32% of this country's GDP. Such significant foreign financing plays an important role in the advancement of the U.S. economy.

World War II also provided the U.S. with advantages in science and technology. Science requires an enormous financial investment (first for adequate education and then for providing resources to educated specialists for research) and is a luxury. As the U.S. was the only major nation not damaged by the war, it had a larger budget for research, science and development than any other nation. Besides being able to finance its own scientific research, it could also attract the brightest minds from all over the world, especially when the priority of the ruined countries was simply rebuilding. For example, the American space program was established entirely by scientists from Germany: when the war was over, the U.S. recruited the whole team of Nazi scientists, which was one of the most advanced in rocket technology at this time. As the U.S. continued to provide more funding for science, the brain drain from around the world into this country continued, and still goes on today.

Besides all of the above, it is a known phenomenon that wealth attracts more wealth. Although this seems obvious to almost anyone, economists have yet to figure out the mechanics of how it works. In the U.S., it works in several ways, two examples of which are below.

First, American wealth attracts highly educated technical specialists, or what is called human capital. It takes a lot of resources to prepare highly skilled specialists; for example, it costs hundreds of thousands of dollars to acquire a Ph.D. or M.D. degree in the U.S. But foreign specialists holding various degrees come to the U.S. by the millions, saving the U.S. a lot of capital investment in their education. They come to the U.S. mainly from poor countries, for many reasons, but primarily for the much higher salaries. Thus, money attracts skilled human capital, and saves the U.S. resources.

The second example involves immigration law. As the U.S. is flush with money and life in this country continues to be comfortable, many people from poorer non-Western countries are willing to come to live there. But who can get immigration documents and move there easily? It's mostly rich people who are looking for more comfort and safer places to keep their wealth. And U.S. law facilitates the influx of rich immigrants by issuing visas based on the value of bank accounts (so-called investment visas). Moving to the U.S., these people bring money and investments, and help the American economy. Thus, they move money from poor emerging economies such as China into the U.S. In 2013 alone, the Chinese spent $22 billion on U.S. homes, [15] which greatly supported the fragile American real estate business. And money outflow from China seems to be accelerating. Bloomberg Television estimated that in August-October of 2015 it reached the rate of about $200 billion per month!

Much of this money left China illegally. The Washington-based Global Financial Integrity Group estimates that from 2002 to 2011, about $1.08 trillion left China this way. [16] Most of this illegal money went to the U.S., the country that refuses to cooperate with China and became a safe haven for "economic fugitives." And the Chinese are not alone – Russians, Indians, and many others are doing the same thing.

Thus, the U.S. economy is more successful than economies of other Western countries not because of its antisocialist policies, but rather due to its fortunate geographic location, which allowed it to avoid the devastation of World War II.

However, the unwillingness of the U.S. to introduce socialist programs like free public education and healthcare began to drag on its economy. Currently, U.S. healthcare is the most expensive in the world and consumes almost 18% of its GDP. Despite the high cost, it is rated only 70th among 132 nations in health and wellness, [17] making it one of the least efficient systems in the world. Similarly, the highly privatized U.S. education system is also among the most expensive and inefficient in the world. Despite the fact that it consumes about 7.3% of GDP – compared with the average 6.3% in the world's most developed countries – U.S. students trail their rivals on international tests. [18]

In order to improve its system and reduce costs, the American government has begun to socialize its healthcare system. And as the role of education in economic success grows (and will continue to grow), the U.S. will also have no choice but to adopt a more successful model, which is a tuition-free (including college) education system, moving the country one step closer to communism.

Moreover, the facts on the current state of the economy in the U.S. are not very clear and can be deceiving. Official data is presented in a way that looks much better than the reality. Using unemployment figures as an example, most nations show a number that includes all the people who have no jobs. But in the U.S., the government only counts individuals who receive unemployment benefits, which only last for a maximum of six months after an individual has lost his or her job; after this, individuals are not considered unemployed even if they are still jobless. As a result, in February 2015, instead of the 5.5% unemployment claimed by the U.S. government, the actual unemployment figure was estimated to be 23%. [19]

Regarding taxes on income, most nations present them as one final figure that includes all taxes – but not in the U.S. Besides the tax to the federal government, paychecks of Americans include a number of additional tax duties, such as state tax, OASDI (social security), Medicare, etc. Most people think that federal tax is the only tax they have, while other contributions combined can be as substantial as federal tax; thus, the real tax is about twice as big as most people think.

As for prices displayed in stores, these never include sales tax, which can add up to 10%; thus, one pays up to 10% more than is advertised. The situation worsens if one goes to restaurants: menu prices not only omit sales tax, but also don't include tips, which are considered to be obligatory and are suggested at about 20%; thus, one pays up to 30% more than is shown on menus.

A number of other facts suggest that the situation in the U.S. may not be as good as official data portrays it. Some data suggests that the American economy is actually sinking. For example, a recent article in *The New York Times* shows that from the year 2000 to 2013, "real median family income growth has dropped 8 percent, and the number of full-time middle class jobs, 6 percent. The real net worth of the 'bottom' 90 percent has dropped by one-fourth. The number of food stamp and disability aid recipients has more than doubled, to 59 million, about one in five Americans." [20] American social mobility (the ability of individuals or groups to move upward or downward in status based on wealth, occupation, education, etc.) now ranks among the lowest in the Western world. [6] More than that, some analysts predict that the American economy is on the verge of a major collapse for several reasons, the most critical of which is the continued borrowing from future generations and the accumulation of debt. For example, U.S. federal debt by 2016 reached $19 trillion, which is more than 100% of GDP, and the country has $127 trillion of unfunded liabilities, for which there is no way to pay. [19,21]

To make things worse, the modern world is undergoing a political-economic transition toward so-called "digital capitalism." The system of digital capitalism operates with imaginary wealth (future earnings, future prices, etc.) and makes economic estimates very subjective and distorted. According to Daniel Schiller's book *Digital Capitalism: Networking the Global Market System*, it allows for the ignoring of reality and serves only powerful economic interests, [22] the first of which is the interest of the U.S. For example, this system significantly distorts stock market evaluations, with the U.S. being among the most overvalued.

One of the most important factors in stock evaluation is the price-to-earnings ratio (p/e); a company is valued more highly when it achieves higher earnings. And yet, a comparison of the evaluation of the stock markets of different countries reveals that this rule is ignored. Based on the p/e and a few other commonly accepted criteria, the U.S. stock market is currently overvalued more than three times as compared to the stock markets of countries like China and Russia. [23] One could argue that business in China and Russia is not very transparent and we have no way to evaluate it correctly. However, several studies indicate that this is not the case. Contrary to expectations, the organizational transparency of Chinese corporations is higher than the transparency of corporations in the U.S.,[24] while the largest corporations of Russia are more transparent than those of the U.S. [25] Moreover, businesses in countries such as Germany and the U.K. are consistently rated as more transparent than businesses in the U.S., but the stock markets of these countries are valued as lower using the traditional criteria. Thus, in general, the U.S. stock market is overvalued. Since the stock market is a very important part of economy, the whole economy of the U.S. also appears to be overvalued.

Lastly, wealth alone is not the best indicator of the success of a nation. Overall prosperity is a better indicator, because prosperity also includes other factors such as governance, education, health, safety and security, personal freedom and environmental protection. Such evaluations are made annually and published by the Legatum Institute. By its criteria, the U.S. is not the most prosperous, and is thus not the most successful nation (see Table 1, Chapter 5). Currently, the U.S. is not even among the top ten most prosperous countries. Contrarily to America's fear of socialism, the most socialist countries, such as Norway and Denmark, are consistently ranked as the most prosperous nations, confirming that the socialization of capitalism results in a better and more successful system. Thus, if anything, the U.S. case demonstrates that a refusal to introduce socialist elements can constrain a country's ability to develop and advance.

Finally, as demonstrated above, the very history of the U.S. shows that the American economy improved after the incorporation of socialist elements, and worsened after these elements were removed; it was stimulated by the socialist reforms of Franklin Roosevelt in the 1930s, while the pro-capitalist reforms of Ronald Regan in the 1980s promoted inequality and directly led to the current downturn.

The Nordic Model

Of course, not all Western countries have followed the same path. For example, Sweden took a more socialist direction almost a century ago. In 1932, the Swedish Social Democratic Workers' Party won control of the government with a promise to turn their country into a people's home based on "equality, concern, cooperation and helpfulness." And soon thereafter, Swedish workers achieved impressive strength. By 1938, both labor and capital came to an agreement to negotiate their differences in a national wage bargain. Then, Sweden developed a model in which economic policies were determined not by state, but through negotiations between organized capital and organized labor. This model became a clear success. For example, Sweden was the first country to recover from the Great Depression and was not as affected by the Great Recession. It is now one of the most economically developed countries and politically balanced societies. There is a lesson to be learned from the Swedish model: socialization is not a bad thing — it can help capitalism avert crises, and turn it into a more balanced system.

Sweden's neighbors took note of its balanced model long ago. They created similar social systems that are a blend of capitalist economy with communist values, a kind of hybrid between capitalism and communism.

In 1954, Denmark, Sweden, Norway, Finland and Iceland created a common labor market. In 1958, they created the Nordic Passport Union, laying the foundation for the Nordic model.

Although the Nordic model can be considered a socialist system, its member countries prefer to be considered a capitalist system that provides citizens with opportunities and economic security. This is quite understandable: first, the word "socialism" has had a negative connotation due to the self-proclaimed socialist/communist regimes in the former USSR and Eastern Europe; second, declaring themselves socialist could provoke isolation from powerful capitalist nations like the U.S.

The Nordic model (also called Nordic social democracy) has a number of common characteristics. First of all, the Nordic model operates through an established partnership between the working class and the bourgeoisie, in which economic policies are determined not by state, but through negotiations between organized capital and organized labor. This model would be impossible without a strongly organized labor force, and all Nordic nations have a high rate of unionization. For example, in 2010, it was the highest in Finland (69.9%) and the lowest in Norway (54.8%). By comparison, the rate was only 11.3% in the United States, and dropping.

As a result of such organization, member countries were able to create an elaborate social and economic safety net that takes care of all of their people. This includes generous unemployment benefits, public pension plans, free education and universal healthcare. For example, in 2001, unemployment benefits were up to 90% of lost wages in Denmark and 80% in Sweden, lasting for several years before reductions. These benefits, of course, come with a price and require a higher tax burden: in 2001, it ranged from 43.3% in Finland to 51.1% in Sweden.

The functioning of this system is facilitated by a high rate of public employment, which makes up about a third of the total workforce. As a result, the Nordic nations have high public sector revenue (see Table 3, Chapter 6) and public spending.

Still, by being a capitalist system, the Nordic model provides strong private property rights, high freedom of market and low barriers to free trade. Alarmed by the dissolution of individualism in self-proclaimed communist countries, the Nordic culture protects individualism and is considered by some to operate as "statist individualism."

Also, the system makes it easy for employers to fire and hire workers, which makes business more efficient. On the other hand, it minimizes stress on the workers by providing generous unemployment benefits, job retraining and even coverage of relocation expenses. This is well illustrated by the International Trade Union Confederation's Global Rights Index, in which the Nordic counties have the highest ranking for protecting the rights of workers.

The Nordic model works exceptionally well and delivers tangible results. All five Nordic countries are consistently ranked among the least corrupt nations, the happiest nations, the wealthiest nations, the nations with the highest social mobility, the nations with the highest healthy life expectancy, etc.

It is clear that the Nordic model greatly benefited from the incorporation of certain elements of communism. But will this trend continue? And if it continues, when will the Nordic model become communist? How far is this model from communism?

The Nordic model will remain a capitalist system until its economy begins to mostly rely on public ownership. Currently, public sector revenues of Nordic countries account for less than 50% of GDP, with the highest in Norway (about 50%). At this point, the Nordic model can be considered in the transitory state from capitalism to communism. When the public sector of the economy exceeds 50%, the Nordic model can become more communist than capitalist. However, when and if this will happen is still a big question. Past performance is not a guarantee for the future. The model may remain in its current state for a long time or even revert back to capitalism. In fact, that is exactly what has been happening in the past few decades. As the world turned back to more inequality and "cut-throat" capitalism, Nordic social democracy was also becoming less "cuddly." Its foundation, the labor movement, began weakening. The public sector of the economy began to decrease and income inequality began to rise. However, most likely, this is just a temporary phenomenon caused by the current trend toward inequality in the world overall. Since the model is undeniably successful, it should eventually continue its course of progression toward communism.

Besides the Nordic model, other capitalist nations have created their own successful models that combine elements of capitalism and communism. For example, Switzerland, which is considered a highly capitalist-oriented country, has incorporated quite a few communist social elements: it is governed without traditional leaders or presidents, and adopts all major decisions through referendums of all its citizens. Although the proportion of public sector revenue in its economy is low, Switzerland has achieved quite a high degree of equality (see Table 3, Chapter 6). Overall, this model has also become obviously successful: Swiss citizens are ranked among the wealthiest and happiest people in the world.

Latin American Model

Socialism is very popular in Latin American countries, although none of them – with exception of Cuba – are labeled as communist. The main reason for this popularity is a significant economic gap between the rich and poor, leading to imbalance in society and the dissatisfaction of the majority. By now, it has been well established that such gaps inevitably lead to revolts of the poor and the search for a better life in communist ideas.

Historically, Latin American nations have tested different socialist systems. Some nations (for example, Venezuela) are not truly socialist, but are merely labeled this way on account of their use of socialist rhetoric. Many analysts divide these systems into democratic socialism and social democracy. The definition of social democracy is well established and refers to the ideology of gradually and peacefully transforming capitalism into socialism through welfare reforms. Examples of social democratic models include Brazil, Chile, and Uruguay. Democratic socialism is a newer term, referring to a political philosophy that decisively breaks with capitalism instead of reforming it. This system advocates that democracy can only work under social ownership of the means of production. Examples of democratic socialist governments include Venezuela, Ecuador, and Bolivia.

These socialist models work in some countries but fail in others. For example, they are failing in some of the largest Latin American nations, such as Brazil and Venezuela. Since these countries are among the most internationally significant due to their size, such failures create the impression that socialism is collapsing in Latin America overall. However, this is not quite the case. For instance, social democratic systems are successful in Chile and Uruguay: Chile is considered to be an economically advanced and socially stable nation; likewise, Uruguay is recognized as one of the most economically prosperous countries in Latin America and one of the most socially advanced nations in the world. Democratic socialist systems can also be considered successful in some countries; for example, Ecuador is succeeding in reducing poverty while Bolivia, although poor, is experiencing some of the fastest economic growth in Latin America. So why is socialism failing in Venezuela and Brazil?

In Venezuela, which was formerly one of the richest countries in Latin America, a form of socialism referred to as the Bolivarian process worked for few decades. But then the country's economy, which was driven completely by oil production and export, began to decline, consequently draining resources from social programs. When oil prices were high, the economy performed well and Venezuelan socialism worked. However, in 2015, when oil prices suddenly collapsed, the economy of Venezuela collapsed with it, putting the country in turmoil and its socialism on the brink of survival.

One could argue that it was bad luck, but the example of Norway – which also is a socialist country that heavily relies on oil – suggests otherwise. Good management navigated the Norwegian economy through the collapse of oil prices relatively painlessly. First, Norway did not spend all its oil money made in good times; rather, it systematically saved a portion for rainy days. Second, the Norwegian government did not solely rely on the oil industry and created a more diversified economy. In other words, the Venezuelan government did not manage its economy as well as Norway. Why? Because the government was not democratic and was led mainly by one person: its president, Hugo Chavez. If economic decisions had been made by professional economists, the economy of Venezuela – and its socialism along with it – would be in better shape today. Then the next question arises: how did it come about that Venezuela turned authoritarian? After all, the country wanted socialism – should it not have become democratic?

Venezuela became authoritarian through a typical scenario. When a state decisively breaks with capitalism for the benefit of the poor, it automatically antagonizes the beneficiaries of the old system, namely the elite and the upper middle class. Thus, the elite united with the upper middle class begin to fight against changes, and the society splits into two opposing camps. As opposition intensifies, the camps antagonize one another more and more to the point that the government employs all means in order to crush the elite and win, which may include accepting dictatorship. This is how Russia ended up with the dictatorship of Stalin and how Venezuela handed over too much power to Hugo Chavez.

Currently, Venezuelan society is neither equal nor free. It is separated into two groups: common people struggling to acquire basic goods and elite individuals enjoying a lifestyle of luxury. For example, out of 157 countries, it is ranked the 84th in income equality, [10] which is below average. This is not socialism – never mind communism. This is a typical collectivist system. The word "socialism" was simply hijacked to cover up totalitarianism. The most common agreement is that the current Venezuelan system is a state founded on Bolivar's ideas in a populist manner and using socialist rhetoric. Nowadays, some ideologues skillfully use the current situation in Venezuela to discredit socialism and communism altogether. They like to say: "If you like socialism, go to Venezuela." In response, tell them this: Go there first yourself, and find out how much socialism Venezuela actually has. But if you'd *really* like to see socialism, visit a country like Norway or Denmark.

Led by the Workers' Party, Brazil took a safer route with social democracy. And yet, it is also not succeeding. Having chosen the moderate path of capitalism transformation, the Workers' Party leadership had to do business closely with the elite. Commonly, this provokes paying under the table and corruption in any country. Brazil, with its significant gap between the rich and the poor, was especially vulnerable to this. Indeed, politicians of all parties in Brazil are currently being accused of corruption. Lula da Silva, the former president and founder of the Workers' Party, was accused of corruption and is in prison. (Please note that no direct evidence of his guilt has ever been presented to the public, and many consider him to be a political prisoner.) His successor, Dilma Rousseff, was also accused of manipulation of certain government accounts and was impeached. (Please note that no direct evidence of her guilt has ever been made public, and many consider this to have been a coup d'état by the judicial system.) This has effectively ended Brazilian socialism, at least for now. The next president, Michel Temer, began reversing socialist reforms, and this is likely to be continued by the current president, Jair Bolsonaro, who is considered to be an advocate of far-right policies.

But that is not all. Regardless of country, one cannot overlook another powerful factor contributing to the failure of socialism: the U.S. government, or as some call it, the "Empire" factor. This factor is especially significant in Latin America, which is the Empire's backyard. The list of affected countries goes on and on, and below are examples. In 1954, Washington backed a military coup that overthrew the socialist government in Guatemala. In 1961, Washington invaded Cuba in an attempt to overthrow its communist government. In 1964, the U.S. government supported the military coup in Brazil, resulting in two decades of dictatorship. In 1965, Washington occupied the Dominican Republic to prevent a communist uprising. In 1973, the Nixon administration managed to destabilize the democratic government in Chile, leading to the installation of the Pinochet dictatorship. In 1976, Washington supported a right-wing coup d'état leading to the installation of a military junta in Argentina. In the 1970s, the U.S. provided money, training, and arms to fight the left-wing Farabundo Marti National Liberation Front in El Salvador. In the 1980s, the Reagan administration helped "the contras" to overthrow the socialist government in Nicaragua. In 2002, Washington supported an attempt to overthrow the government of Venezuela. And right now, as this book is being prepared for publication, the Trump administration is working to overthrow the government of Venezuela yet again.

It is not a secret that Washington has a significant degree of control over the world economy, particularly in the areas of banking and finance. By cutting financing and pressuring international banks to do the same, it has the ability to ruin the economies of smaller countries that don't obey its orders. And that is exactly what is happening to Venezuela. For example, the very next day after the election in 2018, Washington imposed sanctions on the already struggling Venezuelan economy. This included barring all banks (national and foreign) doing business in the U.S. from any transactions involving the Venezuelan economy. Thus, Canada, the European Union, and several Latin American nations have been forced to comply with the sanctions imposed by the U.S. This has had a massively deleterious effect on the Venezuelan economy and has greatly contributed to the crisis of 2019.

Regarding Brazil, information on Washington's meddling in its affairs is scarce. But it is difficult to imagine that the "Empire" did nothing to discredit the Brazilian socialist government for the following reasons: 1) the government and especially its former president, Lula da Silva, promoted the association of the BRICS countries (Brazil, Russia, India, China, and South Africa), which could serve as an alternative or even become dominant to the G7 block led by the U.S.; 2) the government was critical of secret projects that were highly important for Washington, as when Dilma Rousseff accused the U.S. of breaching international law through Internet-based economic espionage and the indiscriminate collection of personal data; 3) Brazil is the largest and thus the most important Latin American nation, a position that could entail a host of sociopolitical complications for the U.S. should social democracy succeed. We probably will not be aware of Washington's role in the current crisis of Brazil for another 50 years, until secret documents are made public, if they are ever declassified. But in any case, it is obvious that communism in Latin America could be more successful if given a fair chance and not assaulted by the U.S.

Summary

At the time of Marx and Engels, the capitalist West had no universal suffrage system, no socialized medicine, no socialized education, no unemployment and no old age insurance; working hours were long, wages were low and paid vacations were non-existent. All of these lacking features are present now, and they are elements of socialism – the first stage of communism. This is a clear indication that Western societies have moved from capitalism toward communism, developing hybrids of capitalism and communism. This transition took place without armed revolutions: the working class movements did not explode into revolts, but were instead tamed by progressive reforms. This demonstrates that those who believed that only an armed revolution could transform capitalism to communism were wrong.

Importantly, capitalism created a degree of class fluidity never seen before, which helped to alleviate the contradiction between classes and make them reconcilable. This makes violent revolutions less likely in the contemporary West, compared to the West of Marx's time. Of course, this was not just a goodwill gesture by the bourgeoisie; it took place as a result of the working class struggle for its rights, and the communist movement was an important component of this. The comfortable life in the West owes much to the communist movement in the East.

Capitalism has proven itself to be a highly fluid and adaptable system. In fact, the capitalist system is so adaptable that, in order to survive, it accepted government interventions and regulations that originally were denounced as Bolshevism. It even began including some elements of communism, such as socialized medicine and free education. Moreover, the experience of the West shows that socialization is a positive benefit for capitalism: it can help to deal with crises, and can turn capitalism into a more balanced system. One cannot ignore the fact that the most socialist countries are also consistently ranked as the most prosperous. This is a direct confirmation that socialization makes capitalism a better and more successful system overall.

References

1. Lenin, V. I. The State and Revolution (1917). *Marxists.org web site* (retrieved July 01, 2015).

2. Marx, K., Engels, F. The Communist Manifesto (1848), published by Verso (1998).

3. Harrington, M. Socialism: Past and Future, published by Arcade Publishing (1989).

4. The Roosevelt Week. *Time, New York* (1932, July 11).

5. Fisher, M. J. Communist Doctrine and the Free World, published by Syracuse University Press (1952).

6. Piketty, T. Capital in the Twenty-First Century, published by Belknap

Press of Harvard University Press (2014).

7. Irwin, N. The Benefits of Economic Expansions Are Increasingly Going to the Richest Americans. *The New York Times* (2014, September 26).

8. Andrews, E. L. Greenspan Concedes Error on Regulation. *The New York Times* (2008, October 23).

9. Zuesse, E. Jimmy Carter Is Correct That the U.S. Is No Longer a Democracy. *The Huffington Post* (2015, August 15).

10. CIA. The World Fact Book (2014), *CIA.gov website* (retrieved 2015, October 22).

11. Smeeding, T. M., Grodner, A. Changing Income Inequality in OECD Countries: Updated Results from the Luxembourg Income Study (LIS). *The Personal Distribution of Income in an International Perspective*, p.205-224 (2000).

12. Kilachand, S. The Forbes 400 Hall Of Fame: 36 Members of Our Debut Issue Still in Ranks. *Forbes* (2012, September 20).

13. Kolko, G. After Socialism, published by Routledge & Francis Group (2006).

14. Terence, P. J. U.S. Government's Foreign Debt Hits Record $5.29 Trillion. *CNS News* (2012, August 16).

15. Weise, K. Why are Chinese Millionaires Buying Mansions in L.A. Suburb? *Business Week* (2014, October 15).

16. Wee, S.-L. China Considers Suing 'Economic Fugitives' in the U.S., Official Says. *Reuters* (2014, November 26).

17. Kantarjian, H. An Unhealthy System. *US News* (2014, May 30).

18. Elliott, P. Study: U.S. Education Spending Tops Global List. *Huffington Post* (2013, June 25).

19. Meyers, S. Many in the U.S. Intelligence Community Fear a 25-year Great Depression is Unavoidable. *Moneymorning.com website* (2015, March 6).

20. Stockman, D. A. Sundown in America. *The New York Times* (2013, March 30).

21. Harmon, M. D. Former Reaganite Offers Dire Economic Warning. *Themainwire.com web site* (2013, April 5).

22. Schiller, D. Digital Capitalism: Networking the Global Market System, published by MIT Press (2000).

23. Caldwell, K. Revealed: The World's Cheapest Stock Markets. *The Telegraph* (2014, June 07).

24. Transparency in Corporate Reporting: Assessing the World's Largest

Companies (2014), published by Transparency International (2014, November 05).

25.   Lossan, A. Rosneft and Gazprom Overtake Google and Apple in Corporate Transparency. *Russia Beyond the Headlines* (2014, November 12).

Chapter 9

What Will Happen in China: The Story of Promise

China has thousands years of history, but its quest for communism only began recently, less than century ago. Monarchy in China had ceased to exist by 1912, when the Republic of China was established by the Kuomintang (the KMT or Nationalist Party, which is a party of the bourgeoisie).

However, at the turn of the 20th century, China was a relatively inert society. Its political awakening was initiated in 1919 by the Versailles Treaty, when Western regimes transferred what China considered to be its territories (Shandong) to Japan without even consulting the Chinese. Chinese intellectuals reacted with resentment and anger that culminated in a violent protest in Beijing on May 4, 1919. The government responded with arrests, to which the public reacted with a wave of additional protests throughout the major cities. This wave helped to spread reformist ideas of the intellectual movement, which became known as the May Fourth Movement. The Communist Party of China (CPC) directly originates from the May Fourth Movement. Its co-founders, Li Dazhao and Chen Duxiu, were leaders of the movement, while the future leader of China, Mao Zedong, became a protégé of Li Dazhao.

One country, Soviet Russia, had a different attitude toward China. In contrast to the capitalist-centric decisions of the Western powers, in

1919, it issued the Karakhan Manifesto, proclaiming that it would give up all rights of czarist Russia gained at China's expense, which included the railway in Manchuria. This affected the Chinese profoundly. It enforced their belief that China needed to model its society after Soviet Russia, and needed a revolution to accomplish that. Thus, one of the main reasons for the rise of the CPC leading to the formation of the People's Republic of China (PRC) was the ignorance and abuse of the Western capitalist regimes.

The CPC was officially formed in 1921, and one of its co-founders, Chen Duxiu, was chosen as its leader. It was accomplished with the help of Russian advisors, and the CPC was modeled as a vanguard of the working class party based on Lenin's theories. In fact, Lenin viewed the liberation of China as an essential stage in the victory of socialism around the world, and in 1927, the Congress of the Communist Party of the Soviet Union declared China to be "the second home" of world revolution.

In the first half of the 20th century, China was a country fragmented by foreign nations and the rivalry struggles of its own military factions. To bring the nation to order and unity, communists (CPC) and nationalists (KMT) had to make uneasy alliances several times. The last alliance resulted in victory over Japan in the second Chino-Japanese war. Nevertheless, after the victory, communists and nationalists (representing the bourgeoisie) went into civil war with each other. These events brought to power Mao Zedong, who helped to found the Red Army and led communists to victory. On October 1, 1949, Mao proclaimed the foundation of the People's Republic of China (PRC) and became its founding father. Nationalists fled to Taiwan.

After scoring the victory, the CPC did not hesitate to experiment and try new things. It made numerous mistakes, but led China to its current success. First, Mao directed China to the disastrous "Great Leap Forward" and "Cultural Revolution." Then, Deng Xiaoping guided it toward a market economy, which worked very well. Today, China is more capitalist than socialist. By some measures, it is more capitalist than many Western countries. However, it is still ruled by the CPC, and the building of communism remains its ultimate goal.

The Great Leap Forward

When communists came to power, China was an agrarian country. The working class, which according to Marx, Engels and Lenin would lead social revolution and transform society, almost did not exist there. Although the working class in Russia when the Bolshevik Revolution took place was already small and industry accounted for about 16% of the national output, industry in China was even smaller and accounted for only around 3.5% of the national output. Thus, Mao, leading the CPC at this time, had no choice but to rely on the agrarian peasantry.

Mao and his followers, Maoists, believed that the working class is not as necessary for revolutionary changes as Marx, Engels and Lenin claimed – the peasantry can do this job just fine. And the absence of industry and the working class did not discourage Mao. In his speech on April 15, 1958, he declared: "Apart from their other characteristics, the outstanding thing about China's 600 million people is that they are poor and blank. This may seem a bad thing, but in reality it is a good thing. Poverty gives rise to the desire for change, the desire for action and the desire for revolution. On a blank sheet of paper free from any marks, the freshest and the most beautiful characters can be written, the freshest and the most beautiful pictures can be painted."

Since only the USSR had experience with the transition to socialism, China turned for experience and help to the USSR, becoming a Soviet-style centrally planned economy. China's first five-year plan was implemented in 1953-1957. It included a very important element without which an economy cannot be successful: industrialization. It was a painful process, especially for peasants, because it channeled about 80% of all investments into urban economy, while about 80% of the population lived in rural areas. The plan seemingly worked, and the economy began to improve. As of 2015, Chinese government official web portals state that "between 1953 and 1956, the average annual increases in the total value of industrial and agricultural output were 19.6 and 4.8 per cent respectively." [1] Encyclopedia Britannica (2015) states that the first five-year plan was "the beginning of China's rapid industrialization and is still regarded as having been enormously successful."

However, after the completion of the first five-year economic plan, China still remained agricultural and poor. This cast doubt on whether the Soviet-style model was the right path for China, and Mao became convinced that China had to develop its own path to communism. First, he came up with a new campaign known as the Great Leap Forward, which was designed to boost agricultural production by collectivization and industrial production by encouraging peasants to develop manufacturing on farms. He saw grain and steel as the base of the economy, and believed that collectives were the best solution to boost the production of both. In 1955, against the wishes of the majority in the CPC, Mao called for accelerated agricultural collectivization.

The Great Leap Forward (1958-1961) included the mandatory process of agricultural collectivization and the mass mobilization of people into the collectives. Collectives were designed as huge rural units that included tens of thousands of peasants from different villages. They had to become autonomous units that produced everything from agricultural to industrial products. They were self-managed and had their own schools and militia. This process went fast. There were only 14.2% of the peasants in collectives in 1955, but 91.2% of the peasants were in collectives by 1966. Surprisingly, the process did not spark the strong resistance and protests it had in the Soviet Union. However, the process also did not produce desirable results, and the reasons for this are as follow.

In theory, agricultural collectivization can increase productivity and provide an advantage because it promotes the formation of larger, more efficient farms. As opposed to small farms, large ones are able to buy heavy machinery and mechanize hand labor, making it more efficient. However, since industry was not yet developed, China could not provide such machinery to newly formed collective farms. Thus, the main factor for stimulating agricultural production by collectivization could not work. In fact, collectivization reduced the motivation of farmers to work and achieve results. Moreover, a portion of the peasantry was taken away from farms to industrial collectives, reducing the farm labor force. For example, 21 million workers were added to non-agricultural state payrolls in 1958. This, combined with possible bad weather, resulted in reduced rather than increased agricultural production, which led to food shortages and severe famine. Chinese industry did not do better and industrial output plummeted.

By 1962, China had completely detached itself from the model of the Soviet Union. Mao turned against Soviet policies of centralized command planning and giant factories. Instead of brining peasants into cities and big factories, Mao decided to stimulate industry by building backyard furnaces in urban neighborhoods and villages. Instead of central government control, the management of these small enterprises was given to provinces. By 1970, the central government controlled only about 8% of industrial output. [2]

However, the mass mobilization of unskilled workers and peasants into the industrial collectives also could not work, as these people had insufficient knowledge and skills in industrial manufacturing. As uneducated workers tried to produce steel on a massive scale, the product was low-quality and useless. To make matters worse, this process was accompanied by the destruction of homes on a massive scale, probably the greatest in human history. As homes were torn down for materials to be used for building canteens, repairing roads or making steel, it is estimated that up to one third of all housing in China was turned into rubble. [3]

Thus, both collectivization and industrialization had failed miserably. They not only did not work — they resulted in catastrophe. The Chinese economy stagnated, and an estimated 18-46 million of a population of 600 million people died, mostly of starvation.

An official Chinese web portal (2015) summarizes the great leap failure as follows: "It was mainly due to the errors of the Great Leap Forward and of the struggle against 'right opportunism' together with a succession of natural calamities and the perfidious scrapping of contracts by the Soviet Government that our economy encountered serious difficulties between 1959 and 1961, which caused serious losses to our country and people." [1] Mao recognized his mistakes and resigned as State Chairman of the PRC. However, he remained Chairman of the CPC and did not leave the political stage. Although he had withdrawn himself from economic decision making, he became more involved in the ideological process that led to the next disaster: the Great Cultural Revolution.

The Great Cultural Revolution

The next of China's troubles emerged with the death of Stalin in 1956, when his successor, Nikita Khrushchev, denounced Stalin's personality cult and initiated reforms in the USSR. Some senior members of the CPC, Deng Xiaoping and Liu Bocheng, advocated that China also needed economic reforms. However, Mao and many members of the CPC became worried that revisionism would end the revolution and turn China back to capitalism. In his polemic titled "On Khrushchev's Phony Communism and Historical Lessons for the World," Mao warned that Khrushchev's revisionism could lead to the restoration of capitalism.

In 1966, to prevent turning back to capitalism, Mao and his colleagues launched the "Great Cultural Revolution," aiming to purify China from revisionism. In 1966, the CPC Central Committee passed its "Decision Concerning the Great Proletarian Revolution" that defined the new revolution. The decision stated: "Currently, our objective is to struggle against and crush those people who are taking the capitalist road, to criticize and repudiate the reactionary bourgeois academic 'authorities' and the ideology of the bourgeoisie and all other exploiting classes and transform education, literature and art, and all other parts of the superstructure that do not correspond to the socialist economic base, so as to facilitate the consolidation and development of the socialist system." Not only that, Chinese leaders advocated support for the anti-colonial "liberation movement" worldwide.

China's urban youth responded to the decision with a massive mobilization and by forming Red Guard groups. The movement became a primarily urban phenomenon that affected large cities the most and remote areas the least. Red Guard groups occupied government buildings and laid siege to foreign embassies in Beijing. All ambassadors, except one in Egypt, were recalled from abroad, which also marked China's self-isolation. Red Guard groups split into factions, each claiming to be the true representative of Mao's thought. All of this produced only chaos and the growth of Mao's personality cult.

Defense minister and prominent leader of the CPC Lin Biao called to destroy the "Four Olds:" old customs, culture, habits and ideas. However, what exactly should be destroyed was not specified. In addition, Mao believed that the masses should find their own direction and make their own decisions instead of relying on the authorities. As a result, the movement spun out of control. It spread all over the country, into all social spheres, including the military and the CPC. For the CPC leaders, Stalin still remained a hero and they adopted many of his ideas and practices. Millions suffered harassment and arbitrary imprisonment. This even included CPC leaders who criticized the movement; for example, Deng Xiaoping, who was later rehabilitated and became one of the most important Chinese leaders.

Following the claims of Marx and Lenin that religion is nothing but "the opiate of the masses" as well as a tool for the ruling class to suppress workers, clergy members were arrested and churches were either closed or even ruined. Many cultural sites were attacked and historical relics destroyed. For example, it is estimated that out of 6,843 cultural sites under protection by 1958 government decision, 4,922 were destroyed. [4] Many intellectuals were either sent to labor camps or fled the country, and the education system came to a halt. Almost an entire generation became inadequately educated for jobs requiring high skills. Prosecutions and political struggles left many local governments, factories and economic institutions short of skilled workers, and the economy had fallen into disarray. From 1966 to 1968, industrial production went down 12%.

The leadership did not pay much attention to the economy, as ideology and the revolution became the priority. As later Chinese governments admitted, the cultural revolution "was responsible for the most severe setback and heaviest losses suffered by the Party, the state and the people since the founding of the People's Republic." [1] The CPC recognized that "the history of cultural revolution has proved that Comrade Mao Zedong's principal theses for initiating this revolution conformed neither to Marxism-Leninism nor to Chinese reality." [1] Yet, the CPC still supported the overall ideology of Mao, putting blame on other leaders: "These erroneous theses, upon which Comrade Mao Zedong based himself in initiating the cultural revolution, were obviously inconsistent with the system of Mao Zedong Thought, which is the integration of the universal principles of Marxism-Leninism with concrete practice of the Chinese revolution. These theses must be thoroughly distinguished from Mao Zedong Thought. As for Lin Bao, Jiang Qing and others, who were placed in important positions by Comrade Mao Zedong, the matter is of an entirely different nature. They rigged up two counter-revolutionary cliques in an attempt to seize supreme power and, taking advantage of Comrade Mao Zedong's errors, committed many crimes behind his back, bringing disaster to the country and the people." [1]

Reforms and Creation of
an Economic Foundation for Modern China

Despite both the Great Leap Forward and the Great Cultural Revolution campaigns having disastrous consequences, not everything was bad. China began the rapid industrialization that is necessary for any successful economy. Mao promoted population growth, and under his leadership the Chinese population grew from 550 to over 900 million. Healthcare was free and standards of living seemed to be improving. During several years of the Cultural Revolution, China advanced in many fields of science and technology, and tested its first hydrogen bombs, launched its first nuclear submarines and launched its first satellite into space.

Although Mao officially declared the end of the Cultural Revolution in 1969, its aftermath lasted until his death in 1976. In fact, it lasted for two more years, as Mao's successor, Hua Guofeng, decided to pursue policies of "Two Whatevers:" 1) "whatever policy originated from Chairman Mao, we must continue to support" and 2) "whatever directions were given to us from Chairman Mao, we must continue to follow." Finally, in 1978, the Eleventh CPC Congress marked dramatic changes. Deng Xiaoping, who was now rehabilitated and a known leader, called for "liberation of thoughts." Mao's successor, Hua Guofeng, recognized that continuing Mao's policies was a mistake. The leadership of the "Gang of Four" calling for a continuation of the Cultural Revolution was arrested, and China entered an era of economic reforms, which owes much to Deng Xiaoping.

This time, the Chinese leadership got Marxism right. In 1978, on Deng's order, the article "Putting into Effect the Socialist Principle of

Distribution According to Work" clarified that China was not yet a truly socialist society and was only in its primary stage. Deng also turned to classical Marxism, suggesting that communism requires an advanced economy. In his speech at the Central Committee plenum in 1984, he clearly went to complete agreement with Marx: "Marxism attaches utmost importance to developing the productive forces. We have said that socialism is the primary stage of communism and that at the advanced stage the principle of from each according to his ability and to each according to his needs will be applied. This calls for highly developed productive forces and an overwhelming abundance of material wealth. Therefore, the fundamental task for the socialist stage is to develop the productive forces. The superiority of the socialist system is demonstrated, in the final analysis, by faster and greater development of those forces than under the capitalist system. As they develop, the people's material and cultural life will constantly improve. One of our shortcomings after the founding of the People's Republic was that we didn't pay enough attention to developing the productive forces. Socialism means eliminating poverty."

Surprisingly, although Deng greatly contributed to the Marxist movement in China, some historians portray him as a nationalist rather than a Marxist. They claim that his motivation was not the building of communism but rather a nationalistic desire to see China on equal terms with global powers. This notion, however, does not disprove that he was Marxist: Deng could have wanted Chinese equality, but he still used Marxist methods. On the other hand, and not surprisingly, Maoists see Deng's reforms as a betrayal of communist ideas and Maoism.

Nevertheless, thanks to Deng, the core idea of Marxism – that communism is based on advanced economy more than the will of the people – was finally recognized. This idea, that economic development should be the main focus, was further supported by Chinese leadership unto our current time. And the leadership became very realistic about this. When asked how long it would take China to pass the primary stage of socialism, one of the CPC General Secretaries, Jiang Zemin, replied, "At least 100 years." This is in contrast to the Soviets, who claimed that the USSR was already in the stage of developed socialism in the 1980s, and that they were about to enter the stage of communism. Preventing any further speculation and misunderstandings, the Chinese constitution was formulated to reflect that "China will be in the primary stage of socialism for a long time to come." To clarify what is needed in order to advance from the primary to the mature stage of socialism, Jiang named three conditions: 1) the emancipation and modernization of the production forces; 2) managing state affairs according to the law and making people the masters of the country (in other words, democracy); and 3) people with high ideals, moral integrity and good education.

The new leadership recognized that China was in a peculiar situation: although the country wanted to build a socialist society, the economic conditions for socialism did not yet exist. This situation was somehow reminiscent of the situation in Russia soon after the revolution, when Lenin realized that Russia needed a stronger economy and introduced the New Economic Policy (NEP) to step back to state capitalism. In Russia, unfortunately, this policy was ended within a few years by Stalin. Thus, it was not Russia, but China who managed to use the advantages of a market economy. In China, Lenin's NEP policies were introduced in the 1980s and remain successful today.

In 1982, the Twelfth Congress of the CPC was directed to "integrate the universal truth of Marxism with the concrete realities of China, blaze a path of our own and build socialism with Chinese characteristics". And what "concrete realities of China" were more important than its economic weakness? And what is "the universal truth of Marxism" other than the foundation of communism is an advanced economy? So, the Chinese leadership became more pragmatic and focused on the economy.

Economy, however, cannot grow without investments, and the leadership appealed to the international community, especially to the Chinese diaspora of about 60 million living abroad. And it did work. Until 2003, about two thirds of all foreign investments to China came from Chinese living abroad. To facilitate the flow of foreign investments as well as experience in technology and management, China established four special economic zones.

To make investors less nervous and to solve the problem of separate territories (Taiwan, Hong Kong and Macao), Deng successfully introduced the concept of "one country, two systems." The concept meant that the socialist and capitalist systems could coexist in one country: while mainland China continued with socialism, Taiwan, Hong Kong and Macao could continue operating as capitalist systems. Further, in 1984, the CPC rejected the concept that a planned economy contradicts market economy, and declared that China would build a planned market economy. Nevertheless, the economy would be based on public ownership, which means that the economic foundation would remain socialist.

The combination of new policies and extremely cheap labor made China a paradise for foreign investors, as manufacturing in this country could be done cheaply and efficiently. All of a sudden, Western enterprises had no choice but to move a lot of their businesses to China in order to be competitive and to survive. China became the world's manufacturing hub and its economy began booming. Still, some analysts criticize Chinese leadership for not being very democratic: "Had the regime been one of genuine Socialist Democracy, with complete freedom of speech and criticism for the workers, this opening up could have been controlled and used to strengthen the socialist system." [5] This, however, is not that simple. More democracy would provide workers with tools to fight for higher salaries and better working conditions, which would make manufacturing more expensive and scare foreign investors away. Thus, if China had indeed installed "genuine Socialist Democracy," it might have been left without foreign financing.

Big changes were also introduced into the countryside, where most Chinese lived, initiating the process of de-collectivization. In the 1980s, land from collectives began to be rented to peasant families. This led to massive privatization through the formation of the so-called township and village enterprises. Price controls were eased, and agricultural production grew quickly.

In 1988, the first stock exchange in China was opened in Shenzhen, followed by the second in 1990 in Shanghai. The economy began a fast growth, lifting people out of poverty. For example, an estimated 150 million peasants were lifted out of poverty in the 1990s.

However, not everyone was happy. Some demanded lower prices, some called to fight corruption and some demanded more political openness. In 1989, students joined by others took to the streets to demand more freedom and changes. This culminated in the protest on

Tiananmen Square in the capital. Was this crowd aware of Marx's discovery that democracy and freedom are based on economy? Probably not; otherwise they would have acted differently. The protest was crushed harshly and swiftly, putting an end to the protest movement and keeping China in order.

Keeping the country in order and stable was another important factor contributing to further economic growth, as investors and businesses don't like instability. And indeed, in 1990s, China became one of the highest recipients of foreign direct investment in the world, and sustained an average GDP growth of 11.2%. Although the Chinese government brutally suppressed the Tiananmen protests, surprisingly, it delivered more democracy and freedom a few decades later. And here is how the government did it: through advancing the economy and lifting people from poverty.

Finally, in 1989, surprising news came to China from abroad: the dissolution of the USSR. Although this was disturbing, Chinese communists had a chance for reevaluation and lessons. And since the main reason for the collapse of the USSR was a stagnant economy, the main lesson of the USSR experience was that economy is the foundation of any society. This further confirmed that China had entered the right path.

Socialist Market Economy

Deng Xiaoping's coalition adopted highly flexible and pragmatic policies: whatever keeps the economy growing is good. The Twenty-Fourth Congress of the CPC named this policy "socialist market economy," elaborating that although "State property remains the base of the national economy, all forms of property – state, collective and private – will have to be used in developing economy." The leadership introduced a system of contract responsibility that facilitated unprecedented autonomy to the managers of state-owned firms. It gave managers control over assets and mergers, which in fact became a form of "spontaneous privatization." Thus, the Chinese state relaxed control over the economy: "In 1978, state-operated enterprises (SOEs) accounted for 78 percent of the industrial output but only 23 percent in 2000. State firms accounted for 82 percent of the fixed assets in 1980 but 55 percent in 1998." [6]

The reforms became very successful. China's economic growth accelerated to a speed unmatched by any Western country. For example, from 1991 to 1995, its GDP increased annually by a whopping 12%. Since reforms began from the end of the 1970s until now, China's GDP has grown an average of 9.4% annually. For the last 35 years, China has become one of the fastest-growing economies in the world, lifting hundreds of millions out of poverty.

Naturally, along with the positives, the capitalist economy also brought some negatives: capitalist relationships and inequality. By 1995, China had become even more unequal than the United States or any other Western capitalist nation. Not surprisingly, members and officials of communist parties have used the chance to benefit from capitalism and abused their power. For example, by 2007, there were "some six million owners of private firms in China; about two thirds are former officials." [2] An estimated one quarter of the 100 richest Chinese were members of the communist party. This raised criticism and questions about whether the party members intended to build communism. This criticism, however, is not quite valid: China does not claim to have a socialist society, much less communism. What China claims is that it is building socialism and eventually communism; this, however, first requires going through the stage of capitalism.

One can imagine that now that capitalism has strong roots and many members of the leadership have become wealthy, China will continue moving toward capitalism. However, when Chinese leadership promised to build communism at the beginning of the reforms, it was not kidding. Despite the fact that China stepped back to a so-called socialist market economy, it remained committed to the Leninist principle of "democratic centralism," maintaining a one-party state and centralized control. It also remained committed to the promise to move from the stage of primary socialism, which requires a market economy, to the stage of mature socialism. After the phases of de-collectivization and privatization, the leadership has recently begun scaling down capitalism and turning in a more socialist direction. By 2005, China began a partial reversal of the market-oriented reforms.

Even when reforms had just begun, the government committed itself to keeping key industries under state control. In 2006, it made clear that such vital industries as armaments, power generation and distribution, oil and petrochemicals, telecommunications, coal, aviation and shipping industries will be under "absolute control" of the state. [7] Moreover, state control over the economy was facilitated through financial systems and money lending: state banks lend money to businesses according to priorities, and at interest rates which are lower for state businesses than private ones. As a result, the state sector of the economy began to grow again, instead of shrinking. For example, the GDP share of the private sector grew from 1% in 1978 to about 70% in 2005, leaving only around 30% for the state sector. However, by 2012, the state sector comprised about half of GDP, and state-backed companies accounted for 80% of the value of China's stock market. [8]

It is known that state enterprises are generally less efficient than private ones. Therefore, in order to keep the state economy more efficient, China developed a model in which the state retains ownership of enterprises but does not directly control their management and operations. Moreover, it seems that although many companies are privatized, "the shareholder and accounting structure is such that at any time the party can regain control if it is necessary." [2] However, it remains to be seen how well this will work. When governments favor certain companies, others are at a disadvantage and suffer. Also, state capitalism favors well-connected insiders instead of well-trained and innovative staff, breeding corruption and making state enterprises less competitive. Last but not least, governments usually back big developed enterprises, while most innovations take place in small start-ups; thus, innovative small businesses remain at a disadvantage and have little chance to grow.

Indeed, the latest data confirms that private firms in China function better than state-owned enterprises (SOEs). In the past few years, as the profitability of private firms has gone up, the profitability of SOEs has fallen. Profits of SOEs in China are now less than half of those of private enterprises. This has not gone unnoticed by leadership, and to fix the problem, a new pilot program of mixed-ownership enterprises has been launched. According to this program, parts of some SOEs will be sold to private investors to see whether this will make SOEs more efficient. The hope is that the reform will help to "better handle the relationship between government and the market."

In general, China and some other communism-oriented countries, such as Vietnam, have chosen free-market economies. For example, "a world-topping 95 percent of Vietnamese say that most people are better off in free-market economies, and 76 percent of Chinese agree, according to a Pew survey of nearly 49,000 people worldwide that might have astonished Ho Chi Minh and Mao Zedong." [9] Thus, some critics claim that Chinese people have chosen the capitalist road. However, why do they think that market economy is incompatible with socialism? China has been building a socialist market economy for many years now, and has done so quite successfully.

Current Success and Challenges

A typical capitalist economy has three main markets: goods plus services, labor and the financial market. China is already a leader in two of these areas: the goods market and the labor market. Its financial market is passing the stage of capital accumulation. Some define this phase of capitalism development as the primitive accumulation of capital. Through discipline and systematic work, China is catching up with the West. It sells abroad more than it buys and raises wealth through a positive balance of trade with other nations, which leads to a constant capital accumulation. In fact, China has already accumulated so much capital that is capable of lending it to other countries and becoming one of the main world creditors. By 2013, China "had four of the world's top ten banks in terms of capitalization and possessed the largest foreign exchange reserves (3.2   trillion)." [10] Thus, China has already acquired the main characteristics of developed capitalist economies, and theoretically is ready for transition to communism.

Chinese leadership has already initiated the transition from capitalism to the first stage of communism, which is socialism, and the Chinese economy is currently a mixture of both public and private ownership of the means of production. It is largely market-based, but the government actively intervenes in the economy through macroeconomic policies to correct market failures, and to keep inflation and unemployment low. A central government that controls a massive financial system continues to provide the country with general political and economical direction.

With the possible disadvantages named above, this centralized system also has an advantage: it can mobilize large resources and remove obstacles fast. The successful handling of the recent Olympic games in China illustrates this well. Also, as much as Western ideologues generally dislike centralized governments, they have to admit that, due to centralization, China was able to build one of the best infrastructures in the world.

However, not everything is extremely centralized in China. Although government revenues are highly centralized, local governments have been delegated a broad range of authority and resources at their own command. In fact, recent studies show that "China is among the most decentralized countries in the world when it comes to government expenditures." [11]

Led by the communist party, China achieved impressive success. It "had the highest average annual growth rate in the world over the preceding two decades (10.2 percent in constant price terms), accounting for about 40 percent of global economic growth." [10] As Marx said, economy is the foundation for everything else. And following the economic advances, China has advanced in many other fields: since 1980, China has lifted about 400 million people – which is a massive amount – out of poverty. [12] (Of note, 150 million people are still living on less than $1 USD per day.) Lifting people out of poverty was accompanied by improving their education, health care and social security. This is reflected by the annual Human Development Index, according to which China has been continuously advancing for the past few decades.

Compared to the rest of the world, China has risen above the average prosperity level and, in 2014, ranked 54th out of 142 rated countries according to the Legatum Prosperity Index. For comparison, its comparably sized neighbor, India, is ranked only 102nd. In 2008, China surpassed the U.S. as the world's top producer of Ph.D.s; it is becoming the top world innovator. For example, in a 2011 report, the U.K.'s Academy of Sciences (Royal Society) cited that China's growing share in the total number of articles published globally is now second only to the long-time scientific world leader, the United States. [13] In 2012, the Chinese accounted for the largest number of patents filed throughout the world. [14] China is also becoming the leader in emerging technologies. For example, it now publishes the biggest share of academic papers in the field of nanotechnology.

Today, China is independent from foreign investments and content with its development. The manufacturing boom brought China independence from foreign financing. Chinese exports far exceed its imports, and China has a huge annual trade surplus. And this is going to continue, as foreign businesses still prefer to manufacture goods in China that are then exported back to their home countries.

Out of the 500 top multinational corporations, 470 currently operate in China. With the rapid growth of Chinese industry, the working class has grown too. The Chinese working class is now the biggest in the world, and it continues to expand. Importantly, its living conditions have been continuously improving. This improvement is well illustrated by the materialistic approach of Chinese people to marriage. In the 1970s, married couples were expected to own a watch, a sewing machine and a bicycle; in the 1990s – a mobile phone, a computer and a motorbike; and now – a home, a car and cash. This rapid improvement in living conditions did not go unnoticed by mainstream China: according to a series of surveys, 80-95% of Chinese express extreme satisfaction with their central government. [15] This number is higher than in any Western country, and Chinese are very optimistic about the future. For decades now, Western ideologues have kept predicting and warning that China is heading toward social unrest and even revolution; [2] however, considering the levels of public satisfaction, the reality is very far from such predictions.

Recent success does not mean that China has no serious problems and challenges. Having the world's biggest population, China also has the greatest challenges. Whether it will be able to solve them is an important question. If not, as suggested by Western ideologues, then the Chinese model will not work, and the country will have to retreat to capitalism and forget about communism. If yes, then China will develop a successful model for the transformation of developing economies to communism. Since this question is crucial for our understanding of future world development, let's discuss the main problems of modern China and the possibility of their solution in detail. The most serious problems are as follow:

1) China needs to build its own research, development and scientific potential, which is the basis for progress, innovation and economic growth. Chinese analysts recognize this: "Currently, there is a bad trend in China's science policy. It is geared toward a desire for quick returns. The priority should be for China to encourage a curiosity for pure science, and promote exploring unknown worlds. We must strengthen basic scientific research in order to promote original technological innovation, because China cannot find its place in the new economic order merely by following or imitating technologies developed elsewhere." [16] So far, China has mostly been a supply chain for foreign companies and a global manufacturing hub. In 2009, according to the WTO, manufacturing comprised 93.6% of China's exports. In order to be self-sufficient and self-sustainable, China needs to change its role from "Made in China" to "Made by China" or "Designed in China." Currently, too many of China's exports – especially high-tech products – are made by foreigners. Deng brought it to public attention as long ago as 1977: "First of all we must recognize the gap between China and the rest of the world in the area of science and technology. We cannot fool anyone because you can't visit our country without seeing how backward we are. We can only fool ourselves by saying that we are not backward." [11]

2) China requires the ability to maintain economic growth, as growth due to cheap labor is coming to an end. This growth is necessary to employ massive amounts of people without jobs. As one senior Chinese economist put it: "The whole world is talking about jobs going to China, but we are talking about where to get another two hundred to three hundred million jobs." [11] China became the manufacturing hub of the world because production there could be executed cheaply and efficiently. Workers in China used to be paid wages at least 10 times lower than in the West. They did not have legally recognized rights, they did not form unions, and their working conditions were poor. This is now changing. Workers now protest more, their conditions are improving, and their salaries are growing rapidly.

3) There is too wide a gap between people – between rich and poor as well as between people living in urban and rural regions. In China, people who live in urban regions have significantly higher incomes than those in rural regions. On the other hand, urban regions are mostly located in coastal areas while rural regions are located in inland parts of China. Thus, incomes are closely associated with location, and solving income inequality would help to solve location inequality: urban/coastal versus suburban/inland. Unfortunately, China's income inequality, and urban/suburban inequality along with this, has been widening since the 1980s. Of note, in 2014, it was ranked below the U.S. level. [17]

4) Another problem is environmental damage. Air pollution in many Chinese regions, especially in industrial eastern cities, routinely exceeds safe levels. According to a 2012 Asian Development Bank report, less than 1% of China's 500 largest cities meet air quality standards of the World Health Organization. About 300 million Chinese have no access to safe drinking water. Environmental damage also has big economic costs. Depending on the source, it is estimated at between 3% and 9% of the nation's GDP. The West had it easy: it first became rich by exploiting natural resources and the environment, and then began fixing environmental damage. Due to its massive population and industry, China cannot afford to follow the easy path of the West, because pollution may grow to catastrophic proportions.

5) The growth of an aging population presents another serious problem for China. First, the aging population has no safety net. Second, due to the one-child policy adopted in 1979, it will put big pressure on families of workers, as one family will have to take care of four elderly people (the "4-2-1 Problem"). Mao encouraged population growth in China because he thought that this would empower the country. But then economic reforms began, and Deng advocated changing this policy in the opposite direction in order to raise income per capita. At present, China's total working population – aged between 15 and 64 – has just hit the peak and turned downhill. [11]

6) Corruption is a huge obstacle in advancing the economy and progress of any country, and China is no exception. As the Chinese state put some of its enterprises on sale and many state enterprises have mixed state/private ownership, it is easy for officials to abuse their power in

order to enrich themselves. The following example well illustrates this: by 2007, there were "some six million owners of private firms in China; about two thirds were former state officials." [2]

7) The outflow of wealth and capital from China to the West poses another serious issue. As the overall quality of life in China is lower than in the West, many rich Chinese immigrate to the West and move their wealth along with them. For example, Bloomberg Television estimated that in August-October of 2015, Chinese were moving out of the country a staggering $200 billion per month, mostly illegally. If this continues, China may never be able to accumulate sufficient finances to become a wealthy nation.

Chinese leadership is well aware of these problems. It works hard to address them and China is already making very promising steps in the right direction. First, it is building a solid scientific and research base. As cited above, China's growing share in the total number of articles published globally is now second only to the U.S., and it is probably overtaking the U.S. as this book is being written. In 2012, Chinese accounted for the largest number of patents filed throughout the world, and China is becoming a leader in new emerging technologies. China's spending on information and communications technology was projected at more than $465 billion in 2015, a growth rate of 11%.[18] This is far above the average 5% growth rate worldwide. And the country is already succeeding. Out of 500 fastest computers in the world, China has 167, overtaking the U.S. at 165. In 2016, China announced the world fastest supercomputer that is built entirely on homegrown processors.

Second, China is no longer relying on cheap labor in order to keep the economy growing. It increasingly relies on innovation and it has its own advanced technologies. For example, "In 2015, IDC estimates that nearly 500 million smartphones will be sold in China, three times the number sold in the United States and about one third of global sales. Roughly 85 percent of the smartphones sold in China will be made by its domestic producers like Lenovo, Xiaomi, Huawei, ZTE and Coolpad." [18] New Chinese technology companies already successfully compete with the American big four: Google, Apple, Facebook and Amazon. The Chinese company Alibaba has already overtaken Amazon and become the world's largest online merchant. Chinese Lenovo is already the number one PC maker in the world. Huawei has surpassed Apple as the world's second largest smartphone maker, while Xiaomi and Oppo are the fourth and fifth largest smartphone makers in the world respectively. The Chinese social network Tencent is catching up with Facebook, and the Chinese Internet search engine Baidu is catching up to Google. This is not to mention that some technological inventions of China are now copied by the West. For example, while some media sources refer Letv as the Netflix of China, it is actually the opposite: Netflix is the Letv of the USA, because Letv launched its video streaming service several years before Netflix. To make things even easier for Chinese companies, in the wake of scandals revealing the cooperation of American high-tech businesses with the government to spy on citizens worldwide, American companies have lost their privacy edge and credibility. Overall, the expansion of the China tech market is projected to account for 43% of tech-sector growth worldwide. [18] Not only that, but China is also building a good macroeconomic environment. In 2013, it was ranked 10th in macroeconomic environment, 32nd in innovation, and the 29th most competitive economy in the world. [19]

Third, as mentioned in Chapter 8, the world is competing for highly skilled and knowledgeable specialists and managers, offering them super-salaries and feeding inequality. Of course, China had to follow. Otherwise, it would not be able to hire these individuals, and would lose in economic competition with the West. However, Chinese leadership took note of growing gaps between rich and poor as well as urban and rural populations. Recently, at the beginning of the 2000s, China began implementing a new policy of accelerated urbanization that aims to increase the proportion of people that lives in cities. Since incomes and locations are closely associated, this should help to shrink both gaps.

Moreover, China recognized that it had policies that favored urban over rural residents, and these policies are now undergoing changes – changes which are already producing promising results. A recent study published by the World Bank shows that instead of widening, the gaps between rich and poor as well as urban and rural standards of living seem to be shrinking. [20] Beginning in 2008, both income (Figure 9.1) and urban-rural (Figure 9.2) gaps have slightly decreased. This study also revealed another important piece of information: inequality in China is

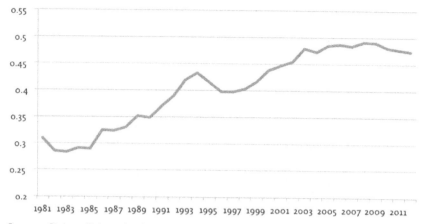

Sources: Gini coefficients for the years 1986–2001 are from Ravallion and Chen (2007), 2002 from Gustafsson et al. (2008), 2003–2012 from the National Bureau of Statistics.

Figure 9.1. Income inequality in China (1980-2012).
Inequality is measured by the Gini coefficient from 0 to 1.0. Zero represents perfect equality, while one indicates perfect inequality. Inequality rose from about 0.3 in the 1980s to 0.49 in 2008. Since then, it has slightly declined to about 0.45. The illustration is taken from a World Bank publication. [20]

not the result of stagnant or declining income among poor groups (as it is in the West), but of the more rapid growth in the income of richer groups. In other words, all groups of people saw their incomes rise – it's just that the incomes of the rich have been rising faster than those of the poor. Also helping to close the gaps, the urban population in China is constantly growing: at the end of 2011, the urban population rose above half of the total population, and it is expected to reach 68% of the national total by 2030. [11] This is driving the growth of the middle class, which currently accounts for about 12% of the total population and is likely to double in the 2011-2021 period. [11]

Fourth, environmental issues are taken very seriously by the Chinese public and its government. In fact, environmental damage has been a source of social unrest and numerous protests. China has been working to address environmental problems for years now with some success. For example, World Bank data shows that the proportion of the population with access to safe water sources in rural regions of China increased from 82% in 2008 to 85% in 2012. The central government has

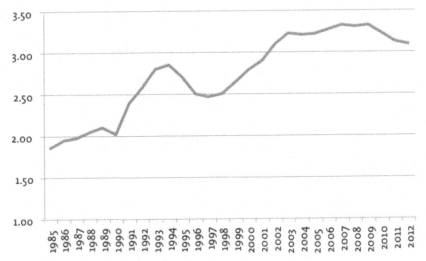

Source: National Bureau of Statistics, 2012.

Figure 9.2. Urban-Rural income ratio in China (1985-2012).
Urban-rural income ratio is measured by the average income per capita of urban households divided by the average income per capita of rural households. The urban-rural income gap rose from less than 2.0 in the 1980s to well over 3.0 by 2008, which is very high by international standards. Since then, the gap has slightly declined. The illustration is taken from the World Bank publication. [20]

strict regulations regarding environmental issues. However, the problem was that, in the past, the monitoring and enforcement of these regulations were undertaken by local governments more interested in economic growth than in the environment. This is now changing. In 2014, China revised its protection laws to fight environmental damage. The new law provides environmental authorities with more punitive powers and a broader range of actions. Also, the latest Chinese five-year plan now includes a budget equivalent to 277 billion USD to fight environmental damage. Particularly, this plan aims to reduce air emissions by 25% between 2012-2017. Finally, China heavily spends on alternative sources of energy and is becoming one of the biggest investors in renewables.

Fifth, although China simply cannot afford to provide the aging population with a decent safety net now, there is hope that it will be able to do this in the near future due to growing economy and wealth. Also, the leadership is working to address the aging population problem. In 2013, the Third Plenum of the 18th Central Committee of the Chinese Communist Party made the decision to relax the one-child policy. Of note, this may not solve the problem because more and more families in China – similar to many developed countries – don't wish to have more than one child. Thus, this situation is not unique to China but rather attributed to modern life.

Sixth, China has been working to address the corruption problem for many years now. It regularly cracks down on corruption regardless of rank. For example, in just half of 2014, China probed about 25,000 people. [21] This included the arrest of an official of the highest rank, "a tiger." Recently, the Chinese president announced a comprehensive anticorruption program that will be extended beyond individuals to include organizations and state firms. [22] Although the situation is still unsatisfactory, it is becoming better, as rated by a corruption perception index that is annually published by the Transparency International organization. In this rating, the perceived level of public sector corruption is scaled from 0 to 10, where 0 means that a country is perceived as highly corrupt and 10 means it is perceived as very clean. In 1995, the index was 2.2, in 2000 – 3.3, in 2010 - 3.3, and in 2014 – 3.6, suggesting that the system is becoming less corrupt.

Seventh, the outflow of wealth presents a serious challenge to China. Although Chinese leadership comes up with new laws and regulations designed to alleviate the problem, capital always finds new ways to escape. For example, the Washington-based Global Financial Integrity Group estimates that from 2002 to 2011, about $1.08 trillion left China illegally. [23] However, the main reason for the outflow of money from China to the West is poor quality of life. Thus, since the quality of life in China is gradually improving, the problem of wealth outflow should also gradually be alleviated.

Finally, the biggest challenge and threat for China is currently the U.S. Since the collapse of the USSR, Washington has been guided by the Wolfowitz Doctrine, which clearly states: "Our first objective is to prevent the re-emergence of a new rival." As China is growing to become the world's largest economic and political power, Washington perceives the country as a grave threat to its ambition to rule the world, and is attempting to derail Chinese development. Will Washington succeed? It is difficult to tell, but success seems unlikely. If Chinese leadership peacefully and patiently continues its current course, China will eventually grow so big and powerful that Washington will have no choice but to accept its preeminence on the world stage.

As the economy improves, China also becomes more politically liberal and democratic. The Chinese government listens to the voices of the people more carefully, and things that were impossible a decade ago are now taking place: villagers are able to prevent building enterprises that would destroy their environment and the government no longer hides such facts as the real figures for air pollution. In fact, Chinese can now track air pollution levels in real time using their mobile phones.

In general, China is gradually becoming more democratic. However, it remains a one-party state, while democracy means that all parties are allowed. Therefore, some critics argue that this gradual improvement will eventually stop and gradualism will ultimately fail, because this will threaten the survival of the Communist Party. [24] This argument seems logical and valid. However, it is possible that the Communist Party may become so democratic and sensitive to the needs of the people that no other party would do a better job and would thus not be necessary. No one can predict if this will happen, but it is possible. After all, democracy and freedom is a goal and a necessary condition for communism.

Overall, Chinese leadership has demonstrated its determination and ability to adhere to classical Marxism. Although China has been influenced by Western ideologies, president Xi has recently stressed the importance of adherence to Marxism and its philosophy, [25] which is dialectical materialism and historical materialism (see Chapter 3). Although China is currently more capitalist than socialist, its leadership has not forgotten that its goal is to build a socialist and then communist society. Still, its leadership remains realistic about China's development, and its president, Xi Jinping, has recently "reiterated that China will remain at the primary stage of socialism for a long time to come." [25]

Chinese Development as a Model for Others

Overall, it seems that the CPC tackles all problems systematically and successfully. There is no reason to believe that some Western-style government would do a better job. In fact, China's neighboring country of about the same size, India, which has Western-style democracy, is not so successful (see Table 6). The only thing that may be slightly better in India is the situation with income inequality: according to data available from the World Bank, it stood at 33.9 in India as of 2009 and at 43.1 in China as of 2010 (scale 0-100, from the lowest to highest inequality). However, this is hard to compare, as neither country published complete data. (In fact, some analyses show the opposite: as of 2000-2010, India had higher income inequality than China.) [17]

Infrastructure, such as social safety nets, are equally bad in both countries. With the corruption perception index at 36 in 2014, China is slightly less corrupt than India, which scores 38 (scale 0-100, from the least to the most corrupt). China has a much better education system and crushes India in university rankings. [26] The percentage of the adult population with primary education in 2010 was 84.4% in China and only 65.4% in India. [11] The Chinese economy grew much faster than the Indian economy and is more competitive. In 2010, Chinese GDP (PPP) comprised 13.5% of the world, while Indian GDP accounted for only 5.6%. According to the 2014 Global Innovation Index, China is rated 29th in innovation, while India is ranked 76th. Finally, and most importantly, China also crushes India in prosperity: according to the 2014 Legatum Prosperity Index, China is ranked 54th, while India is only 102nd.

As one can see, democracy and attempts to copy successful Western systems do not automatically bring prosperity. Policies of "copy and paste" or "plug and play" prescribed by Western ideologues simply don't work. In his book *The End of Poverty*, J. Sachs notes that the position of Western leaders in recent eras, "ushered in by a conservative turn in the United States under President Ronald Reagan and in the United Kingdom under Prime Minister Margaret Thatcher, was based on a simplistic, even simpleminded, view of the challenge of poverty. The rich countries told the poor countries: Poverty is your own fault. Be like us (or what we imagine ourselves to be – free market oriented, entrepreneurial, and fiscally responsible) and you, too, can enjoy the riches of private-sector-led economic development." [27]

Unexpectedly, China, which did not follow the Western model,

Table 6. Comparison of China and India in 1980 and 2010

Country	GDP(PPP) % of world		GDP per capita, PPP (constant 2005 $)		Share of world trade (%)		Infant mortality (per 1,000 birth)		Hospital beds (per 1,000 people)		Life expectancy (years)		Urban population (% of total)		Adult population with primary education (% of total)	
	1980	2010	1980	2010	1980	2010	1980	2010	1980	2010	1980	2010	1980	2010	1980	2010
China	2.0	13.5	524	6,810	0.9	7.8	46.1	16.6	2.2	4.1	66.0	73.3	19.6	44.0	54.6	84.4
India	2.3	5.6	895	3,240	0.6	1.9	103.2	50.3	0.8	0.9	55.1	64.1	23.1	29.8	28.4	65.4

Note: Data for this table comes from the book *Following the Leader* written by David M. Lampton. [11]

became more prosperous than India, which did follow it. And we saw in Chapter 6 that Vietnam, which followed China's model, became more prosperous than Nicaragua, which followed the Western model. One size simply does not fit all. This is being increasingly recognized by more ideologists. Thus, China has developed its own successful model of development, and some countries that followed it are becoming successful too. It seems that the Chinese model, which employs a one-party government, can perform better than Western-like models, which employ multiparty (democratic) governments.

Why does this happen? The key to the success of China lies in fast industrialization. In the modern world, only countries that have developed industry are rich and successful. Countries that rely on agriculture are poor. This was clearly understood by the Soviets, and China took note of this. As described above, the very first Chinese five-year plan of development implemented industrialization. This process channeled about 80% of all investments into urban economies, although about 80% of the population lived in rural areas. Because of that, it was painful for the rural majority of the population. Thus, this would be less likely to happen in any democratic country, because people would not like to make tough sacrifices for the sake of future development, and would vote against it. However, in China or any other country ruled by one party, such tough decisions are possible. Therefore, while Western-style democracy provides some clear advantages in developed countries, it is not always helpful in developing ones. A one-party system can accelerate building the foundation of the economy in developing countries, as was the case in China.

Summary

China went through the disastrous "Great Leap Forward" and "Great Cultural Revolution," but found out that Marx was right: the basis of communism is advanced economy. Simply waving red flags is not socialism – lifting people out of poverty is! Some communists criticize Chinese leadership for insufficient provision of food, housing, education and medical care. But where would all of these come from? They do not come miraculously as the result of our wishes. They have to be created by human hands and are a part of the economy! China is successfully building an economy and has lifted hundreds of millions of people from poverty already. Its leadership came to concurrence with Marxism that society has to progress through certain developmental stages before entering communism. First, it needs to go through capitalism and develop its economy. Then, when the economy is strong enough, society can afford to enter socialism, which is a transitory stage between capitalism and communism.

In the name of communism, China first had to unleash capitalism. Following this path, it successfully acquired the main characteristics of developed capitalist economies and theoretically is ready for transition to communism. Indeed, the Chinese government has already initiated a transition from capitalism to socialism, and the Chinese economy is currently a mix of both public and private ownership of the means of production. Overall, the CPC tackles all the problems systematically and successfully, and there is no reason to believe that some Western-style government would do a better job. In fact, its neighboring country India, which has a Western-style government, is not as successful as China. On the other hand, countries that follow the Chinese model, such as Vietnam, have become more successful. This confirms that, at a certain point, the infusion of some elements of socialism into capitalism can provide society with advantages, which is in agreement with Marxism. It also demonstrates that China may succeed in its quest for communism, showing the path for others to follow.

References

1. Chinese Government. China: A Country with 5,000-Year-Long Civilization. *English.gov.cn website* (retrieved 2011, September 3).
2. Hutton, W. The Writing on the Wall: China and the West in the 21st Century, published by Abacus (2008).
3. Dikotter, F. Mao's Great Famine, published by Walker & Company (2011).
4. Yan, J., Gao, G. Turbulent Decade: A History of the Cultural Revolution, published by University of Hawai'i Press (1996).
5. Fabbri, M. China - "Socialist Market Economy" or Just Plain

Capitalism? *Marxists.org website* (2006, January 20).

6. Kolko, G. After Socialism, published by Routledge & Francis Group (2006).

7. Huanxin, Z. China Names Key Industries for Absolute State Control. *China Daily* (2006, December 19).

8. The Rise of State Capitalism. *The Economist* (2012, January 21).

9. Wiseman, P. Study: Vietnamese, Chinese Choose Capitalist Road. *Associated Press* (2014, October 09).

10. Shambaugh, D. China Goes Global, published by Oxford University Press (2013).

11. Lampton, D. M. Following the Leader, published by University of California Press (2014).

12. The World Bank. *Worldbank.org website* (retrieved 2014, November 21).

13. The Royal Society. New Countries Emerge as Major Players in Scientific World. *The Royal Society* (2011, March 28).

14. World Intellectual Property Organization. Global Patent Filings See Fastest Growth in 18 Years. *WIPO.int website* (2013, December 9).

15. Jacques, M. A Point of View: Is China More Legitimate Than the West? *BBC News Magazine* (2012, November 2).

16. Kuang, P. Poor Quality Scientific Research Fetters China's Strength. *Global Times* (2010, March 08).

17. Piketty, T. Capital in the Twenty-First Century, published by Belknap Press of Harvard University Press (2014).

18. Lohr, S. In 2015, Technology Shifts Accelerate and China Rules, IDC Predicts. *The New York Times* (2014, December 02).

19. Perlberg, S. The 35 Most Competitive Economies in the World. *Business Insider* (2013, September 04).

20. Sicular, T. The Challenge of High Inequality in China. *Inequality in Focus,* published by the World Bank (2013).

21. Lopez, L. China's President Just Proved How Serious He Is. *Business Insider* (2014, December 05).

22. Lopez, L. Chinese President Xi Jinping Just Took His War on Corruption to a Whole New Level. *Business Insider* (2015, January 15).

23. Wee, S.-L. China Considers Suing 'Economic Fugitives' in the U.S., Official Says. *Reuters* (2014, November 26).

24. Pei, M. China's Trapped Transition: The Limits of Developmental Autocracy, published by Harvard University Press (2008).

25. Xinhua. Xi Stresses Adherence to Dialectical Materialism. *People's*

Daily (2015, January 25).

26.   Hajani, A. China Crushes India in BRICS University Ranking. *CNBC* (2013, December 17).

27.   Sachs, J. D. The End of Poverty, published by The Penguin Press (2005).

Chapter 10

Elements of Communism Improve Capitalism

Defenders of capitalism point out that capitalism has now existed for a few centuries and no other economic system has been as beneficial for working people. Although this is true, it cannot be accepted as proof that capitalism is the best and the last stage of societal development, because each successive social system is generally superior to the previous one: feudalism was better than slavery, and capitalism is better than feudalism.

On the other side, defenders of communism point out that despite living standards of the working class having improved in some countries, they have worsened in others. Although this argument may appear reasonable, it is difficult to identify capitalistic countries in which the life of the working class is continuously getting worse. About 30 years ago, "communists" were naming Spain, Portugal and Saudi Arabia as examples. However, as of about 10 years ago, the life of the working class in these countries had dramatically improved, making these examples no longer valid. Of note, the standard of living in Spain and Portugal recently worsened due to the Great Recession, but is rebounding as this book is being written.

On the other hand, it is very easy to identify capitalist countries in which the life of the working class has improved over the past century: for example, the U.S., Canada, Germany, Australia and others. Thus, the argument that living conditions of the working class in some capitalist countries have deteriorated cannot be accepted. Moreover, by 1991, about 30 countries representing about a third of humanity attempted to become socialist/collectivist, but none of them could achieve more prosperity than capitalist nations. This is clearly illustrated by the annually published Legatum Prosperity Index, which is based on a variety of factors, including quality of life and personal well-being. Year after year, the top 20 ranked countries on the list are all capitalist (see Table 1).

"Communists" also argue that those capitalist nations that achieved a better standard of living did so at the expense of developing countries in Asia, Africa and Latin America. In other words, Western Europe and the United States used their power to extract wealth from poorer and weaker countries. Nevertheless, this notion does not match up with reality, and is refuted in the book *The End of Poverty*:

> "This interpretation of events would be plausible if gross world product has remained roughly constant, with a rising share going to the powerful regions and a declining share going to the poor regions.

> We can see that is not at all what happened. Gross world product rose nearly fiftyfold in the last 200 years. Every region of the world experienced some economic growth both in terms of the overall size of the economy, and even when measured per person, but some regions experienced much more growth than others. The key fact of the modern age is not the transfer of income from one region to another, by force or otherwise, but rather the overall increase in world income, and at different rates in different regions." [1]

It is true that capitalist nations extracted benefit from developing countries. For example, they used their natural resources and cheaper labor. However, it is also true that developing countries have benefited from doing business with developed capitalist nations that brought money, better paying jobs and new technologies. Thus, both sides have benefited from each other, and the argument that capitalist nations achieved their better standard of living at the expense of the Third World is not convincing. One can even argue that the opposite may have happened; for example, the dramatic progress in the living conditions of Chinese workers that we witness today would not have been possible without the business from Western Europe and the U.S.

Defenders of capitalism also point out that the capitalist system has improved so much since the time of Marx that his idea of an inevitable crash is no longer applicable. For example, M.J. Fisher in her *A Critique of Communist Theory* writes: "[The] Marxist-Leninist exposé of the ills of capitalism was based upon the *laisse-faire* system which prevailed in the mid-nineteenth century. Marx made the dogmatic prediction that capitalism must necessarily proceed toward its own downfall, according to the immutable laws of history. Capitalism could only be destroyed, not improved. This is an absolutist assumption which denied the possibility that the capitalist world would recognize its own weakness, and would proceed to adopt curative and ameliorative measures." [2]

In other words, capitalism's defenders say that the system has become so much better that it is no longer self-destructive. This may be true. But let's not overlook the fact that the system improved by adopting socialist measures such as universal suffrage (equal right to vote), higher working class salaries, reduced working hours, a free education system, etc. In other words, capitalism gained strength by becoming more like communism!

Most developed countries today have one foot in capitalism and the other already in communism. At this point, the capitalist world has recognized its own weaknesses, and Marx was a major contributor to this process. As Michael Harrington puts it: "One of the main consequences of the socialist movement has been not socialism but a more humane, rational, and intellectual capitalism, usually in spite of capitalists." [3]

So why don't Marxism's critics see this? The answer may lie in a phrase painting Marx and Engels as dangerous pessimists who believed that "capitalism could only be destroyed, not improved." It is true that many of their writings suggest this. But it is also true that Marx and Engels valued the process of a peaceful transformation of capitalism into communism, and they even proposed it for certain countries (see details in Chapter 5). To people who believed that armed fighting was the only way to get from capitalism to socialism, Marx famously replied: "If that is Marxism, then I am not a Marxist." But, most importantly, Marxism's cornerstone theory that communism will be brought about by advancements in economy rather than by people's wishes suggests exactly that: capitalism will be transforming to communism gradually, naturally and peacefully.

Due to Inequality, Capitalism Is Not the Best Economic System

Unequal distribution of wealth is one of the main drawbacks of capitalism. Recent detailed analysis by Piketty demonstrates that the decreased inequality observed in capitalist nations in the 1940s through the 1970s was an exception rather than the general trend. It was the result of special circumstances: the two World Wars and the Great Depression.[4] Indeed, inequality in the capitalist world is back on the rise. It is especially prominent in Anglo-Saxon countries, where it has spiked in the past few years.

Piketty's analysis also demonstrates that the theory of marginal productivity and the race between technology and education do not explain the spike. First, he demonstrates that the spike is mostly due to unequal pay for labor and the rise of super-managers with their super-salaries. Then he proposes that the super-salaries were a result of the complexity of evaluating the contribution of super-managers due to the uniqueness of their positions: "When the job is replicable, as in the case of an assembly worker or fast-food server, we can give an approximate estimate... But when an individual's job functions are unique, or nearly so, then the margin of error is much greater." Thus, one can conclude that overpayment to super-managers is the result of errors, which are impossible to avoid. The problem with this logic, however, is that if those where just random errors in judgment, then the salaries of super-managers would be sometimes over-valued and sometimes under-valued. But the salaries are almost always drastically over-valued; therefore, the explanation cannot merely be attributed to error.

There is a much more fundamental reason: the super-managers get super-salaries because they can. They simply take as much as they can, and an unregulated capitalist system allows this. Modern governments attempt to regulate the excesses and extremes of capitalism by applying certain rules to certain institutions, but economists admit that "the rules are generally ambiguous and flawed." [4] On the other hand, one has to recognize that more regulation of capitalism means more socialization. If governments begin to regulate business completely, then society will be transformed from capitalist to communist. Therefore, super-salaries are simply a byproduct of the inequality inherent in capitalism.

The other interesting phenomenon, a sharp spike in inequality in Anglo-Saxon countries, also confirms that capitalism and inequality go hand in hand. Piketty demonstrates that, for some reason, the rise of super-salaries is an Anglo-Saxon phenomenon, and income inequality in continental Europe is nowhere near as extreme as in the U.S. and the U.K. His reason for the super-salaries and rising inequality is the revolution in technology. But then he notes that technology has affected Germany, France, Sweden, Denmark and Japan just as much as the U.S., Britain and Canada.

So why is there a difference in the U.S. and the U.K.? The explanation lies in differences in culture and social norms: "Executive compensation of several million Euros a year is still more shocking today in Sweden, Germany, France, Japan and Italy than in the United States or Britain." And yet, the question remains: where do social norms come from and why are they different in different countries? The answer is simple: social norms are based on the structure of a society. In a capitalist society, norms are capitalist and they allow for inequality. In a communist society, they are communist and they don't allow for inequality. In a socialist society, they are in-between, allowing some – but not too much – inequality. Thus, inequality is higher in the Anglo-Saxon countries because the people have a more capitalist mindset; it is lower in continental Europe because people there have a more socialist mindset. If inequality is above the social norms, then a socialist revolution may take place, as happened in Russia in 1917. If inequality is below the social norms, then capitalist reforms may take place, as occurred in Russia with the dissolution of the USSR.

It is clear that capitalism and inequality are inseparable. But what effect does inequality have on the economy? A recent global study of OECD countries clearly shows that rising inequality is dramatically holding back economic growth: "An increase in income inequality between 1985 and 2005 knocked 4.7 percentage points off cumulative growth between 1990 and 2010 on average across a range of its 34 member countries, the OECD said." [5] The report also suggested that the countries with the highest inequality lost the most: the U.K. and the U.S. lost 6-9% of GDP over this period due to rising inequality. Moreover, a widely recognized analysis by Piketty determined that inequality was one of the main reasons for the recent Great Recession. [4]

Capitalism is Using Elements of Communism
to Save Itself

The theory of capitalist crises is one of the keys of Marxism. In his major work, *Capital,* Marx devoted several hundred pages to it. The theory suggests that crises are the inevitable result of the normal activities of capital. And yet, Marx did not imagine that capitalist governments would listen to him and learn to avoid them. However, the methods that these governments use to avert crises are by their very nature socialist: bailing out businesses using public funds, large-scale projects that are initiated with public money, etc. The reason capitalism has not met its fatal crisis as Marx predicted is not because capitalism is such a successful system *per se*, but rather because capitalism is using elements of communism to correct itself. As we already saw in Chapter 8, public property plays a much greater role in capitalist systems than most people realize. Capitalism has greatly benefited from the use of public property and, as time goes by, incorporates more and more socialist elements in order to become more successful.

At present, it seems that there is a general consensus among economists that the secret to a successful society is a balanced incorporation of capitalist and socialist elements in the economy. In other words: capitalism benefits from elements of communism. And no truly serious economist can suggest that capitalism in its pure form works best. In fact, Chapter 6 of this book demonstrates that the countries with the most socialism (the greatest equality and public sector revenue) are the most prosperous. On the other hand, unrestrained capitalism always creates inequality, which harms economies.

In his acclaimed analysis, Piketty comes to the conclusion that a progressive global tax on capital would be the ideal tool in resolving the problems of modern capitalism. [4] Naturally, he understands that "a truly global tax on capital is no doubt a utopian idea." But what would such a tax do to capitalism? The author suggests that it would "promote the general interest over private interest," which means that it would promote socialism and communism. Thus, this is yet another recognition of the fact that socialist and communist elements improve capitalism.

Socialist measures in capitalist countries are especially welcomed in times of crisis. For example, when the Great Recession came in 2007, the biggest defenders of the free market and capitalism in the U.S. and the U.K. were the first to demand governmental intervention in order to pump money into the banks and save the economy.

Could the introduction of socialist measures be the secret to the survival and success of capitalism? Will the further introduction of these elements make capitalism even more viable? If so, then won't socialism/communism eventually take over capitalism?

One could argue that this theory has already been tested and failed miserably: an attempt to build socialism/communism was made in Russia after the 1917 revolution, followed by many Eastern European nations. The attempt did not last, and after about 70 years, these countries were back to capitalism. But let's not forget that real socialism was never built there in the first place. Instead, a kind of pseudo-communism was created; some classify it as a bureaucratic collectivism that was destined to fail from the very beginning.

Some bourgeoisie ideologists still believe that capitalism in its pure form works best. They came up with the so-called trickle-down theory of wealth, suggesting that when money goes into the pockets of the rich, it inevitably spills into the pockets of the poor. Some also describe it as a theory of tides: a rising tide lifts all ships – rich and poor alike. But as we saw in Chapter 8, this is a delusion – only the rich ships were lifted in most capitalist economies in the last few decades. This was especially the case in the largest capitalist economy: the U.S. Even worse, when the Great Recession struck, the rich ships were lifted even higher, while the poor have drowned in debt and bankruptcy (see Figure 8.1, Chapter 8).

Inequality was among the chief causes of the Great Recession, and if it continues to rise, it will lead to other crises. Unregulated capitalism does not have a decent economic track record and the regulation/socialization of capitalism helps to avert crises and improve its functioning overall. Countries in Northern Europe (Norway, Sweden, Denmark and Finland) are perfect examples of this. They are among the most socialized – and the most prosperous – countries in the world (see

Chapter 6), confirming that socialization helps capitalism perform better. Other contrasting examples also confirm this; for instance, China versus India (see Chapter 9) and Vietnam versus Nicaragua (see Chapter 6).

The Russian anarchist Peter Kropotkin tried to justify the idea of communism in his book *Mutual Aid: A Factor in Evolution* (1902). Using biological and sociological data, he showed that cooperation benefits society more than competition. He may have been right all along.

Summary

Inequality is inseparable from capitalism. Because of this, a capitalist economic system is not ideal, and runs into periodic crises. To improve and save itself from self-destruction, capitalism introduces more and more elements of a communist nature. Thus, in the long run, capitalism will eventually replace itself with communism.

References

1. Sachs, J. D. The End of Poverty. Published by The Penguin Press (2005).
2. Fisher, M. J. Communist Doctrine and the Free World, published by Syracuse University Press (1952).
3. Harrington, M. Socialism: Past and Future, published by Arcade Publishing (1989).
4. Piketty, T. Capital in the Twenty-First Century, published by Belknap Press of Harvard University Press (2014).
5. Keller, G. Rising Inequality Holding Back Economic Growth, Report Warns. *Associated Press* (2015, May 21).

Chapter 11

The Path to Communism: Revolution or Evolution?

The philosophy of Marxism, dialectic materialism, supports either a peaceful or revolutionary path to communism (see Chapter 3). Chapter 5 demonstrates that Marx and Engels believed that communism could arise through reforms or revolutions. However, the state of the world in their time made revolutions more likely than reforms. And because Marx and Engels discussed revolutions more than reforms, they created the impression that they only advocated the revolutionary way.

According to Marxism, social revolution is unavoidable in an antagonistic class society. Capitalist society was increasingly antagonistic in the time of Marx, Engels and Lenin (the end of the 19th and beginning of the 20th century). This led to the formation of two beliefs: 1) with growing antagonism, capitalism will eventually become such a hostile society that it will burst and will have to be replaced by a more progressive social organization – communism; and 2) since the bourgeoisie does not show any signs of goodwill in sharing wealth and power, there is no other way to change society except through violence and revolution – this became the core doctrine of Marxism-Leninism.

Considering the difficulties of that period, it would have been hard to disagree. Crises in capitalism and public revolutions seemed inevitable. And yet, somehow, capitalism became a less instead of a more antagonistic class society. The distance between classes in capitalist nations became smaller. The gap between the rich and the poor began to shrink. Moreover, class fluidity grew and individuals began moving from the working class to the aristocracy and vice versa. Some workers were able to save money, invest and become rich within years. Others came up with great ideas, started new businesses and became rich within months. The reverse scenario also became common: some aristocrats lost their money and moved to the working class. Unexpectedly, antagonism between classes shrank, reducing the chances of revolts and revolutions. Capitalist nations incorporated more and more socialist elements into their systems (see Chapter 8), and the transformation of capitalism to communism became possible through reforms and gradual evolution, as originally suggested by social democrats, rather than through revolution, as suggested by Leninists.

Even the Soviet ideologists, who were supposedly Leninists, began to recognize the possibility of a peaceful transformation of capitalism into socialism. A good example is provided in one of the most important Soviet textbooks, *Marxist Philosophy*, which has undergone 11 editions and has been translated into dozens of languages. After criticizing reformists and revisionists of Marxism in the first 300 pages, its 329th page suddenly states: "After the February Revolution in 1917, Lenin and the Bolsheviks raised the question of a peaceful development of the revolution. This did not happen, but not through the fault of the proletariat. Now the situation is different. The new correlation of forces between capitalism and socialism which arose in the world after the last war (World War II) greatly extended the possibilities of a peaceful transition to socialism … In these conditions, the working class of some countries, relying on the broad movement of the people against imperialism, has greater opportunities than ever to take power into its hands without bloodshed. The parliamentary road can be one of the ways for the peaceful development…" [1]

Unfortunately, the trend of growing equality, alleviation of class contradictions and incorporation of communist elements into capitalism only lasted until the 1970s. A recent book, *Capital in the Twenty-First Century*, demonstrates that it was not a normal development of capitalism. Rather, it was created by the two World Wars and the Great Depression.[2] Afterwards, as the consequences of the wars and depression were overcome, capitalism turned back to its natural course. From the 1970s until the present time, inequality has been on the rise in all major capitalist countries. In the U.S., it grew especially fast and now stands at the level of Europe in 1910 (see Chapter 8). The gap has now grown largest in the U.S. and the U.K. – ironically, the two countries that Marx considered to be among the most democratic and, therefore, the most able to move from capitalism to communism through peaceful reforms, and now the least likely to do so. Whether or not this rise in inequality will continue is a big question. If the answer is yes, then the peaceful transformation of capitalism will again become impossible, and armed revolutions may follow.

Peacefully or not, communism still cannot arise in most of the modern world, as the basis for communism – economy – is not yet sufficiently developed and strong. Even more so, communism was not possible in the past. And yet, socialist revolutions took place and attempts to build communism were made. They took place under the guise of Marxism and yet contrary to its very core idea that communism would arise as a result of advancements in economy. Why did this happen and why has such an obvious contradiction between theory and practice been ignored? Let's analyze the most significant examples: Russia and China.

In general, the reason for revolutions is a crisis of society. Many factors can contribute to communist revolutions: injustice, corruption, poverty and others. But the primary cause is the gap between groups of people constituting a particular society. The gap could be educational, cultural or political — but the mother of all gaps is wealth. A gap between the rich and the poor can cause all the other disconnects and misunderstandings. And who is to blame for this? Is it the members of working class or the people who lead them? The question seems rhetorical: obviously, leaders and the ruling class, who make the key decisions, are responsible.

Clearly, the Russian economy was not ready for communism in 1917, when the Socialist Revolution took place, as capitalism was just beginning to take hold there and most of the population lived in poverty. The Chinese economy was even less ready for it in 1949, when the People's Republic of China (PRC) was proclaimed. Rather than economic readiness, these events were caused by gross mismanagement of these countries by their ruling classes. Some Western ideologists like to blame revolutionaries for these events, and they present Lenin and Mao as evil geniuses who created these communist movements. But they ignore the fact that the rulers and aristocracy must be held responsible – they established the horrible conditions that exploded into revolutions in the first place. While it cannot be denied that Stalin was responsible for the atrocities that took place after the revolution, it was the Russian czarist regime that was initially responsible for creating the conditions for the revolution.

In Russia, the aristocracy widely abused its power and appropriated most of the wealth, leaving the workers struggling to survive (see Chapter 7). Indeed, Russian workers could readily connect to *The Communist Manifesto*'s statement that they had nothing to lose in fighting against the rulers except their chains. It was not only the situation in Russia, but also the world situation and the policies of other capitalist powers that made the revolution possible. The revolution was unlikely to succeed without help from the German government, which financed the communist movement and its revolutionaries in order to distract Russia from World War I.

The situation that initiated the communist movement in China was slightly different. Although the workers were poor, it was not the unequal distribution of wealth that ignited the revolutionary movement. It was abuse by Western capitalist regimes, which colonized and fragmented China with no consideration of the country's interests, and the ruling class of China was not fit to do anything about this (see Chapter 9).

Thus, in both Russia and China, incompetence and abuses by the ruling aristocracy, as well as by external capitalist regimes, were the primary culprits in communist movements and revolutions. At the same time, the ruling classes in the Western countries were cooperative with their workers, and this spared those countries from revolutions. Therefore, whether revolutions take place or not depends on the ruling class. If a rich minority can share its wealth reasonably – as happened in most of the West in the 20th century – the balance will be maintained, the majority will be content and revolutions will not take place. If the aristocracy tries to take too much – as happened in czarist Russia – the poor majority will have nothing to lose and will revolt. Heads that go out of control usually get chopped off, as happened to Nicolas II of Russia and Marie Antoinette of France.

A society's path of revolution or evolution comes down to the choices made by the workers and the bourgeoisie. However, the workers' choice depends on the aristocracy's behavior, and not the other way around. What happened in the 20th century should be a warning for the ruling class: its choices will lead to reforms or revolutions. In fact, signs of possible revolutions are now surfacing in the countries with the highest inequality: in the U.K. and the U.S., where the "social contract" – the agreement between the rulers and the workers – has now been broken (by the rulers). In the U.K., Jeremy Corbyn, who identifies himself as socialist and openly admires Marxism, was recently elected as the Leader of the Opposition, a position considered to be that of an alternate Prime Minister. In the U.S., Bernie Sanders, who was one of the frontrunners in the presidential election of 2016, openly called for more equality in the distribution of wealth and a socialist revolution.

This is not to say that the working class movement has no effect on the behavior of the bourgeoisie: capitalist rulers will improve the conditions of the working class when they are forced to do so. And that force is usually communist in its origin. However, a communist movement will not become active unless the ruling class (bourgeoisie) makes the working class extremely unhappy.

History indicates that, at the current stage of development in human society, capitalism is the most efficient social system for building and advancing the economy. Other systems have tried and failed. Russia, followed by several Eastern European countries, attempted to skip capitalism by going straight to the first stage of communism – socialism – but failed. China made the same attempt, but realized that it still needed to develop its economy and reintroduced capitalism (see Chapter 9). Currently, it appears that no one can run the economy better than capitalists. So, let's let them do their job and help them when we can, so that communism can arise sooner!

Capitalism contains the potential for transformation into communism. The development of the Western capitalist nations in the 20th century clearly illustrates this: willingly or unwillingly, they have gradually become the most socialist countries (see Chapters 6 and 8). Of course, capitalism does not automatically transform into communism. As the last few decades have shown, inequalities can return and this development can slow down or reverse. Certain controls of capitalism must be exercised in order to keep its development in the proper direction. As American socialist Michael Harrington expressed it: "There is no such thing as a socialist apocalypse, a sudden leap, to use the classic Marxist formulation, from the 'kingdom of necessity to the kingdom of freedom' … 'All' that socialists have to do in order to forward that emancipatory potential is to make this process transparent and subject to democratic control." [3]

There are different schools of communism, and communism has been pursued in different ways: through social revolution in an individual country, through an international movement, through a national liberation movement and through reforms. Which way is the best? The revolutionary way in Russia was painful and did not work. The revolutionary way in China was also painful but, after returning to capitalism, it appears to be working. Ironically, the reformist way, which was pursued by the West and is not considered to be a useful path to communism, seems to be the least painful and most effective way. Thus, revolutionary (as in China) and evolutionary (as in the West) ways can lead to socialism and then to communism. We don't have to choose a particular way because any of them could work, and Marx and Engels recognized this. But one fact is crystal clear: regardless of the way, communism cannot arise without a developed capitalist economy; therefore, one cannot skip capitalism in the development toward communism.

Can the Rise of Communism
Be Accelerated by Revolutions?

Some people claim that they are socialists but not communists, that they support socialism but are against communism. Since socialism is the first phase of communism, can one be a socialist but not a communist? Strangely, yes: there is a substantial difference between socialism and communism, and one can accept some elements of communism but reject the others. For example, one can accept that everybody should be paid according to contributed work (the principle of socialism), but reject that everybody should be paid according to needs (the principle of communism).

Nonetheless, let's not forget that socialism is the first stage of communism. Also, since communism is so distant in the future, why even ask whether one approves or disapproves of communist ideas? Socialism is in the present and immediate future and society should focus on that. As socialism is developed, society will see how it works and will be able to decide if moving further toward communism is beneficial. People can accept that, theoretically, communism would make an ideal society, but this does not mean that this society should be created immediately.

Currently, there is no superabundance of goods, which is the prerequisite for communism, in any country. In poor countries, people still starve and do not have even basic goods. In rich countries, people don't starve but they still want more goods: bigger houses, more cars, etc. Since materialistic conditions are not even close to those necessary for communism, the approval or the disapproval of communist ideas is not a pressing matter. Communism cannot be forced onto a society through desire – society must be ready for it, if it will ever be. The only way to accelerate the arrival of communism will be to work on advancing the economy. This does not mean that we should quit politics altogether, because politics affect the economy. And, as this book illustrates, the introduction of elements of a socialist/communist nature improves capitalism and advances an economy.

Here we return to the reality: only advances in economy can make communism possible. Capitalism cannot transform into communism by desire or revolution. Poor countries that desire communism the most are the farthest from it, and there is not much they can do to bring it into existence other than patiently working to improve their economies. It is nearly guaranteed that with a strengthening economy, the rise of communism is inevitable.

Ironically, when the working class rushes into revolutions in order to speed up the transformation to communism, the opposite effect can occur, and the transformation can be delayed. Armed revolutions are destructive and negatively affect the economy; they can be a hindrance to building the foundation for communism. Therefore, the quickest path to communism is through reforms, not armed revolutions.

Is Communism in an Individual Country Possible?

The question of whether communism could arise in a solitary nation, separate from the rest of the world, became a very relevant topic with the socialist revolution in Russia. Some revolutionaries argued that the revolution should spread to other countries as quickly as possible – if it didn't, the united forces of capitalism would crush the revolution in Russia. The most vocal of these revolutionaries was Trotsky. However, Stalin took the view that communism could be built in Russia and the Soviet Union alone, regardless of what the rest of the world was doing. Indeed, for a period of time after the revolution, the economic situation in the Soviet Union improved, and it looked like the five-year plan was working and Stalin was right. But history later proved him wrong: the USSR was dissolved in 1991 and Russia returned to capitalism. This return was caused by the isolation of the Soviet bloc from the rest of the world, which in turn led to a stagnant economy (see Chapter 7).

Another factor, which is often overlooked, also makes creating communism in a separate country very difficult. If communism is forced onto a country, then capital will flee from that country into more capitalist countries. France in the 1980s is a perfect example: when the government tried to introduce more social programs, money and capital left France for other nations, forcing France to retreat from its course. Naturally, a communist country can close its borders and cut off business with other nations in order to avoid capital outflow. However, this leads to the isolation of a country and its businesses, leading to economic stagnation and a probable collapse.

In fact, France recently tested this direction again. In 2012, it instituted a tax of 75% on income earned above one million euros. At the time of the proposal, British Prime Minister David Cameron sarcastically offered to "roll out the red carpet" to the rich willing to avoid the tax. Two years later, the Associated Press reported that "faced with a stalling economy and rising unemployment, the government reversed course in 2014 with a plan to cut payroll taxes by up to 40 billion euros ($49 billion) by 2017, hoping to boost hiring and attract more investments... Ultimately, while the super tax affected only a small number of taxpayers, it triggered huge protests in business, sporting and artistic communities." [4]

If a country decides to redistribute wealth from the rich to the poor excessively, then the rich, who hold the money, will simply move wealth away from that country to countries that allow them to keep more of their profits. Thus, in order to permanently redistribute wealth from the rich to the poor, most countries must take similar measures at the same time, so that money has fewer or no safe options for leaving.

One can argue that this also may depend on the size of the economy of the country trying to pass such social reforms. France has an average-sized economy, but a bigger country with a larger economy could do it. Nevertheless, the economy should probably control close to half of the world's wealth, so that the money has few places to escape if wealth is redistributed. It is unlikely that even the largest economies, such as the U.S. or the EU, could do it alone. At present, the EU and the U.S. understand this and coordinate with each other on even the smallest changes in their economic policies. For example, their central banks consult each other before they change interest rates. Jointly, however, the EU and the U.S. probably hold about half of the world's finances, and together they would be able to pass any major socialist reform.

History demonstrates that capitalist countries have not accepted a world in which some countries choose a communist orientation. Indeed, when the revolution took place in Russia, several capitalist nations attempted to reverse it with military force (see Chapter 7). Similar reactions were observed when communist forces grew in power in other countries: Vietnam was bombed, Cuba was blockaded, etc. In the end, even Russia was unable to stand against capitalism despite its large size. Smaller countries have even less chance of survival on their own. Time and time again, history shows us that communism cannot be built in a solitary country because it will be weakened and destroyed by global capitalist forces.

The core problem here is that no country has ever been on the proper path to communism. So far, not a single country with a self-proclaimed communist orientation can be classified as truly communist. In reality, these countries can only be classified as "bureaucratic collectivist" (see Chapter 6). It is not that capitalist nations could not accept the existence of communist countries. Rather, they had trouble accepting the "bureaucratic collectivism" that leads to authoritarianism. Capitalist nations may react differently to the emergence of truly communist countries in the future. More than that, what we see today is that the most advanced capitalist countries themselves are progressing toward communism without really noticing this.

There are other reasons why true communism is impossible in a solitary country, beginning with the very nature of communism. First, the transformation of capitalism to communism is a gradual process. This process is taking place right now, as this book is being written. There can be no sudden leap because the transformation is based on advances in the economy, which has to provide a superabundance of material goods. As the economy develops gradually and the economies of most countries become more and more interconnected, they will achieve levels of superabundance and reach communism simultaneously. Second, let's imagine that one solitary country has entered communism on its own. Now, let's not forget that, theoretically, communism is a perfect society where people live in what could be considered a paradise. Then it is logical to expect that all nations would immediately follow the example of such a country, so that they can be paradises too. This would lead to most nations becoming communist simultaneously.

Summary

With or without revolutions, human society is gradually but inevitably moving toward communism through reforms and evolution. Armed revolts and revolutions are not necessary to advance communism, unless, of course, the ruling class blocks reforms and makes them impossible. On the contrary, armed revolutions can actually slow down economic advances and the rise of communism. Waving red flags does not advance communism – improving the economy does! By its very nature, communism in an isolated country is impossible – it will rise all over the world gradually and simultaneously.

References

1. Afanasiev, V. G. Marxist Philosophy, published by Progress Publishers (1978).
2. Piketty, T. Capital in the Twenty-First Century, published by Belknap Press of Harvard University Press (2014).
3. Harrington, M. Socialism: Past and Future, published by Arcade Publishing (1989).
4. Corbet, S. France Drops Its Super Tax on Millionaires. *Associated Press* (2014, December 31).

Chapter 12

Is Communism Feasible?

Can the communist system work? One could argue that the idea is wonderful, but it does not work: every society that has tried to create communism has failed so far. The problem with this logic lies in the very word "tried": the word is in the past tense and expresses a previous action. Creating a communist system in the past was impossible, because communism could only arise as the result of an advanced economy, which had not yet existed. Such an economy that provides a superabundance of material goods does not exist presently either, but hopefully will develop in the future.

It is easy to imagine that, if its economic model performs better than a capitalist model, communism will replace capitalism. People have always adopted the system that performs better, unless prevented by force of arms. Moreover, the replacement of capitalism with communism logically should not be resisted by capitalism – capitalism always adopts economic systems that perform better. And vice versa, if the economic system of capitalism outperforms the system of communism, then why would people adopt communism? Any attempts to install communism without consideration of the state of the economy will fail, and this is exactly what has happened so far.

But can communism ever outperform capitalism economically, and are there any indications that this will happen? In addition to this doubt about communism, there are several others. Communist society is drastically different from all previous social systems, and it raises many questions. For example, money, classes, private property and the state will disappear in a communist society. It is possible to imagine a society without money and classes. But it is harder to imagine how a society can function without a state organization. Also, if people will only work voluntarily, will they work at all, and who will do the jobs that nobody wants? Finally, will any kind of ownership exist and will people even desire equality? But probably the most important question is whether economies will ever reach levels that will completely satisfy the material needs and wants of each and every person. In other words, is the superabundance of material goods possible? One could argue that humans are naturally greedy: they will always want more material goods than they have, and there will never be enough. Below is a discussion of each topic in more detail.

Can Communism Outperform Capitalism Economically?

Indeed, as was demonstrated earlier in this chapter, as well as in Chapters 6 and 8, there are signs that this can happen. First, capitalism is not a perfect economic system, due to inequality. Inequality slows down economic growth and is one of the main reasons for major economic crises. Second, capitalism that incorporates elements of socialism performs better. Those measures include more equal distribution of incomes, social programs such as free education and socialized medicine, etc.

But can an economy successfully function without an owner/capitalist? Can a business be successfully self-managed by workers? Numerous examples show that it can. Prototypes of such communist businesses already exist and successfully operate in many capitalist countries. They are called worker cooperatives, and they are no less than businesses owned and managed by the workers. In cooperatives, each worker is a partial owner. Thus, each worker can equally participate in decision-making and the selection of managers. And cooperatives have been proven to be as functional and successful as typical capitalist businesses. The Mondragon Corporation in Spain is a good example. It was started by a Catholic priest, José María Arizmendiarrieta, in 1956, and grew to become the tenth largest company in Spain. Another example, Arizmendi Bakery, also named after this priest, was formed in 1997 in San Francisco, California. It has grown into a chain of bakeries and was named the city's best bakery by local newspapers. In fact, worker cooperatives are becoming more and more popular. In Europe, they've grown to number 85,000, employing about 1.5 million worker-owners.

Besides being successful businesses, worker cooperatives have an important advantage over typical capitalist businesses: by nature, they are more conscious of the environment and of the needs of the people. For example, let's imagine that a new technology has been developed to manufacture certain products. This technology can dramatically cut manufacturing expenses but produces toxic substances that would pollute the environment around the factory. A typical capitalist business would adopt the new technology regardless of the possible health risks from pollution, such as cancer, lung issues, birth defects, etc. Why? Because owners usually live far away from their factories, and they and their families would not be personally exposed to the pollution. On the other hand, out of necessity, owners of cooperatives (workers) usually live close to the factories where they work, which would directly expose them and their families to the pollution. Therefore, cooperatives are very unlikely to adopt such risky new technology, ensuring the continued health of people living around the factory, saving money on potential medical treatments, and preserving the environment for future generations.

A communist economy can successfully compete with capitalism, but a capitalist economy may simply be incompatible with the future. Marx foresaw this almost two hundred years ago in his book *Grundrisse (1858)*. Unfortunately, like some of his other works, this book did not find a publisher until it was discovered by the Soviets in 1939. In the part of the book titled *"The Fragment on Machines,"* Marx imagines an economy in which everything is produced by machines with only supervision by people. With new technologies and improvements, machines could be made more and more cheaply while lasting longer and longer. Eventually, new machines would cost almost nothing and would last almost forever. In such a situation, he concluded, machines would cut labor costs, prices and profits with this to almost zero. But how can capitalism work without profits? The driving force of capitalism is profit. Thus, capitalism would lose its driving force and disappear. Simply put, there is no place for capitalism in an advanced future economy.

Today, we have more and more evidence that Marx was right. Technology has already made some parts of capitalism disappear. For example, remember the stores selling music albums? They are almost gone now. Most albums are now available either for free or almost for free through the Internet. Or remember libraries and encyclopedias? How many people go to libraries now? Most people in advanced countries get their information through the Internet from their homes for free. How many people are willing to pay for a set of encyclopedia books that are quickly out of date when Wikipedia is available to everyone for free and is always up to date?

In his recent book *Postcapitalism (2015)*, Paul Mason argues that information technology is ending capitalism and comes to the same conclusion as Marx: "Information goods are replicable. Once a thing is made, it can be copied/pasted infinitely. A music track or the giant database you use to build an airliner has a production cost; but its cost of replication falls towards zero. Therefore, if the normal price mechanism of capitalism prevails over time, its price will fall toward zero, too." [1] According to Paul Mason, "The business models of all our modern digital giants are designed to prevent the abundance of information." However, if our free market economy leads to the underutilization of information, "then an economy based on the full utilization of information cannot tolerate the free market." Thus, again, free market capitalism will become incompatible with future economies.

Also, it is important to keep in mind that the goal of communism is to provide each individual with complete freedom. Because of such maximal freedom, communist society should be the most diverse, the most flexible and, ultimately, the most economically successful system.

Can Society Function Without State Organization?

According to Marxism, the main reason for the existence of the state is the existence of classes: it supports the political power of the ruling class and serves to enforce class dominance. Since there will be no classes in communist society, the state will no longer be necessary. But is it possible? The state is an organization with a centralized form of government. It supports the legal system, administrative bureaucracies and the military. Thus, in order for the state to disappear, one has to have a community without military, legal and administrative systems.

Since the main function of the military is to engage in battle with other countries, in order for the military to disappear, all countries must merge and disappear so that there is nothing to fight against. This is possible, as the world appears to be moving toward unification: most European countries are merging into the European Union (EU), some European and Asian countries are merging into the Eurasian Economic Union (EEU), South American nations are merging into the Union of South American Nations (USAN), etc.

Having countries function without legal and administrative systems is a much more challenging endeavor. Eliminating the legal system would require that all crimes disappear. Eliminating the administrative system would mean the elimination of all kinds of regulations and planning. However, legal and administrative systems can exist as local and global non-political agencies without a state, making a stateless society possible. When and how "the state will wither away," as Marx and Engels suggested, is not known, but it will be a gradual and spontaneous process.

Will Private Ownership Exist?

There are different types of property: private, public and personal. Conflicting views on what is private property and what is personal property creates confusion in understanding how communism will work. For example, most anarchist philosophies don't make a distinction between the two. As a result, some believe that a communist society will have neither private nor personal property and everything will be held in common, which is not an easy pill to swallow.

However, political and economic science refers to private property as the means of production, and defines personal property as consumer goods and services. The means of production, which include tools, factories, natural resources, etc., are used to create economic value. In a capitalist system, they are privately owned by capitalists and can serve as the foundation for the exploitation of workers. Thus, private property is incompatible with communism. Whatever is considered private property in capitalism will become public property in communism. In a communist society, all means of production will belong to the public and will be used to benefit all members of society equally.

And yet, communism does not take issue with personal property that includes any items intended for personal use; for example, clothes, food, homes, vehicles, etc. Thus, individuals can have their own cars and homes in a communist system. The only question is how many of those items can one possess? For example, does communism permit just one home or several, just one car or many, etc?

Communism does not limit how many possessions one person can have. However, the amount should be reasonable – it all depends on a person's needs. For example, if someone lives in a city with great public transportation, then this person may not need even one car. On the other hand, if someone lives in a place with poor public transportation and uses a car as a tool for work, then this person may need two cars: one specifically for work and one for leisure and family use. If a city dweller owns a big house with a nice garden, then this person probably does not need a second home. On the other hand, if a city dweller owns a small apartment, then this person may need a second home in the countryside.

Communist society will accept and approve whatever is reasonable and makes people more productive. However, huge displays of wealth, such as owning ten houses or ten cars without any logical or rational reason, but simply to have them, would be rejected. Even though private property will disappear in communism, personal property will remain and be readily encouraged in moderation.

Will People Work Voluntarily?

If people have everything they need, will they still work and will they work hard enough to maintain their communist lifestyle? This question was first raised a long time ago. In fact, in his famous book *Utopia*, Thomas More doubted this by saying: "I don't believe you'd ever have a reasonable standard of living under a communist system. There'd always tend to be shortages, because nobody would work hard enough."

If one asks working people whether they like to work, most of them would say "no." They would rather take long vacations or quit their jobs and retire. Of course, some people like their jobs and want to continue working, but they are in the minority. Then the question arises: If given the chance to take long vacations or to retire, why would people still choose to work? If everyone has everything they need and no one has to work, why would they continue working?

First, many people think that they don't want to work, but when they are retired and do nothing for one or two years, they get bored and want to work again. Second, most people want to quit their jobs because they don't like their current jobs or careers and would rather work at a job that they would enjoy more. Third, it is inherent in people's nature to want to accomplish something and be useful to society; thus, people will always want to do something, to work and to achieve the best results possible, in order to have a sense of fulfillment in their lives.

However, in order for communism to be possible, all jobs must be performed. And truthfully, not all jobs are popular. Ask people what they would like to do, and many would answer that they would like to just travel around the world and take photos. Many people would like to be photographers, designers or writers. Some people would like to be doctors, scientists or chefs. But it is not as easy to find people who would rather be cleaners, maids or factory workers. There aren't too many people who want to clean sewers or mine iron ore just for fun. If there are no volunteers to perform some of these essential jobs, how would communist society function? The answer lies in advancements of the economy.

In today's world, many jobs would be unclaimed, making communism impossible. However, in the future, robots will perform these jobs. With continued progress in technology, robots that are able to perform all kinds of jobs will eventually be created (for more details, see the section below), which will make a communist society possible. Robots that can walk and even dance have already been created. Humanoid robots already work as receptionists in department stores in Tokyo, while Dubai is planning to introduce robots working as police officers – so-called robocops – by 2017. An article in the New York Times raises the possibility that robots may even replace doctors. [2] Thus, creating a robot cleaner, maid or factory worker should also be possible.

Is the Superabundance of Material Goods Possible?

Up until the 21st century, the world GDP was doubling every 25 years. All three figures – the growth rate of world output, world population and per capita output – have been increasing from antiquity until modern times.[3] If this continues, there is hope that this could provide an economic foundation for communism. Unfortunately, contrary to projections, all of these figures have recently slowed down and are expected to decrease for the next hundred years, unless certain events occur and change this. One such event could be a revolution in robotics/artificial intelligence, and there are credible reasons to believe that this revolution will take place within the next few decades.

Computers can already understand human speech and communicate with each other using human speech. As mentioned in the section above, robots that can work as receptionists or police officers will soon be used in practice. The automobile industry is getting close to manufacturing cars that can be driven by computers (robots). The first steps in manufacturing artificial human organs such as the pancreas and eyes have already been taken, and science is now on track to simulate the most complex human organ – the brain. The recent book *Emerging Medical Technologies* finds that "the European Union assigned €1 billion for the Human Brain Project aiming to replicate the brain in a supercomputer and eventually produce a synthetic mind. But even bigger resources are now pouring into this field of science. Big technological companies are currently working to imitate functions of the brain. The military also joined the quest. For example, a new chip, called TrueNorth, that functions like a brain has been reported in 2014 by IBM. This chip was developed for drone technology using money from the Pentagon. Taken together, military and technology giants control huge financial resources. With all the resources directed to this field, there is a good chance that the last frontier of the human body, the brain, will soon be understood and its functions will be artificially simulated." [4]

This means that robots will be able to function as humans and replace them at work. And this could mean that humans would not need to work anymore. All jobs, or at minimum the undesirable jobs, will eventually be performed by the workers of the future – robots.

Clearly, robotization can dramatically accelerate the economy. In fact, when one can manufacture unlimited numbers of robots and the robots can then manufacture themselves, the growth of the economy can become unlimited. Robotization has the potential to provide an unlimited amount of material goods and wealth, which is the foundation of communism. Now one can see how the economic base of communism can be created and communism can be possible!

Not everyone agrees with this scenario. For example, David Harvey, in his recent book *Seventeen Contradictions and the End of Capitalism*, argues that since "social labor is the ultimate source of value and profit" in a capitalist system, capitalists would not allow the replacement of human labor with robotic labor. [5] Although it appears to be logical, this conclusion is surprising and not very convincing for this reason: if the process was fast and sudden, then yes, capitalists might unite and resist in order to ensure their profits. However, it is clear that the switch to robotic labor will be made slowly and gradually. In fact, it has already begun. Although capitalists may already be aware of this, they will not begin to prohibit robots out of fear that some abstract capitalists will not be able to make profits in the far future.

In reality, robots are the dream of every capitalist. When the use of robots gives an advantage to one capitalist over another, then all capitalists rush to use them. However, as global robotization progresses, profits will begin to decrease, eventually arriving at zero and making capitalism no longer possible. Thus, capitalism is programmed at the core level to transform itself into communism, and it will simply wither away naturally. Paradoxically, it is headed toward extinction by virtue of its ever-increasing efficiency in production.

We are clearly moving toward the replacement of the current mode of production with a higher one that makes unlimited use of computers and robots. As historical materialism suggests, the history of society is a natural process of the replacement of lower modes of production with higher ones (see Chapter 3). The mode of production is independent of man's will and consciousness. It conditions and determines the social, political and intellectual life process. Thus, this process should inevitably change our society and will lead to the replacement of capitalism with a higher social system, which is communism.

In this book, Harvey also warns that, by replacing humans, robots will create an unemployment crisis. This will likely happen, but why is this a problem? Humans will no longer need to be employed. Robots will provide everything needed so that humans can do what they like, just as Marx and Engels imagined over a century ago in *The German Ideology*. People in a communist society would "do one thing today and another tomorrow, to hunt in the morning, fish in the afternoon, rear cattle in the evening, criticize after dinner... without ever becoming hunter, fisherman, herdsman or critic."

Lastly, one has to keep in mind that the main principle of communism is "to everyone according to needs," but not "to everyone according to wants." While human "wants" could be unlimited, which makes the possibility of communism questionable, human "needs" are limited. Of course, the line between "needs" and "wants" is very thin and difficult to define. However, it clearly exists; for example, having one car per person can be a "need," but having more than one car per person should generally be considered a "want," not a "need." With this practical mindset, the economy can definitely reach sufficient levels to satisfy all human needs, making communism possible.

This is supported by data on the correlation between income (which translates into material goods) and happiness. For example, a well-known 2010 study by Daniel Kahneman and Angus Deaton found that income/money make people happy only up to a certain point (around $75,000 per year), after which other factors become more important. This was confirmed in 2018 by Fast Company, which surveyed 1.7 million people in 164 countries. The survey revealed that happiness correlates with incomes of up to $40,000-$125,000 per year around the world, depending where people live. Understandably, in places with a low cost of living, such as sub-Saharan Africa, $40,000 income was sufficient, while in places with a high cost of living, such as Australia, income has to be $125,000 to achieve the same result. In the U.S., this figure was $105,000. Since the only purpose of money is to acquire material goods, these studies confirm that after a certain level of abundance has been attained, people can stop fighting over material goods and become motivated by other factors, such as social relationships.

And yet, we must realize that there will never be a point at which all people are completely satisfied and not competing for material goods. When new things and new ideas emerge, new needs emerge with them. The attempt of productive forces to catch up with demand is like chasing one's own tail. Thus, there will always be need and desire for new things, and these things will not be readily available to everyone immediately. In other words, there will never be a final stage of communism. However, this does not contradict Marxism, but is rather in agreement with its philosophy that everything is developing and there is no end of this process.

Like everything in life, superabundance is relative and hard to measure. What is important is that as material goods become more abundant, we become less stressed in acquiring them and more free to do the things that we like. In his recent book, Terry Eagleton puts it as follows: "To enjoy a sufficiency of goods means not to have to think about money all the time. It frees us from tedious pursuits. Far from being obsessed with economic matters, Marx saw them as a travesty of true human potential." [6]

When superabundant economies will be created is unknown and can be debated. However, there is more and more agreement that, with new technologies, this may happen sooner than we think. Western intellectuals, who don't know the meaning of communism, agree that communism is coming but give it different names. For example, some name it "trekonomics" [7] after the *Star Trek* TV series and movies in which the characters live in an advanced communist-like society. Others simply call it "postcapitalism." [1] But there is no need to invent new terms – the term has already been invented by French socialists in 1840. This term is "communism"!

Can the Superabundance
of Material Goods Improve Human Morals?

Will material goods ever be so plentiful that humans will stop fighting and competing for them? Observations of the current era suggest the opposite. If people have a three-bedroom home, they want to move to a four-bedroom, while some don't stop until they get to 10 or even more bedrooms in their homes. If a person has a ring with a one-carat diamond, he or she will want a ring with a bigger diamond, while some get 10 or even more rings. It seems that people never have enough and they always want more. In other words, people will always fight over material goods and "Man is a wolf to man." If this is so, then there will never be a sufficient amount of material goods to completely satisfy everyone. This would mean that some people will always have more than others, making communism impossible.

Some other people (so-called "communists," who are collectivists in reality) believe that communism is possible because human nature is such that people can always share; in other words: "Man is a friend, comrade, and brother to man." In practice, however, one can see a lot of examples confirming that humans never have enough: the strongest get the most, and "Man is a wolf to man." But are there any indications that the opposite is possible: that humans can be reasonable in their materialistic needs, that they can share and that people can be "friends, comrades and brothers"?

Believing that people can improve their morals and share in an economy of scarcity is nothing but utopian. Over a dozen countries have tried this by now, but to no avail. In an economy of scarcity, people don't share easily, and morals don't improve. Of course, some individuals have the morality of the "New Man" regardless of economy. For example, a wealthy Italian Catholic friar and preacher from the middle ages, St. Francis of Assisi, gave away all his possessions to the poor and joined them. Nevertheless, this was the exception and not the rule. Francis became a saint for this very reason: the phenomenon was so rare and exceptional that the Catholic Church canonized him.

But will people share more readily when material goods are abundant. Is there any indication of this? Surprisingly, such indications do exist. Many people have heard that one of the richest men in America, Warren Buffett (who lives modestly), keeps calling on the rich to share their wealth. And there are more and more people like this. The author of this book personally knows a rich man who lives like an average-income person, and wants to share his wealth to the point that his bank account is empty before he dies.

In 2010, *USA Today* reported: "In an unprecedented show of generosity, a band of 40 American billionaires have pledged to give at least half of their fortunes to charity." [8] The same year, National Public Radio reported: "A recent Quinnipiac University poll showing nearly two-thirds of those with household incomes of more than $250,000 a year support raising their own taxes to reduce the federal deficit." [9] Thus, as material goods become more abundant, the ability to share the wealth is becoming more common. In fact, this principle applies equally to both humans and animals. When a pack of wolves kills a small animal, sharing is a problem: the strongest will eat it all, leaving nothing for the others. When the pack kills a large animal, sharing is not a problem: the strongest cannot finish it all, thus leaving enough food for every member of the pack. Likewise, communism does not require altruism and the transformation of man to a better being. It is possible even if "Man is wolf to man." All it takes is a superabundant economy!

But what if man is morally inferior to animals? Normally, animals only kill what they can eat; and if they cannot finish the food, they share it. What if humans cannot share no matter how much they have?

One of the main reasons why people are unreasonable in their material needs, such as the desire to possess grandiose houses or multiple cars, is not due to actual material needs *per se,* but rather a desire to show off wealth in order to impress or make jealous the people who surround them. Such practices are supported and work well in poor countries — as well as in some not-so-poor countries like the U.S. and Russia. However, such practices are no longer supported by many rich societies in Europe. In many European countries, showing off wealth is considered to be in bad taste or a form of primitivism. Thus, one of the main reasons for the obsession with possessing as much as possible is already disappearing in Europe, resulting in people being more reasonable in their material needs. This trend is growing and, eventually, may spread to the rest of the world. In fact, humanity has no choice but give up its obsession with material desires: our planet simply cannot support a growing materialistic population without being destroyed.

It is not only individuals, but also the governments of rich nations that have now changed their attitudes and are attempting to help poor nations – something unheard of one or more centuries ago. In 2005, the

UN Millennium Summit came to an agreement that rich nations should increase their international aid to 0.7% of their GDP. (Of note, it appears that rich nations collect more wealth from impoverished nations compared to the aid that they give, [10] but this is a whole separate topic.) What is important is that rich nations are seriously looking for the best ways to help poorer countries.

Remarkably, the most socialized and rich countries, mostly located in Northern Europe, help the most. For example, in 2013, Norway gave away 1.07% of its GDP for international aid, Sweden gave 1.02% and Denmark gave 0.85%, which is far above the longstanding UN targets. [11] All these facts indicate that, as an economy becomes more abundant, morals indeed improve and the rich become more willing to share their wealth. This suggests that the human appetite for material goods is not endless, and communism is possible.

Here we come to the key misunderstanding of communism. Many people assume that one can only accept that communism is possible if one believes in the good nature of humans as altruistic beings who help and share with each other. They think that all you need for communism is a better man. History has already confirmed that this is not true. Wishful thinking and ideas cannot change human nature. What always changes it is the economy. "All" we need for man's ability to share and communism to take root is the superabundance of material goods! In fact, in communist society, sharing becomes unnecessary and even theoretically impossible, because each and every person already has everything he or she needs. Thus, the alteration of human nature is not a prerequisite for communism – it actually works in reverse, and as communism arises, it will inevitably change human nature for the better.

The views of Marx and Engels on this subject may be confusing and must be clarified. Some of their statements are not very clear and can be interpreted as contradictory. For example, in *The German Ideology* they write: "Both for the production on a mass scale of this communist consciousness, and for the success of the cause itself, the alteration of Man on a mass scale is necessary, an alteration which can only take place in a practical movement, a revolution; this revolution is necessary, therefore, not only because the ruling class cannot be overthrown in any other way, but also because the class overthrowing it can only in a revolution succeed in ridding itself of all the muck of ages and become fitted to found society anew." [12]

This sounds like they suggest that communism is impossible without the alteration of humans to a species with better morals. And yet, they don't say that the alteration of humans is all that is needed. If they did, they would not be Marxists, because this would suggest that the foundation of communism is human morals, leading us to idealism. Marxism, however, is based on materialism (see Chapter 3). It suggests that the foundation of communism is an advanced economy, and as economy progresses, human relationships will follow. This means that economic progress will inevitably cause the positive alteration of humanity, but not the other way around.

In fact, if the Bible is correct that "the love of money is the root of all evil," then when money in a communist society disappears, then evil should also disappear. Thus, as communism progresses, human morals will inevitably improve.

Do People Want to Be Equal?

A society with complete equality may sound like something grey and boring: everyone is the same. Do people really want to be equal? By nature, humans are competitive creatures: they want to be better than others.

But what does it mean to be better? For people living in contemporary capitalist societies, better is tightly associated with richer: better singers sell more albums, better doctors charge more for their services, etc. Money becomes a universal measure of human value. If one is not richer, how can one be better?

Additionally, money gives power to one person over another. Humans like to have this power, and the ones that have it don't want to give it up. On the other hand, people that don't have it still support it, because they hope that one day they will have this power too.

Not only that, human happiness can be a relative thing: often, we appreciate what we have only when we see that others are suffering. If everyone is considered equal and no one suffers, can we still be happy?

Table 7. The Happiest Countries (as of 2010-2012)

Rank	Country	Score
1	Switzerland	7.587
2	Iceland	7.561
3	Denmark	7.527
4	Norway	7.522
5	Canada	7.427
6	Finland	7.406
7	Netherlands	7.389
8	Sweden	7.378
9	New Zealand	7.364
10	Australia	7.350
11	Israel	7.301
12	Costa Rica	7.257
13	Austria	7.221
14	Mexico	7.144
15	U.S.A.	7.143
16	Brazil	7.088
17	Luxembourg	7.082
18	Ireland	7.076
19	Belgium	7.054
20	U.A.E.	7.039

The report is published by the United Nations Sustainable Development Solutions Network. It surveyed over 150 countries over the period of 2010-2012. The score includes six factors: GDP per capita, social support, healthy life expectancy, freedom to make life choices, freedom from corruption and generosity. The scale is from 10 (the highest happiness) to 0 (the lowest happiness). Names of the countries with the highest equality are underlined.

Indeed, we hear examples of rich and famous people who seem to have everything one could desire for happiness, and yet they commit suicide instead of continuing to live their lavish existence.

Fortunately, besides being richer, there are other ways to be better. We don't need to see a bank account to recognize a talented singer or doctor. Also, people don't need to see that others suffer in order to be happy – they can be happy despite being surrounded by other happy people. In fact, people in countries with more equality seem happier than people in places with high inequality. For example, in 2011, nations with the highest equality (as shown in Table 3, Chapter 6) have been ranked as the happiest nations (see Table 7). The top four happiest countries are among the countries with the highest equality. Out of the 20 nations with the highest equality, eight were on the list of the top 20 happiest nations. Therefore, there is a strong correlation between equality and happiness.

Also, it is important to keep in mind that communism does not mean treating or calling everyone equal. Picturing communist society as a grey, boring society in which everyone is the same is simplistic and incorrect. The main principle of communism is to give to everyone "according to needs." People's needs are not equal: a single mother with a baby has more material needs than a single woman without children; a healthy young man needs less material assistance than a sick old man, etc. Addressing equally everyone's needs means providing everyone with the opportunity to realize their full potential and talents. And when everyone can fully express themselves, we will have more ideas and a more diverse society overall. As this transition occurs, communism will end up being more diverse and colorful than any other previous social system.

Robotization Can Lead to Communism – But Will It?

Fears that machines and automation will take our jobs are not new. They came with the appearance of machines over a century ago. What is new is that machines are becoming intelligent. As the field of artificial intelligence develops, there is now a growing fear that robots will become as smart as or even smarter than humans, taking our jobs completely and rendering human workers unnecessary. Most people will become extraneous to business operations and will be thrown on the unemployment pile. This would make the poor even poorer while making the rich – who own robots – even richer. At first, this seems logical. But a closer look suggests that this does not make much sense. Let's analyze all possible consequences of robotization.

1. The rich get richer and richer. It would initially seem that there is no inherent problem with the rich getting richer; however, in this case it would mean that the poor will get poorer. But to what extent will the poor continue to become poorer – until death of starvation? This does not make sense. Clearly, the poor will not just lay down and die. Poor people will revolt and take what they need before dying. This is natural and makes common sense. Of course, the rich might resist and employ robots that would simply kill the revolting poor. But then how many people would survive to the future world: 1000, 100, or merely 10? Living alone with machines would not appeal to any human. Furthermore, such a scenario would lead humans to genetically in-breed and eventually die out as a species.

2. The rich elite plays a game, in which it doesn't share the total wealth, but rather gives the poor just enough to prevent revolts. This seems like a very possible scenario. Actually, this is the scenario in which we live right now. In most Western countries, the rich have become richer and the poor have become poorer since the 1980s. This is especially pronounced in the U.S. and the U.K. And yet, the elite have shared part of the wealth and managed to keep the poor from revolting. For how long this can continue, however, is a significant question. Indeed, there are already signs of revolt in the U.S. and the U.K. – both countries with the highest income inequality in the developed world. Namely, voters in the U.S. elected Trump as their president against the will of the establishment, while citizens in the U.K. voted for Brexit against the will of the establishment. On the other hand, Jeremy Corbyn, who identifies himself as socialist and openly admires Marxism, was elected as the Leader of the Opposition in the U.K., a position considered to be that of an alternate Prime Minister. And in the U.S., Bernie Sanders, who was one of the frontrunners in the 2016 presidential election, openly calls for more equality in the distribution of wealth and what is essentially a socialist revolution. Thus, even this scenario seems problematic.

3. Wealth becomes evenly distributed. (This, indeed, would mean communism). Theoretically, such a scenario is possible and could make all individuals happy. But not everyone agrees. Currently, there is a strong opinion that communism has never worked and will never work. Many argue that human beings simply cannot share, because they have competition built into their DNA and will always attempt to gain a position of superiority. This position suggests that all the material excess in the world won't change human nature. However, there is a counterargument to this: if we have competition in our DNA, we may have cooperation and sacrifice hardwired as well. Indeed, Peter Kropotkin in the book *Mutual Aid: A Factor in Evolution (1902)* demonstrated this over a century ago. Using biological and sociological data, he showed that cooperation benefits society more than competition. He may have indeed been right, validating the more optimistic view that human nature is not necessarily an obstacle to communism.

Importantly, let's not forget that according to Marxism, communism can only arise as the result of a superabundance of material goods, which in turn would change our consciousness and morals. At this point, people would stop fighting over material wealth, instead sharing it freely and becoming driven by moral and social values, such as usefulness to society and the achievement of creative goals. People would begin to realize that wealth is more about social status than about things – the wealthy will be those whom others want to assist when they need something, rather than those who have accumulated a great deal of material possessions, since most material possessions will be very easy to come by.

It is important to distinguish between "material wealth" and "social wealth." In the future, material wealth may become so abundant that everyone will be able to satisfy their physical necessities. Some even suggest that our capacity to produce will eventually outstrip the capacity to consume. But it is harder to make such a claim about social wealth. There will never be a limit to the human desire to create or achieve something. Undoubtedly, individuals who take from but do not contribute to society may always be with us. They have always existed and certainly exist now. But we should not derail life for the functional majority on account of the dysfunctional minority.

Philosophical Feasibility of Communism

Given the circumstances of reality, communism was and still is impossible, just as capitalism was impossible a millennium ago. The material conditions have not yet existed and still don't exist for the success of communism.

Compared to other systems, communism is the ultimate, perfect, ideal and final society. To build communism is to reach for something absolute. But is it really possible to reach it? Absolute phenomena are known in the natural sciences: absolute zero temperature (-273.15^0C), absolute speed of light (300,000 km/sec) and others. These are states that one can approach, but never actually reach. Communism may be a similar phenomenon: society can move toward it, but can never reach it completely. It is hard to imagine that such a perfect society as communism could ever be finalized.

Everything in the world is changing and nothing is final. In assuming that communism could be built to its perfection, one would also have to accept that there would be nothing left to improve or change. This would also mean that, after reaching communism, society would stay the same forever, which contradicts Marxist philosophy recognizing that all things change and nothing lasts forever. Philosophically, one can move ever closer to communism, but never achieve it completely. As human societies enter the first or even later stages of communism, there will always be elements to improve, and there may not be a final stage.

Summary

Communism is feasible but distant. It is feasible because it can outperform capitalism economically. Communism will arise as the result of advances in economy and a superabundance of material goods. Its prerequisite is not a new (more altruistic) human. Instead, it is the economy, which will inevitably transform human morals and spirit, creating a more altruistic and conscious mankind.

References

1. Mason, P. The End of Capitalism Began. *The Guardian* (2015, July 17).
2. Hafner, K. Could a Computer Outthink This Doctor? *The New York Times* (2012, December 4).
3. Piketty, T. Capital in the Twenty-First Century, published by Belknap Press of Harvard University Press (2014).
4. Ermak, G. Emerging Medical Technologies, published by World Scientific Publishing Co. (2015).
5. Harvey, D. Seventeen Contradictions and the End of Capitalism, published by Oxford University Press (2014).
6. Eagleton, T. Why Marx Was Right, published by Yale University Press (2011).
7. North, A. A 'Star Trek' Future Might Be Closer Than We Think. *The New York Times* (2015, July 10).
8. Swartz, J. Band of Billionaires Pledge to Give to Charity. *USA Today* (2010, August 6).
9. Noguchi, Y. Some of the Rich Ask for Higher Taxes. *NPR.org web site* (2010, April 14).
10. Hickel, J. Aid in Reverse: How Poor Countries Develop Rich Countries. *Newleftproject.org website* (2013, December 18).
11. OECD. Aid to Developing Countries Rebounds in 2013 to Reach an All-Time High. *OECD.org website* (2014, April 8).
12. Marx, K., Engels, F. The German Ideology (1846), published by Progress Publishers (1964).

Conclusion

The idea of communism is now passing through its lowest point: the Soviet Union collapsed, China turned to capitalism, and it appears that capitalism continues to flourish. Some ideologists see this as an obvious indictment of communism: look what happened in the USSR, China, and other pro-communist countries – is that what you want? They publish books in which they have collected all atrocities associated with communism. Impressively, they estimate that communist practices are responsible for as many as 25 million deaths in the former Soviet Union, 65 million in China, etc.[1] On the other hand, look what happened in the West! Adherence to capitalism brought the world prosperity, freedom, etc. So the choice must be clear: human society must bury this harmful idea of communism and stick with capitalism.

It is not so simple. This book may simply backfire on its creators. First, to say that communism caused terrible atrocities but that capitalism did not would be a falsification of history. In fact, capitalism may have caused as many, or even more, atrocities than "communism." Historically, capitalist systems have thrived on slavery and the extermination of indigenous people around the world. This is especially true for such vanguard capitalist countries such as the U.S. and the U.K. In North America, entire tribes were annihilated. From the colonial era through the 1900s, the U.S. government authorized over 1,500 military actions on Native Americans, many of which have amounted to genocide.

The history of British capitalism is no better. During British rule from 1765 to 1947, tens of millions people in India starved to death while the British Empire sent millions of tons of food abroad. Even more have been killed during civil wars ignited by the British partition of the country. By some estimates, the British Empire is responsible for over 100 million deaths in India alone – more than all estimated atrocities of "communism" combined. This does not even begin to broach the idea that, in the case of "communism," the Soviets or Chinese inflicted suffering on their own soil, whereas the British inflicted suffering on other countries: impoverished, defenseless nations.

Crimes of capitalism are often hidden from the public, but they are numerous. No one has yet written the book compiling the atrocities associated with capitalism. If such a book had been written, it would show that capitalist societies also gave birth to fascism (in Germany, Italy, etc.) and dictatorships (in Chile, Saudi Arabia, etc.). Capitalist societies are responsible for unleashing World War I with up to 20 million killed, World War II with over 60 million killed, and the Vietnam War with over three million killed. Somehow, atrocities associated with capitalism outnumber atrocities associated with "communism." Yet, "communist" atrocities have received far more attention than capitalist crimes.

Where Did the Misunderstanding of Communism Come From?

The misunderstanding of communism was the result of a misunderstanding of Marxism. Marx and Engels made several major discoveries, including the leading role of economy and class struggle in human relationships. They found that human history was filled with class struggle, and that class struggle was an important element in society's progress. However, their most important idea was that human relationships are based on the economy and that the economy is the foundation of any society; thus, as the economy advances, communist society will inevitably arise. The origin of this idea lies in the philosophy of Marxism – dialectic materialism (see Chapter 3), which recognizes that the development of a society depends on material causes but not on people's ideas or wishes.

Marx and Engels established the foundation of this philosophy in a set of manuscripts, written in 1846 and united in one book *The German Ideology,*. Amazingly, this work did not find a publisher for almost a hundred years, until it was translated into Russian and published in 1932 in the USSR. This explains why these major philosophical ideas are little-known to the world audience. It also explains why Russian revolutionaries distorted Marxism: they were not familiar with some of its main ideas, because *The German Ideology* had not yet been published.

Believing that communism can arise at any time, regardless of the economy, depending on people's ideas and wishes, is idealism, which is incompatible with a Marxist worldview. Although it has already been cited, the following quote of Marx and Engels is so important that it bears repeating: "...in general, people cannot be liberated as long as they are unable to obtain food and drink, housing and clothing in adequate quality and quantity. 'Liberation' is a historical and not a mental act, and it is brought about by historical conditions, the development of industry, commerce, agriculture..." [2]

Unfortunately, the core idea of Marxism has been ignored and the focus has been on the class struggle. The socialist revolution took place in Russia followed by revolutions in other countries. They all failed and, according to Marxism, they could not have succeeded. In fact, the economies of those countries were not ready for communism then, and there is still no economy that is ready in any country in the world. Even the economies of the Nordic countries that are the closest to communism are not there yet (see more details in Chapter 8).

So why did the revolutions take place? For three main reasons: 1) in some countries, workers lived in such misery that they simply could not tolerate it anymore, and were not willing to wait until their economy was ready. They had nothing to lose and the revolution became their only hope for a better life; 2) revolutionaries did not want to wait until their economy was ready either. They became too excited about communism's bright future and wanted to see it as soon as possible. They wanted immediate action instead of settling for a long, agonizing wait for generations until the economic foundation of communism was built; and 3) critically, Marx and Engels were not clear on the role of revolutions in the transformation of capitalism into communism. Sometimes they envisioned the transformation taking place peacefully through reforms (see Chapter 5), and at other times they suggested that violent revolutions were necessary. In their defense, they lived in a different time – a time when the rich were continually getting richer while the workers lived in misery. At the time, it looked like this situation would never end and would only keep getting worse and worse, until finally bursting into a storm of protests and revolution. But this did not happen. Instead, capitalism developed a humane face: reforms were initiated and the conditions of the working class began to improve all over the world. Contradictions between the working class and the rulers eased and became reconcilable, making revolutions unnecessary. Can we blame Marx and Engels for not foreseeing this? Of course not – they were scientists, philosophers and thinkers, but not prophets.

As one can see, the misunderstanding of communism was brought about by so-called "communist" revolutionaries, who essentially hijacked Marxist theory. At times, this was committed purposefully in order to justify a string of brutal, totalitarian regimes throughout the world. As expected, such revolutions did not deliver the desired results, and unfortunately damaged the credibility of one of the world's great philosophies along the way. Using Marx's words, the revolutions brought "the old crap in new form." They installed some kind of bureaucratic collectivism, which was sold to the world under name of communism. Even some of them did realize the mistake, they were invested into this system too much to admit it. And capitalist ideologists were happy to buy this, because it helped (and still does) to discredit the whole idea of communism. That is how both communists and anti-communists got it wrong.

Fortunately, not everyone got it wrong. The social democratic movement, which took its roots from Marxism but split from its militant "communist" stream (see Chapter 4), got it right. Social democrats recognized that capitalism did not develop as Marx projected, and could be slowly reformed into a more balanced society such as socialism. Not surprisingly, countries in which the social democratic movement is the strongest have the most socialism today (see Chapter 6). China first got it wrong but then corrected its course, staying on the correct path to this day. First, led by Mao, China hoped that it could jump from feudalism straight into communism. But under Deng's leadership, China turned back to capitalism with the intention of building the economic foundation for communism first, as required by Marxism (see details in Chapter 9).

A New Look at the History of Communism

This book demonstrates that many aspects of communism have been misunderstood. This also means that many events in the history of communism have been misunderstood: some were more important, others less important, while some had nothing to do with communism. Thus, the history of communism has to be reevaluated and reviewed. Below is a list of the most important events in the history of communism that takes into account the findings in this book:

380 BCE: A communist-like society was described for the first time in the book *The Republic* by Plato.

490-520 CE: The first communist movement took place. It happened in what is now Iran. It was initiated by a religious activist, Mazdak, and was named after him: the Mazdak movement.

1516: Thomas More wrote the book *Utopia*, which describes a utopian society based on wealth equality. This book marked the beginning of the criticism of private ownership.

1535-1536: An attempt to establish a communist community/theocracy took place in the city of Münster, Germany.

17th century: A puritan religious group called "Diggers" tried to establish communes with common ownership of land (agrarian communism) in England.

18-19th century: French intellectuals, German philosophers and British economists laid the foundation for the rise of Marxism. French socialists (Jean Jacques Rousseau, Sylvain Maréchal, Francois-Noël Babeuf, Francois Marie Charles Fourier and others) came to the conclusion that if capitalism inevitably leads to exploitation, it should be replaced with communism. French economist Henri Saint-Simon laid the groundwork for the core idea of Marxism that economy is the foundation of social relationships: in order to have a better society, one must build a stronger economy. German philosopher Georg Hegel developed dialectic views of the world, while Ludwig Feuerbach developed materialistic views. British economists David Ricardo and Robert Owen developed the economic understanding of capitalism.

1846: Marx and Engels wrote a set of manuscripts that later became known as the book *The German Ideology*. This work developed the philosophy of dialectic materialism and historical materialism, which became the foundation for Marxist views on communism.

1848: Marx and Engels wrote *The Communist Manifesto,* which popularized the idea of communism and became one of the most influential political manuscripts of all time.

1848: The first major international organization of the working class, the International Workingmen's Association, was founded. In 1864, it unified communist, left wing socialist, trade union and anarchist organizations to form a single association named the First International.

1867: Marx wrote the first volume of *Capital*. The book analyzed how a capitalist economy functions and demonstrated that capitalism is a precursor to communism.

1871: The first proletarian revolution (Paris Commune) took place in France but failed.

1917: The Socialist October Revolution took place in Russia and succeeded. The first pseudo-communist state, which could actually be classified as bureaucratic collectivist, was established.

1919: Social democracy split from communist movements.

1919: The reformist May Fourth Movement began in China. This movement later formed the Communist Party of China.

1922: The Union of Soviet Socialist Republics (the USSR), based on

Soviet Russia, was formed.

1949: The second major self-proclaimed communist state, the People's Republic of China (PRC), was established.

1978: China's leadership turned to classical Marxism. After the failures of the Great Leap Forward and The Great Cultural Revolution, China turned to economic reforms (socialist market economy). These reforms initiated rapid economic growth, which could create the foundation for communism.

1991: The first self-proclaimed communist state, the USSR, was dissolved due to its under-performing economy. All member states of the union returned to capitalism.

Present Day: China is prosperously developing toward socialism and communism. The Chinese model was successfully adopted by Vietnam and can be adopted by other developing countries. Western capitalist countries, especially Nordic nations, which did not pursue communism, have become much closer to achieving it than the countries that actively pursued it.

References

1.   Panne, J.-L. et. al. The Black Book of Communism: Crimes, Terror, Repression, published by Harvard University Press (1999).

2.   Marx, K., Engels, F. The German Ideology (1846) published by International Publishers, p. 61 (2007).

Index

About the Author

Gennady Ermak was born and raised in the former Soviet Union. He holds a Ph.D. in Biology, and for many years conducted research at the University of Southern California. He is the acclaimed author of 45 scholarly articles and the book *Emerging Medical Technologies*. Upon realizing the extent to which the idea of communism is misunderstood in contemporary society, he paused his research career in order to address it and write this book. He currently resides in Los Angeles, California.

Made in the USA
Coppell, TX
14 January 2020